Spinoza's Authority Volume I:
Resistance and Power in *Ethics*

Also available from Bloomsbury

Conflict, Power, and Multitude in Machiavelli and Spinoza, Filippo Del Lucchese

Spinoza and the Specters of Modernity, Michael Mack

Between Hegel and Spinoza, edited by Hasana Sharp and Jason E. Smith

Spinoza: Ethics of an Outlaw, Ivan Segré

Spinoza's Authority Volume II, edited by A. Kiarina Kordela and Dimitris Vardoulakis

The Role of God in Spinoza's Metaphysics, Sherry Deveaux

Bloomsbury Companion to Spinoza, edited by Wiep van Bunge, Henri Krop*, Piet Steenbakkers and Jeroen van de Ven

Spinoza's Authority Volume I: Resistance and Power in *Ethics*

Edited by
A. Kiarina Kordela and Dimitris Vardoulakis

Bloomsbury Academic
An imprint of Bloomsbury Publishing Plc

BLOOMSBURY
LONDON • OXFORD • NEW YORK • NEW DELHI • SYDNEY

Bloomsbury Academic
An imprint of Bloomsbury Publishing Plc

50 Bedford Square	1385 Broadway
London	New York
WC1B 3DP	NY 10018
UK	USA

www.bloomsbury.com

BLOOMSBURY and the Diana logo are trademarks of Bloomsbury Publishing Plc

First published 2018

© A. Kiarina Kordela, Dimitris Vardoulakis and contributors, 2018

A. Kiarina Kordela and Dimitris Vardoulakis have asserted their right under the Copyright, Designs and Patents Act, 1988, to be identified as Author of this work.

All rights reserved. No part of this publication may be reproduced or transmitted in any form or by any means, electronic or mechanical, including photocopying, recording, or any information storage or retrieval system, without prior permission in writing from the publishers.

No responsibility for loss caused to any individual or organization acting on or refraining from action as a result of the material in this publication can be accepted by Bloomsbury or the author.

British Library Cataloguing-in-Publication Data
A catalogue record for this book is available from the British Library.

ISBN:	HB:	978-1-4725-9320-7
	ePDF:	978-1-4725-9322-1
	ePub:	978-1-4725-9321-4

Library of Congress Cataloging-in-Publication Data
A catalog record for this book is available from the Library of Congress.

Series: Bloomsbury Studies in Continental Philosophy

Typeset by Integra Software Services Pvt. Ltd.

Contents

Preface *A. Kiarina Kordela and Dimitris Vardoulakis*	vi
Acknowledgments	vii
Reference Guide	viii
Authority in the *Ethics*: An Introduction *A. Kiarina Kordela*	1
1 Equality and Power: Spinoza's Reformulation of the Aristotelian Tradition of Egalitarianism *Dimitris Vardoulakis*	11
2 Spinoza's Ethics and Politics of Freedom: Active and Passive Power *Aurelia Armstrong*	33
3 Grammars of *Conatus*: Or, On the Primacy of Resistance in Spinoza, Foucault and Deleuze *Cesare Casarino*	57
4 Beyond Legitimacy: The State as an Imaginary Entity in Spinoza's Political Ontology *Juan Domingo Sánchez Estop*	87
5 The Cold Quietness of the Stars: Proof, Rhetoric and the Authority of Reason in the *Ethics* *Joe Hughes*	113
6 Spinoza: A Different Power to Act *Antonio Negri*	135
7 Commanding the Body: The Language of Subjection in *Ethics* III, P2S *Warren Montag*	147
8 Interrupting the System: Spinoza and Maroon Thought *James Edward Ford III*	173
9 Spinoza's Biopolitics: Commodification of Substance and Secular Immortality *A. Kiarina Kordela*	197
Biographical Notes	218
Index	220

Preface

A. Kiarina Kordela and Dimitris Vardoulakis

Just as in the 1960s the pessimism about dialectical materialism was giving way to a new hope that Marxist dialectics can be amended or augmented by Spinoza's anti-teleological philosophy, a new, seemingly intractable problem arose. Namely, the problem that the more one opposes regimes of power, the more this opposition strengthens the structural system that makes such regimes possible. As Foucault puts this point somewhere: "Anyone who attempts to oppose the law in order to found a new order … will encounter the silent and infinitely accommodating welcome of the law. The law does not change: it subsided into the grave once and for all, and each of its forms is only a metamorphosis of that never-ending death." This problem is even more acute in neoliberal governmentality, where it becomes increasingly difficult to identify even a target to oppose or resist, given that executive government cedes a lot of its power to capital.

This may suggest that optimism of the will in the face of the pessimism of the intellect is even more urgent today—and yet such a stance is precarious for a Spinozist who would be suspicious not only of any concept of the will but also of the very idea of hope, given what Spinoza has to say about the will and about hope in his works.

The wager of the present two collections is that we may be better served by paying close attention to what Spinoza says about authority. Examining Spinoza's authority in the full range of its significations—as prophetic authority or as sovereignty, as power or as authoritative process of interpretation—we may be able to evade the dilemma between pessimism and optimism. In fact, we may be able to steer a path that shows how resistance is possible because authority is ever present as obedience or as the sad emotions that decrease our power.

Acknowledgments

We are thankful to all of our contributors as much for the final products that appear in the form of these thoughtful essays as for what came before that: their enthusiastic engagement in conference panels and workshops that have helped us all shape our ideas as we were putting them down in essay forms. These events include: the seminar on "Spinoza's Authority," organized by Dimitris Vardoulakis, which took place at the University of Western Sydney, in Sydney, Australia, in August 2012; the thematic stream on "Spinozan Politics" at the *London Conference on Critical Thought*, organized by Filippo Del Lucchese and Dimitris Vardoulakis, which took place at the Royal Holloway, University of London, in June 2013; the seminar on "Spinoza's Authority: Resistance and Power" at the conference of the *American Comparative Literature Association*, organized by Siarhei Biareishyk and A. Kiarina Kordela, which took place at the New York University in New York, in March 2014; and the workshop on "Spinoza's *Theologico-Political Treatise*," organized by Stathis Gourgouris and Dimitris Vardoulakis, which took place at Columbia University in New York, in November 2015.

Reference Guide

References to Spinoza's works

The various translations of Spinoza's works offer often significantly different interpretation of the meaning of his original Latin text. For this reason, the contributors have been free to choose their preferred translation, or to translate themselves the Latin from the established text of Spinoza's works in the Gebhardt edition of the *Opera*.

The following abbreviations of specific works have been used:

E = *Ethics* [*Ethica*]

The Roman numeral in capital following *E* indicates the part of the *Ethics*. For example, *E* I is *Ethics*, Part I, *E* II is *Ethics* Part II, and so on. The following abbreviations have been used here:

A = Axiom
Ap. = Appendix
C = Corollary
D = Definition
L = Lemma
P = Proposition
Pr = Proof
Pref = Preface
S = Scholium

So, for instance, *E* II, P7 refer to *Ethics*, Part I, Proposition 7. And, *E* IV, P34S refers to *Ethics*, Parts IV, Scholium to Proposition 34.

Other abbreviations to Spinoza's works

TIE (Treatise on the Emendation of the Intellect): cited by paragraph number.
Ep. (The Letters): cited by letter number.
PC (Principles of Cartesian Philosophy).
ST (Short Treatise).

TP   (Tractatus Politicus): cited by chapter followed by paragraph number.
TTP (Tractatus Theologico-Politicus).

The contributors indicate in each chapter which edition of the above works they prefer to use.

Authority in the *Ethics*: An Introduction

A. Kiarina Kordela

Barely a reader of Spinoza's *Ethics* could fail to notice that this work far exceeds the scope of its title. Already by reading the first pages we find ourselves enwrapped first of all in a theology—and one might add, a secular theology—which quickly reveals itself to be simultaneously an ontology and an epistemology, to mention only the most eminent subject matters of Spinoza's rather short book. The first of the two volumes of our collection on *Spinoza's Authority* brings to the foreground another, perhaps less conspicuous, aspect of the *Ethics*, namely, that it is also a work on political philosophy.

The itinerary of the nine essays in this volume could be briefly described as follows. (1) We begin with Dimitris Vardoulakis introducing us to two of Spinoza's many unorthodox positions, and specifically his intertwining of equality and power, and his politicization of the ontological, with which Spinoza opposes the entire Aristotelian tradition of egalitarianism and the assumption of an ante-political space. (2) Spinoza's next heresy concerns his concept of freedom, which, as Aurelia Armstrong argues against its liberal political interpretation as a product of self-perfection, can emerge only as an effect of internal (individual) and external (social) relational interactions. (3) Such interrelations between singularity and the common bring us to the issue of *conatus*, whose interconnections with *potestas* and *potentia* are unfolded in Cesare Casarino's reading of Gilles Deleuze's thesis that resistance (*potentia*) comes before power (*potestas*) through the Spinozan principle that truth is the standard both of itself and of the false. (4) One of the most fundamental concerns of *potestas* and the state is legitimacy, which, as Juan Domingo Sánchez Estop shows, in opposition to the dominant contractual theories of political legitimacy, Spinoza considers to be an effect of the imagination, so that the state has essentially no proper existence. (5) The centrality of the imagination to the political culminates in Joseph Hughes' essay which argues, against Alain Badiou, that Spinoza's method of proof involves discovery, historicity and the potential of radical retroactive reconstitution of sense, so that neither proof nor the political can be reduced to mathematical logic. (6) Antonio Negri returns to his distinction between *potentia* as constituent power and *potestas* as transcendent sovereignty, and to his critics, to argue that *potentia* is a non-teleological productive engine and a permanent source of laws that builds virtue from below, and that politics is not a mediator but the origin and rupture of society. (7) The same horizontal architectonics of power is also reflected in Spinoza's conception of body and mind, which, as Warren Montag shows, opposes the entire Christian-Cartesian tradition and its conception of the mind as the master and the body as the slave, to raise the question: what can the body do when liberated from the master? (8) James Edward Ford III brings the problematic of the master and the slave squarely within (post)colonial theory to argue that effective resistance can occur not through solitary acts of revenge but through a shared life in the common, just as authority manifests itself in sharing power with the multitude. (9) Lastly, my essay functions as a bridge to the second volume, as its thesis regarding Spinoza's anticipation of hegemony and biopolitics, including the possibility of their radical reconceptualization, is based on both the *Ethics* and the treatises.

Below are summaries of the essays contained in the present volume.

* * *

In "Equality and Power: Spinoza's Reformulation of the Aristotelian Tradition of Egalitarianism," Dimitris Vardoulakis argues that Spinoza gives us an alternative to Western political philosophy and its Aristotelian conception of "geometric equality" which "utilizes a value or merit to determine equality by analogy." In this tradition, authority always privileges one of three types of equality—"procedural, material or desertful"—which are always at odds with each other and therefore cause "bloody conflict that is destructive of the polis." Drawing on Spinoza's axiom in his *Ethics*—"There is no singular thing in Nature than which there is not another more powerful and stronger. Whatever one is given, there is another more powerful by which the first can be destroyed" (*E*, IV, A1)—Vardoulakis argues that Spinoza "co-posits being and power" and "introduces an inequality of power" that entails that "everyone will be overpowered by an external cause." In its affirmation of differential power relations, this axiom denies absolute authority itself and opens up "a common space where democracy unfolds because of the power interaction of citizens." This is an "agonistic democracy" marked by "an equality in the participation of engagement of contestation."

Vardoulakis' further target is the "oft-repeated move" in Western political philosophy to suppose "an ante-political space of equality" in order to justify some form of sovereign authority. Augustine's Eden, Hobbes' state of nature, and Kant's kingdom of ends—which correspond to the logics of "three types of sovereignty: ancient, modern and biopolitical," respectively—all represent presupposed spaces of absolute equality that help justify their different political frameworks. Spinoza rejects this ante-political space because "the political is not confined to human relations regulated either by formally instituted laws or transcendental laws," since for Spinoza the ontological is itself already political. Therefore, the political "does not require a transcendent authority to supervise over…and regulate" itself, "since it is the immanent unfolding of power relations." In Vardoulakis' conclusion, the "Spinozan position allows for a conceptualization of equality which is not dependent on authority, but consists rather in the equality of access to participation in the differential unfolding of power."

Aurelia Armstrong's essay, "Spinoza's Ethics and Politics of Freedom: Active and Passive Power," critically examines the grounds for the claim made by a number of recent liberal political theorists that Spinoza's conception of freedom belongs to a self-perfectionist tradition of autonomy. This claim easily dissociates Spinoza's freedom from politics since it includes as its constitutive condition that freedom is achievable only by the individual's own intellectual activity. Armstrong argues that this claim mischaracterizes Spinoza's conception of ethical liberation insofar as it fails to account for the impact of the different concrete forms of existence on the way essences exist. While the liberal view invites us to imagine freedom as the self-realization of essential power and, thus, as a function of the internal causal activity of singular essences considered in abstraction from the relations that determine how they operate in existence, the alternative view sketched in this essay emphasizes the centrality of relational interaction to Spinoza's account of activity. Armstrong argues that the degree of freedom and activity we enjoy as existing individuals must be understood as the combined effect of internal causal force and external causes in their interactions. Thus, how we are related to one another, whether through relations of agreement and mutual support or disagreement and opposition, becomes crucial to determining individual and collective prospects for empowerment and liberation. The more we manage to agree, Spinoza suggests, the less subject we are to the arbitrary power of external things, and consequently, the greater our power to act from the necessity of our own natures. In this light, and against the liberal interpretation, Armstrong suggests that if we are freer in a state this is not just because the state protects us from relationships that threaten our power, but also because a state constitutionally constrained to take the welfare of all citizens into account acts positively as a vector for building relationships of agreement, which enhance individual and collective power and freedom.

In "Grammars of *Conatus*: or, on the Primacy of Resistance in Spinoza, Foucault, and Deleuze," Cesare Casarino illuminates Gilles Deleuze's formula that "the final word on power is that *resistance comes first*"—that is, before power—by tracing the relationship between resistance and power in the *Ethics*. Just as "truth is the standard both of itself and of falsity," "resistance," Casarino argues, "is the standard of itself and of power." To locate the concept of resistance in Spinoza (since it is not explicitly stated), Casarino turns to *conatus*, "the striving to persevere *in one's being*." The question then becomes: "What being is at stake in such a perseverance?" In Spinoza, being has two facets, essence and existence, and because on the level of modes, the two do not coincide, being is the non-identity of essence and existence. *Conatus* is the striving to persevere, "against all odds," in the non-identity of essence and existence, and it is this striving that invests and constitutes the realms of the ethical and the political. Further, Casarino argues, "*essence is singularity*"—hence "to each its own *conatus*"—while existence is common—"we can never bring it about that we need nothing outside ourselves to preserve our being"—so that *conatus* has also always "included the outside and the common as its own condition of possibility." Having established the above, Casarino is then able to describe the three aspects of *conatus*. (1) The first is the "form of relation," in other words, "the historical formations, or 'social field,' which in this case bear the name of mercantile capital." (2) The second aspect of *conatus* involves a "relation of force expressed as power," or *potestas*, which aligns with "capitalist exchange relations," relations among "modes of thought and modes of extension." (3) Finally, *conatus* involves a "relation of force expressed as resistance," or *potentia*, the singular essence which always "comes first" insofar as it operates on the level of the "entire plane of immanence," or the "absolute outside." This third aspect of *conatus*, or resistance, is realized via Spinoza's third kind of knowledge, "intuition," which is "knowledge from the standpoint of eternity," that is, outside of time, so that here "the striving to persevere in one's being turns into the striving to resist." Thus, resistance (*potentia*), operating under the species of eternity, is *both* first *and* last in the formula of power.

In "Beyond Legitimacy: The State as an Imaginary Entity in Spinoza's Political Ontology," Juan Domingo Sánchez Estop takes as his starting point Antonio Negri's distinction between two lines in modern political philosophy, the one being predicated on a transcendent conception of legitimacy, the other viewing legitimacy as an imaginary effect of real power. The former constitutes the "mainstream tradition of Western political philosophy, from Hobbes to Hegel, through Locke and Rousseau," which "sought to produce a consistent theory of legitimate power and legitimate obedience based on the concepts of consent, legal power, authority and legitimacy." Spinoza, belonging to the other line of thought along with Machiavelli and Marx, can be seen as a reversal of this logic, in his claim that "authority is not the basis for legitimate *potestas*, but an effect and a means of the actual exercise of *potestas*, that is, of the production of obedience." Drawing further on Louis Althusser, Sánchez Estop argues that for Spinoza, "the most effective power is the one founded on the subjects' inner obedience," and that "power generates its legitimacy not by means of its action on subjects but through the production of subjects." Crucial to the production of subjects is the imaginary, a concept which in Spinoza is intimately tied to the political insofar as "law, power and obedience" are "needed in order to correct the effect of human passions" which are "rooted in imagination" rather than reason. In Spinoza, Sánchez Estop concludes, political legitimacy is the "product of imagination, as a necessary illusion produced by political power, as a means to reproduce its constitutive relations of force." Concomitantly, the state is not "constitutive of the political community," rather it is the "result of the imaginary transformation of a social relation into a substance through the common mechanisms of imagination," and therefore "has no proper existence"—a position that, as Sánchez Estop shows, Spinoza shares with Marx.

In "The Cold Quietness of the Stars: Proof, Rhetoric and the Authority of Reason in the *Ethics*," Joe Hughes engages with and critiques Alain Badiou's "movement from a mathematics of proof to a logical politics," that is, the intention "to perform a transfer of the authority of reason from the sphere of mathematical rationality to that of practical and political rationality." While Badiou, following Descartes' interpretation of the geometrical method, claims in his "What is a Proof in Spinoza's *Ethics*?" that "a proof explains the proposition in terms of what has gone before," that is, what is already known, Hughes argues that to attend to a proof is "to notice that it is not merely a recuperative gesture which becomes clear only after everything is already known." Rather, for Spinoza, attending to a proof requires "an inescapable apprenticeship through which thought learns *to create*." Hughes grounds his thesis on an attentive comparison of Spinoza's conception of method to its respective conceptualizations by the two major figures between which he is historically situated, Descartes and Leibniz. This comparison reveals that Spinoza's concept of proof exceeds the "merely logical proof" because it includes an *inventive* dimension, an aspect of thought "which constituted for a long time the zone of indiscernibility between rhetoric and philosophy." For Spinoza, true ideas "can only be *discovered*, in so far as they are *invented*, and once invented they will ground, at a later stage of history, the discovery of still more." This means, Hughes continues, that for Spinoza, (1) method "has a history which is the history of invention," (2) "science must be invented," (3) both reading and demonstrating are "discovery," and—what is presupposed for the above three—(4) "there is a temporality to the process of demonstration," because of which "there always persists, in any given utterance, a horizon of potentiality, specifically the potentiality for radical, perhaps savage, future specification." In short, Hughes historicizes proof and method in the most Spinozan and psychoanalytic sense, that is, he shows that the temporality of demonstration is not linear—proceeding from one known to the next—but rather involves retroactivity—bringing a present known back to a past unknown so as to render it known and available to future specifications. This is why "the movement of proof is never only repetition" of the known—as is conceived in canonical logic, Descartes and Badiou—"but difference as well." Against the mathematizing "fantasy that the proof can be formalized" in the form of letters or other symbols "and clarified by virtue of deductive relations between them," Hughes proposes that a Spinozan "practical and political rationality" should embrace the inventive dimension involved in its demonstrations.

In "Spinoza: A Different Power to Act," Antonio Negri begins with five theses which attempt to differentiate Spinoza's conception of constituent power (*potentia*) from the traditional notion of transcendent power (sovereignty/*potestas*), especially in its political application. First, Negri argues that "it is impossible to reduce Spinoza's concept of power to the individual, or to the individual power to act," so that Spinozan power differs in that "it is socially constituted, and innovates on simple interaction, being always oriented toward the common." Second, this constituent power cannot be analyzed with the "various forms of transcendental understanding of power," but rather falls into the "excessively monistic perspective" of accumulation. Thus, the "*positive* identity of [constituent] power and right can't be reduced to a *positivist* perspective," because, unlike an actualized legal system, power as *potentia* is productive. Third, Spinozan power is non-teleological despite the fact that "the defence of freedom [...] represents the *telos* for [Spinozan] thought and politics." Fourth, *potentia* is different from *potestas* in that it is marked by an excess of "the rational expression of *amor*," which itself is produced by the movement from *conatus* to *cupiditas* (desire); *cupiditas* is the core of this movement in that it produces the imagination, which, in turn, "leads the singularity from resistance to the common." Lastly, Negri concludes, "politics is not the mediator of society, but its permanent origin as well as its continual rupture" because of a consistent surplus of constituent power which perpetually "opposes nothingness and builds the common." Negri's description of *potentia* (and politics) is followed by his responses to past and anticipated criticisms. First, he responds to the critique that he has "created an absolute antinomy between *potentia* (ontologically creative) and *potestas* (fixed and/or parasitical)," claiming that their relationship is rather "a continuously produced struggle, a conflict that keeps being posited and resolved," and in which "*potentia*, as *cupiditas*, is never bad, and is always excessive." Next, Negri responds to the criticism that his advocated program of absolute democracy would be an "undue interruption of the continuous process of conflict among singularities," as postulated by Spinoza. Rather, absolute democracy is necessarily constituted by *potentia* insofar as "a constitution is an engine and not a result, it is a 'constituent power' as permanent source of laws." Negri further avoids teleological guarantees by rejecting a utopian destination for the common and arguing, instead, that "the multitude, and not us, has to decide what it wants to be." Thus, Negri is able to conclude that what differentiates Spinozan *potentia* from theories of sovereign power is that "it builds virtue from below."

In "Commanding the Body: The Language of Subjection in *Ethics* III, P2S," Warren Montag argues that the ultimate function of the proposition and scholium in question lies in revealing the very "prejudices" because of which their explicit message had to remain non-apprehensible to Spinoza's contemporary readers. With Montag, Spinoza takes the term "prejudice" in its literal, legal sense, as a judgment already made as the very precondition for everything that follows. Far from being simply errors or purely imaginary, "prejudices" iterate previous judgments that are now materialized within the existing practice of law, and are, thus, co-extensive with each historical society and its specific apparatuses of subjection—in Spinoza's case, the line from Christianity to the seventeenth century. Apostle Paul encapsulates the logic of this apparatus as follows: "do you not know that your body is a temple of the Holy Spirit who is in you and that you are God's and not your own?" Descartes reiterates this dictum in his declaration of the mind as the *dominus* that decrees its *servus*, the body, with benevolent God crowning this cosmic hierarchy. For Spinoza's imaginary interlocutors, the body can no more engage in the work of production without a master than the actual slave seized in Palestine in the first century or in West Africa in the seventeenth. Against this Christian-Cartesian tradition, Spinoza dares to raise the revolutionary question—what is the body capable of doing when it is liberated from the master's command?—with *E* III, P2: "the body cannot determine the mind to think, nor can the mind determine the body to movement or rest." This statement cuts the Gordian knot of causality between body and mind—in which the lines of individuality, freedom, accountability, guilt, authority and subjection are so entangled as to seem inseparable and inescapable—thereby obliterating the theoretical opposition of command and obedience on both levels, mind and body *and* political authority and people. The "absolute sovereignty" of the mind is impossible, nothing more than a "forensic" fantasy that renders us "absolutely" accountable for affects and actions—including, crucially, (not)remembering—that we cannot entirely control; and the same fantasy conceives of political power as "absolute sovereignty." The demolition of this fantasy constitutes Spinoza's Machiavellianism. The scholium's intertwining of the lexica of natural philosophy, causality, legislation, military and politics, entails a Moebius-strip-type relation among nature, humans and politics, whereby the outside folds back upon itself as its own interior, and thus reminds us that, irrespective of their truth, "beliefs" produce real effects.

In "Interrupting the System: Spinoza and Maroon Thought," James Edward Ford III disputes Antonio Negri's hypothesis that a "certain black and leprous Brazilian" in Spinoza's "unpleasant dream" is Caliban from *The Tempest*. Rather, Ford III argues, the Maroon is "a more effective figure for hypothesizing about Spinoza's dream, his materialist shift, and the global reach of the multitude." The Maroon—"an African who has joined a community of other Africans escaping enslavement in the New World"—complements Spinoza's active immanent materialism, whereas "Caliban symbolizes individual acts of the subordinated that remain mired in what Franz Fanon would call *ressentiment*," and his defiance "works strictly within the confines Prospero [his master] has set." Furthermore, Caliban, a solitary figure, "dreams of but does not pursue a shared life in the common," and "will forego freedom for revenge because, as Spinoza says, revenge is the slave's *modus operandi*." By contrast, the Maroon productively and resolutely reaches for "a new sociability," and his active "remaking" potentiality, like Spinoza's own excommunication, constitutes a historical actualization of Spinoza's ontology. As Ford concludes, "Spinoza's authority manifests in sharing power *with* the multitude, which cannot be fully understood without understanding racial complexity," and, in light of "the resurgence of fascist elements," along with the persistence of global capitalism and its effects, it is an imperative "to rethink authority."

A. Kiarina Kordela approaches Spinoza's conceptualization of political power as a system that negotiates authority and freedom in ways that parallel his theological distinction between fearful obedience to biblical laws and the love for God. She shows that this intertwining of authority and freedom anticipates modern hegemonic and biopolitical forms of power, while, importantly, offering insights into biopower that far exceed its hitherto theorizations. By being predicated on a monistic relation between Body and Mind, as well as on the third kind of knowledge—as the kind of knowledge in which the Mind conceives of itself and the Body *sub specie aeternitatis*—Spinoza's conception of biopower reveals that its object extends beyond the biophysical body (Foucault) or "bare life" (Agamben)—which are modes of substance—to include Body and Mind as attributes of substance and, hence, as eternal. Linking Spinoza's substance to Marx's labor-power (the potential of labor to actualize itself) Kordela suggests that in capitalist modernity it is substance itself that is politicized, as it is commodified, thereby becoming an object of political economy. From then on, biopower can, and must, constitute itself as a form of power that directly intervenes in the relationship of the human being to eternity, while also setting in motion that modern biopolitical mechanism which triggers the slippage from eternity to its distorted underside: the secular fantasy of immortality.

1

Equality and Power: Spinoza's Reformulation of the Aristotelian Tradition of Egalitarianism

Dimitris Vardoulakis

Equality in the Axiom to Part IV of the *Ethics*

There is an almost unanimous agreement on Spinoza's democratic credentials, which is surprising, given, the wildly divergent interpretations on Spinoza's philosophy.[1] And yet, it is next to impossible to find any discussion of equality in Spinoza's work.[2] Partly this is due to Spinoza himself, who refers to equality sporadically but never systematically.[3] For instance, Spinoza mentions in Chapters 16 and 17 of the *Theological-Political Treatise* that both in democracy as the "most natural constitution" and in the "theocracy" of Hebrew state people enjoyed equality, but this does not seem to suggest much more than that in both of these cases the citizens do not transfer their natural right to another human person. This absence of a sustained discussion of equality in Spinoza raises a problematic: Is it possible to defend a theory of democracys without a sense of equality? Or is it perhaps the case that Spinoza never thematizes equality explicitly because it is included within another concept? I will argue that the latter is the case. Spinoza's sense of equality is inextricably linked to his conception of power and the production of state authority.

One could point out, of course, that equality has always been an aspect of state authority, at least since the Solonian reforms that lead to the writing of the first ever democratic constitution. As Aristotle explains in *The Athenian Constitution*, the cause of these reforms was the violent dispute between the rich and the poor parties due to stark inequalities within Athens.[4] Around 594 BC, the Athenians turned to Solon—widely regarded as both wise and impartial—to find a solution to these constant struggles. Solon instituted three fundamental reforms to promote equality. First, he canceled the debts and redistributed the wealth (this is the famous reform of *seisachtheia*, the shaking of the burdens). Second, he extended citizenship to all, whereas in the past citizenship was confined only to the rich. And lastly, everyone was expected to participate in public office through a process that relied on chance—election by lot.[5] In these three reforms, we can discern the three senses of equality that have dominated Western political discourse ever since. Namely, there is the material equality of wealth redistribution; the procedural equality before the law by granting everyone citizenship; and, the equality of worth whereby one is deemed to deserve to hold office.

I will return to these three senses of equality in the next section. I need to point out here three points: First, it is Aristotle who thematizes the three senses of equality under the rubric of geometric equality in *Nicomachean Ethics*, which has had an enormous influence in how equality has been thought ever since in the Western political and philosophical tradition. Second, the three senses confine equality within state authority, or, to put it different, equality is raised to a significant political virtue. It is for this reason that I call the various permutations and combination of the three senses of geometric equality *state equality*. Third, Jacques Rancière has made a pivotal contribution is highlighting the origins of the modern thinking of equality and its links to state power.[6] (For reasons of space I cannot deal with Rancière in this chapter.[7]) My argument concentrates on Spinoza to show that he is skeptical of the authority produced by state equality, which explains why he both avoids an explicit thematization of equality, and why equality is in fact subordinated to his conception of power.

Further, my contention is that the central axis of the thinking of equality in Spinoza is provided by the Axiom to Part IV of the *Ethics*. Many have noted the importance of this axiom. For instance, Antonio Negri in *Savage Anomaly* insists that "this axiom constitutes the dynamic center of Spinoza's philosophy."[8] Negri's assessment is related to the fact that the Axiom to Part IV posits an imbrication of the ontological and the political. My further assertion is that this imbrication resonates with a thinking of equality—moreover, a thinking that will appear to be incompatible with the Aristotelian extrapolation of geometric equality, which has dominated the Western philosophical tradition.

Let us examine the axiom, which at first glance may appear deceptively simple. The Axiom to Part IV of the *Ethics* reads:

> There is no singular thing in Nature than which there is not another more powerful [*potentior*] and stronger [*fortior*]. Whatever one is given, there is another more powerful by which the first can be destroyed. (*E*, IV, A1)

The first noticeable aspect of this axiom is that it coposits being and power. The axiom expresses the imbrication of the ontological and the political. This imbrication, significantly, introduces inequality of power. Ultimately, everyone will be overpowered by an external cause. For an attentive reader of the *Ethics*, this should come as no surprise. Already Proposition 28 of Part I of the *Ethics* announces that every finite mode has a cause, which entails that there is always something more powerful than us because we are all subject to external causes and something acts upon us as a cause if it is stronger than us.[9] The difference from the earlier Proposition 28 is that in Part I the idea is discussed from the perspective of the modes, whereas the Axiom to Part IV articulates the idea in terms of how power unfolds within the totality of the single substance, or Nature. This consolidates the interdependence of power and the ontological. Power is not simply a political concept—it is not solely *potestas*. Power also has an ontological dimension—it is *potentia*. Being, for Spinoza, is political.

To delineate Spinoza's critique of equality, we need to elaborate on the three senses of equality mentioned above. These are the senses of procedural, material and desertful equality. These three senses work in tandem to produce political authority. But the image of the authority presented is different, depending on whether the three senses are presented as working in tandem, or as being in conflict, or, finally, whether a sense of harmony or equilibrium based on equality is posited as an ante-political space. By positioning himself against these three different ways that the three senses of equality have been organized in the Western philosophical thought in order to produce state equality, Spinoza suggests his own conception of equality.

The three senses of equality in collaboration: The production of authority

To discern both the critical aspect of Spinoza's reworking of equality and the positive articulation of his position, it is necessary to start with Aristotle, who developed in the *Nicomachean Ethics* the earliest sustained discussion of equality that has survived in the philosophical canon and which has had a profound influence in subsequent elaborations of state equality in theory and in politics. According to Book V of the *Nicomachean Ethics*, equality is a species of justice.[10] Aristotle distinguishes two types of equality. One is referred to as arithmetical equality or corrective justice (διορθωτικό δίκαιον).[11] This equality pertains to justice in private transactions (τὸ δ' ἐν τοῖς συναλλάγμασι δίκαιον).[12] Aristotle's example is of a judge who needs to determine reparations for damages. The judge's job is to determine the equality between the loss and its compensation. For instance, if someone steals $10 he should repay exactly the same amount. From a political perspective, geometrical equality is the significant one.[13] This is a distributive justice (τὸ ἐν διανομῇ δίκαιον) that utilizes a value or merit to determine equality by analogy.[14] "All are agreed that justice in distributions must be based on desert of some sort."[15] Equality in a political context is not determined by a mathematical formula but by what one deserves.

The sense of geometric equality has dominated the Western philosophical tradition—or, to be more precise, a problem about geometric equality that Aristotle is acutely aware of has been the major source of thinking about state equality in political theory. Aristotle immediately qualifies his assertion about the universal agreement on desertful equality: "although they do not all mean the same sort of desert." Geometric equality gives rise to a fundamental political dispute—to which we will turn later. Aristotle continues: "democrats make the criterion free birth; those of oligarchical sympathies wealth; … upholders of aristocracy make it virtue."[16] These three different senses of geometric equality provide, then, three different determinations of the desert or merit of political equality. I pointed out in the previous section that all three were present in Solon's reforms, which established state equality, and I identified them, respectively, as the procedural equality, as material equality and as equality of worth. Aristotle is clear that equality is not some kind of metaphysical quality but a way in which the three regimes of constituted power that his system allows—a classification which remains totally unchallenged at least until the development of the social contract tradition two millennia later—anticipate the legal context of power relations between citizens. We can draw an analogy from Aristotle's position of equality as a species of justice to say that within this tradition the different forms of constituted power—democracy, oligarchy, and aristocracy—are species of equality. Equality is the sense of justice that underwrites political regimes of power.

Almost every theory of state equality includes all three forms of equality, but privileges only one of them.[17] The way that the three senses of equality work together determines which regime is preferred. We can give an example by turning to John Rawls' theory of justice as fairness. Rawls indicates that his aim is to use the notion of pure procedural justice as the basis of his theory. This leads him to reformulate the traditional notion of the state of nature to what he calls "an original position." This is envisaged as stripped of all personal interests—in Kantian terms, it is separate from natural causality—and thereby leaves individuals equal to exercise their rationality to form moral principles of justice.[18] At the same time, Rawls distinguishes two principles of justice. The first principle is the articulation of the original equality into a system of rights. This corresponds to what I called "procedural equality." The second principle is concerned with how to deal with social and economic inequalities. Under this second principle, Rawls tackles the issue of material equality and equality of worth (e.g., under the topic of the equality of opportunity). However, consistent with the starting point that expresses a pure procedural justice, Rawls insists on a hierarchy of principles, whereby the first principle strictly precedes the second one. Thus Rawls both deals with all three forms of equality and at the same times privileges one of them, the procedural. This becomes the basis for legitimating political authority—it forms the basis of the kind of liberal democracy that Rawls advocates.

The strategy of utilizing all three forms of geometric justice in legitimizing authority is typical of the way in which Western philosophical thought has approached state equality. It is important to note that the same three ingredients can be—and have been—used to develop anti-democratic positions about equality. The binding element is that the three senses of equality are all retained even though a justification is provided as to why one of them is privileged. For instance, the Greek neo-Nazi party, Golden Dawn, describes its "Identity" in twelve propositions. The last one reads: "The Popular state of Nationalism determines that equal opportunity is based on worth and it does not ignore the law of difference in Nature. Respecting the mental, national and genetic inequality of humans we can build a just society of equality before the law."[19] The three senses of equality are easily identifiable. Both the procedural equality before the law and the material equality of equal opportunity are based on an equality of worth, which is understood in racial terms by appeal to some kind of natural law of difference. I do not want to engage here with the content of this argument but to point out its form, which privileges one while identifying all three forms of geometric equality that Aristotle defines in *Nicomachean Ethics*. In the sense that Golden Dawn uses the three senses of equality in order to legitimate its actions and authority, this neo-Nazi determination of equality aligns itself with the Western philosophical tradition of thinking about state equality in terms of the Aristotelian geometric equality.

The Axiom to Part IV of the *Ethics* speaks of inequality of power in the sense that it is incommensurate with state equality. The "in" of "inequality" is a privative not of equality tout court but of the three senses of equality that we have inherited from Aristotle's geometric equality. But what is it exactly that the Axiom to Part IV rejects? The short answer is: authority. Spinoza seeks to define a sense of equality in democracy that is distinct from the sense of state equality related by the tradition. Spinoza uses the ontological dimension of the Axiom to Part IV—the fact that everyone can be overpowered by external causes—to show the importance of building communities where power is shared. According to Proposition 36, "The greatest good of those who seek virtue is common to all, and can be enjoyed by all equally." Spinoza argues for a common space where democracy unfolds because of the power interactions of the citizens. It is important to recall here that according to Definition 8 of Part IV of the *Ethics*, "virtue and power ... [are] the same thing." The seeking of virtue unfolds within differential power dynamics where power is never distributed equally between the participants. Even though—or, rather, *because*—the power dynamics are never in a state of equilibrium, Spinoza still insists on a sense of equality. Spinoza's is an equality in the participation and engagement of contestation. Or, in Spinoza's terms, virtue as power is not a quality that is given in advance and independently of the particular situation only in order to legitimate authority, but rather the enactment of one's power in a space in common with others. The Axiom to Part IV is the Spinozan expression of equality.

The question, then, becomes: How can Spinoza's equality respond to the political authority produced by the collaboration between the three senses of equality? Or, differently put, how can the imbrication of the ontological and the political deal with consolidated forms of constituted power? Filippo del Lucchese gives a simple and compelling answer in *Conflict, Power, and Multitude in Machiavelli and Spinoza*. At the heart of his account is the Axiom to Part IV understood in ontologico-political terms. The reason is that the axiom establishes a relational ontology, which consists in the mutual limitation of entities. As Lucchese puts it: "Relationship immediately takes precedence over essence and the relationship involved is primarily conflictual."[20] The conflictual nature of this relational ontology leads Lucchese to argue that Spinoza develops a theory of agonistic democracy. As I have argued elsewhere, a relational ontology offers the means both to resist constituted power and to create a space to encounter the other as a partner and agonist.[21] Differently put, echoing Lucchese's vocabulary, there is no essence in the justification of violence characteristic of sovereignty, while at the same time being is conflictual.

As a consequence, the Axiom to Part IV prevents the assumption of an absolute political power. To make this point, Lucchese turns to Proposition 28 of Part I of the *Ethics*, which, as already intimated, is closely linked to the Axiom to Part IV. Proposition 28 holds that every finite mode has a determinate cause—the position which the Axiom to Part IV generalizes to include the whole of nature. In the important Scholium to Proposition 28, Spinoza notes that "God is absolutely the proximate cause of the things produced immediately by him." The insertion of God within the realm of causality that ultimately includes everything that exists opposes a conception of the divine as standing outside the laws of nature and directing at will human affairs. In other words, "the idea of reciprocal determination of finite things" not only rejects "the Aristotelian doctrine of the prime mover and the idea of transitivity in the relationship between cause and effect." In addition, Lucchese continues, it "impedes us from modeling reality in terms of a finalistic explanation."[22] Now, this has clear political implications. Just as Spinoza's God is part of all the relations between beings and cannot be said to stand outside or above these relations, similarly the sovereign is part of the relations between citizens but without standing above the law dictating, as if from above, political actions. A sovereign's authority is delimited by the conflictual nature of relationality. To understand authority from the perspective of the Axiom to Part IV and of equality entails that a sovereign is always subject to be overpowered by the people. A "sovereign power [is] continuously exposed to the judgment ... of its subjects."[23] Or, to provide another quotation that encapsulates the main thesis of Lucchese's important book: "Whenever there is a power [i.e. constituted power], there is also resistance."[24] Such a conception, then, of agonistic democracy, as it arises out of the Axiom to Part IV, necessitates the limitation of political authority. No authority can hold itself to be absolute because it is always liable to be overpowered.

The three senses of equality in conflict: The destruction of the polis

There is also a long tradition within political philosophy, also going back to Aristotle, which does not focus on the production of power through the synergies between the three senses of equality, but rather on how the antagonism between the three senses of equality results in destructive political conflict. It is no longer about how the political authority is produced; rather, it is about which political authority prevails—it is not the genetic question but rather the question of realist politics. This different move is most evident in Aristotle's *Politics*.

In Book V of *Politics*, Aristotle singles out equality as the cause of the most abominable kind of conflict, civil war.[25] In the opening of Book V, echoing the *Nicomachean Ethics*, Aristotle specifies the three constitutions in terms of how each of them defines geometric equality, while also arguing that the dispute about the different determinations of equality is destructive: "Democracy arose from men's thinking that if they are equal in any respect they are equal absolutely, … oligarchy arose from their assumption that if they are unequal as regards some one thing they are unequal wholly."[26] The dispute between the democrats and the oligarchs is about state equality. This dispute about equality between democrats and oligarchs is the "principal cause" of conflict in the city.[27] At the same time, aristocracy is not immune from the influence of equality in precipitating infighting: "And of all men those who excel in virtue would most justifiably stir up faction [στασιάζοιεν], though they are the least given to doing so."[28] The most desertful ones are the most justified in leading a dispute, even though their superior virtue, contends Aristotle, prevents them from doing so.

The tripartite sense of political equality extrapolated by Aristotle asserts political authority. But such a constituted power is not an authority that is universally acceptable. Nor is it an authority immune from attack. It is a contested authority that is liable to change. What happens, however, when such change is resisted by constituted authority or when conflicting interests clash? At this point there arises the possibility of bloody conflict that is destructive of the polis. The notion of state equality has always been accompanied by the threat of such a destruction. And even if equality is not always perceived as the primary cause of civil war, still it is rare to see a call to revolt without support from the concept of equality, in whatever sense it may be configured.

The agonistic description of the political arising from Proposition 36 to Part IV of the *Ethics*—"The greatest good of those who seek virtue is common to all, and can be enjoyed by all equally"—is radically distinct from bloody conflict. Instead, Spinoza sees in it the possibility of collaboration or a space of commonality. Proposition 37 of Part IV asserts: "The good which everyone who seeks virtue wants for himself, he also desires for other men." I will return to this proposition in more detail later, but suffice to say here that for Spinoza the other is not an entity with a distinct identity. One's identity is produced through the other. What one thinks and what one desires are not autonomous activities but rather conditioned in a process of transformation that is precipitated by the other. One's being is always a being with. Here, ontology and power meet, since for Spinoza virtue is power. And this also means that the ontological and the political converge on this site. The political import of this insight is highlighted by Spinoza himself, who asserts in Scholium 1 to Proposition 37 that "I have … shown what the foundations of the state are."

There is one important implication of this reconfiguration of conflict so that it is no longer a struggle *for* power but rather the struggle *of* power: Because no one is immune from being overpowered by external causes, because everyone is subjected to external causes, Lucchese observes, "the collective body holds more absolute power."[29] Here is perhaps a definition of the multitude from the perspective of the Axiom to Part IV: the struggle that takes place in interpersonal relations, and which resists at any point subordination to a single authority. From this perspective, the constitutive characteristic of democracy is not procedural, material or desertful equality, but rather the agon that is possible because of differential power and which creates the multitude. From this perspective, the multitude is the community that is held together by the conflictual relations necessitated by the inequality of differential power.

Equality as ante-political: Equality and the construction of sovereignty

Can a founding account of political authority, which also bypasses the conflict between the different senses of geometric equality, be given? The question of the foundation of political authority is intertwined with the justification of the operation of power. The foundation of political authority that also seeks to resolve the conflict of equality has been a significant and oft-repeated move. It consists in the positing of an ante-political space of equality, which leads to various formulations of state equality. This is a crucial and complex move in political theory, since it develops alongside the conception of sovereign power.

I only have time to discuss here very few facets of this complex move, and I will necessarily have to rely on the genealogy of sovereignty that I develop in my *Sovereignty and Its Other*. I distinguish there between three types of sovereignty—ancient, modern and biopolitical. I argue that each form of sovereignty has its own logic, even though they are all related. I will present here how these three forms of sovereignty are depend on the presupposition of an ante-political space of equality, and how Spinoza's conception of equality counters all three conceptions. I will present the three positions with references to specific philosophers, namely, Augustine, Hobbes and Kant.

Augustine: Ancient sovereignty

Augustine's relating of the Fall is the source of the conception of an ante-political equality in the same move that constructs the free will. What in Genesis was the Garden of Eden, becomes in Augustine paradise (*paradiso*) as a space of perfect happiness: "How happy, then, were the first human beings, neither troubled by any disturbance of the mind not pained by any disorder of the body!"[30] As a result of this harmony and equilibrium, "in Paradise ... there arose in him who dwelt there no desire or fear to hinder his good will. ... A faithful fellowship of honest love existed."[31] The story of the paradise is not simply an allegory, according to Augustine, but a true reality in which such an equality existed.[32] It was only when the protoplasts, through "an act of free will," ate the forbidden fruit that they became subject to sin.[33] There is free will in order for morality to exist, which in its turn underwrites political authority. But the exercise of the free will takes place in a space of absolute happiness and equality. The Augustinian transformation of the Garden of Eden into such a paradise becomes the prototype of the idea of a natural, ante-political space of absolute equality.

It is important to stress the originality of Augustine's account, which resides precisely in the determination of the Garden of Eden as a paradise of perfect happiness and equality and the Fall as the consequence of the original sin of Adam and Eve. This account, the so-called Augustinian theodicy, is not the only account of the expulsion from the Garden of Eden. Besides the well-known fact that the *Genesis* does not describe Eden other than as an earthly garden of pastoral simplicity, John Hick also shows in his classic study *Evil and the God of Love* that there are competing accounts of the Fall in the Eastern Tradition. Hick singles out in particular Irenaeus, who "pictures Adam and Eve in the Garden of Eden as children; and their sin is accordingly not presented as a damnable revolt, but rather as calling forth God's compassion on account of their weakness and vulnerability."[34] According to this alternative tradition, Eden is no paradise where the protoplasts live in blessed equality, nor is there any need for the invention of the free will in order to account for the Fall. Instead, Adam and Eve are weak, vulnerable and easily deceived. Before Augustine, the idea of a natural, ante-political space of equality is absent.[35] This idea now provides the Aristotelian conception of geometric equality with a foundation used by the Western political philosophical tradition to account for the genesis of the political. The ante-political equality is not simply the foundation of state equality but foundational of the entire conception of sovereignty.

Spinoza counters Augustinian theodicy as it is clear from the rejection of the distinction between good and evil in the *Ethics*. According to the preface of Part IV, "good and evil ... indicate nothing positive in things, considered in themselves, nor are they anything other than modes of thinking, or notions we form because we compare things to one another." It is our interpretation of things that makes them good or evil, and this interpretation, as the Axiom to Part IV explains, is part of the relations of power that we form with things and other humans. Spinoza continues: "For one and the same thing can, at the same time, be good, and bad, and also indifferent." Eating the apple is definitely something bad for a resident of the Garden of Eden who does not want to be expelled. And yet, eating an apple in the "fallen world" can be nutritious and appealing to the sense of taste. The rejection of the existence of good and evil in the Preface of Part IV of the *Ethics* is intricately linked both to the Axiom to Part IV and to the definition of virtue as power.

The idea of the natural condition of the human is diametrically different in Spinoza and Augustine.[36] The Christian Father posits the ante-political naturalness of paradise in order to explain the existence of evil in the fallen world. Spinoza's rejection of good and evil subverts the entire structure of the Augustinian argument that invented a sense of equality as a foundational element of the political. For if there is no good and evil, then that space that generates their existence via the operation of the free will—that is, the ante-political space of equality—also does not exist. What is natural is not a paradisiac garden of absolute equality, but rather the fact that nothing escapes causality and hence everything is subject to be overpowered by something else. Differently put, according to Augustine there is no efficient cause for the existence of evil; rather, its existence out of nothing is the creation of the free will. Spinoza responds that nothing can occur without a cause. There is no creation out of nothing for Spinoza. And this means that there is a natural inequality of power since the cause is always more powerful than the effect.

Significantly, Spinoza's rejection of the possibility of a paradisiac ante-political space entails Definition 8 of Part IV. As we saw earlier, this definition holds that virtue and power are one and the same thing. This means that the political is not confined to human relations regulated either by formally instituted laws or transcendental moral laws, which determine in either case what virtue is. Rather, so long as there is an other, there is power. Being is being with. And virtue consists in the participation within this power dynamic. The co-implication of virtue with power and the rejection of good and evil tightly support each other. They show that for Spinoza the ethical is imbricated with the ontological and the political. Conversely, the morality that arises from the supposition of a paradisiac equality and which underwrites Christian conceptions of sovereignty is precisely the rejection of such an imbrication. The combination of the Axiom to Part IV, which shows the differential power that regulates relations, and Definition 8, which links virtue and power, leads to Spinoza's reconception of equality, which consists in participation in the differential power relations within a communal space. The relations cannot be in equilibrium because power is never distributed in equal measure—power is never reducible to geometric equality. Rather, relations unfold in conflict, that is, as the agonistic interactions within a field of relations.

Hobbes: Modern sovereignty

The modern conception of sovereignty transforms the Augustinian paradise into the concept of the state of nature. This is a significant transformation, which has multiple effects. For instance, the state of nature is now not harmonious but rather a state of war and deadly violence. I do not intend to go into the details of this transformation here. I only want to point that one thing remains constant in the transformation of paradise into the state of nature, namely the positing of an ante-political space of absolute equality. The best example here is Thomas Hobbes' description of the state of nature in Chapter 13 of the *Leviathan*: "Nature hath made men so equall, in the faculties of body, and mind ... as that one man can thereupon claim to himselfe any benefit, to which another may not pretend, as well as he." There is an absolute equality, not only of mind but even of body, Hobbes says. "From this equality of ability, ariseth equality of hope in the attaining of our Ends." The coupling of equality with the freedom of desire entails that people might have similar ends—people might want the same thing. What is the result of this coupling? "And therefore if any two men desire the same thing, which neverthelesse they cannot both enjoy, they become enemies; and in the way to their End ... endeavour to destroy, or subdue one another."[37] The result is enmity. Ante-political equality plus freedom—that is, precisely the conjunction that characterizes Augustinian theodicy—is the cause of the war of all against all according to Hobbes. Or, to put the same point in the famous phrase from *De Cive*, "Man to Man is an arrant Wolfe [*Homo homini Lupus*]."[38] For the contractarian tradition, natural man is not a political animal but a carnivore who lusts after its fellow citizen's blood. Only the renunciation of this natural state of equality in favor of the founding of a sovereign state can guarantee order, peace and stability.

Hobbes' extrapolation of the state of nature can be understood as a combination of the Augustinian paradise with the sense of stasis found in Thucydides' *History of the Peloponnesian War*. A translation of Thucydides' *History* was the first published work by Hobbes as well as the first ever translation into English of the "father of historiography."[39] Thucydides describes as stasis the conflict that erupted between the different Hellenic city states, thereby leading to their destruction. Hobbes translated this negative sense of stasis not as civil war but rather as "sedition." The choice of words is significant. Even though sedition as a translation of stasis has an established Latin precedent, still sedition is something that cannot possibly be justified. Stasis as sedition is the destruction of the polis. This problem, which Aristotle would have described as the conflict between the different senses of equality, impresses upon Hobbes that what comes before the establishment of the political is not a paradise, but rather the inferno of sedition or stasis. In Augustine's paradise, God can speak directly to the protoplasts. In Hobbes' state of nature, the gods have departed to leave the stage to immanent destruction. And yet, the transcendent element is retained by Hobbes, but now transferred to the commonwealth, which needs a "mortal God" or sovereign to supervise over the cessation of sedition. In this sense, Hobbes' commonwealth is Augustine's Eden. The frontispiece of the *Leviathan* represents the sovereign as the Adam of the state, out of whose flesh the entire body politic is constructed. Except that the Adam/sovereign is given a transcendent dimension with characteristics of the divine. Both Hobbes and Augustine posit an ante-political equality in order to assert transcendent authority. The brute immanence of the state of nature or sedition can only be overcome by the introduction of a transcendent authority, which turns the "arrant wolfe" into a citizen subjected to authority.

The famous sentence from the Scholium to Proposition 35 from Part IV of the *Ethics*, according to which "Man is a God to man," is a riposte to Hobbes. This is not only because of the contrast between the structural similarity and conceptual discrepancy to the statement from *De Cive*. In addition, the development of the argument in Propositions 33–35 points squarely to an engagement with Hobbes. According to Proposition 33, "Men can disagree in nature insofar as they are torn by affects which are passions." The basis of disagreement is not, as in Hobbes, equality and freedom. Rather, it is the presence of passions. The Scholium to the following Proposition clarifies further: "it is far from true that they [i.e. humans] are troublesome to one another insofar as they love the same thing and agree in nature. Instead ... the cause of [their enmity] is nothing but the fact that (as we suppose) they disagree in nature." The fact that they have an equal right and license to love the same thing does not entail enmity, since enmity consists in being slave to passions that blind one from the fact that others have an equal right and freedom toward the same object. Instead, enmity arises from difference in nature, that is, in the differential power relations that can be both productive when pursued virtuously, and destructive when dominated by the passions. And Proposition 35 asserts: "Only insofar as men live according to the guidance of reason, must they always agree in nature." This guidance of reason is not separated from emotions. Indeed, it is bound up with virtue, which, according to Definition 8 of Part IV, is the same as *potentia*. Thus, reason includes the recognition of the differential power presented in the Axiom to Part IV, according to which everyone can be overpowered by an external cause. Potentia entails differential power. But the effect of this inequality of power is that "man is a god to man," which means that we need the other in order to create the space of contestation that makes democracy possible. This agonistic space does not require a transcendent authority to supervise over it and to regulate it, since it is the immanent unfolding of power relations. Thus, Spinoza's affirmation of power inequality is a riposte to Hobbes' supposition of an absolute ante-political equality, which legitimizes a sovereign power. This riposte is conducted in the name of democracy, by transforming the war of all against all to an agon of all against all. Differently put, the Axiom to Part IV precludes the possibility of a Hobbesian state of nature.

Kant: Biopolitical power

For Kant, the moral law produces freedom. But both the moral law and its freedom can never be fully accommodated within being. The fundamental premise of the moral law, as it is conceived by Kant, is that the particular is never the basis of moral judgment. We can see here the fundamental biopolitical move of positing a physical body, which may be capable of cognition, but which nevertheless needs to be supervised and normalized by a higher authority. This higher authority in Kant is the moral law, which, as is made clear in the *Doctrine of Right*, precedes politics. Kant establishes the moral law based on a notion of ante-political equality. In the *Groundwork of the Metaphysics of Morals*, Kant constructs this ante-political equality in the guise of the "Kingdom of Ends": "all rational beings stand under the *law* that each of them is to treat himself and all others *never merely as means* but always *at the same time as ends in themselves*. But from this there arises a systematic union of rational beings through common objective laws, that is, a kingdom, which can be called a kingdom of ends."[40] Treating the other never as a means but only as an end in itself entails that the other is never measured. The other never becomes part of a calculation. This entails, first, that power relations between human beings are never a concern in such a kingdom of ends, which thus remains ante-political. Second, it entails an absolute equality between human beings, in the sense that from the perspective of the moral law, we are all absolutely equal.

John Rawls clearly recognizes the Kantian strategy of asserting an ante-political equality as the foundation for the justification of a biopolitical—and liberal—sense of sovereign power.[41] The first part of the strategy is to assert that moral principles underwrite the political. As Rawls says, with explicit reference to Kant, "Once we think of moral principles as legislation for a kingdom of ends, it is clear that these principles must not only be acceptable to all but public as well." If the kingdom of ends and its categorical imperative point to a notion of humanity, if they are common to every human being, then this commonality itself becomes the basis for the "public," that is, for political authority. But this is not the same as politics itself, since "Kant supposes that this moral legislation is to be agreed to under conditions that characterize men as free and equal rational beings." The kingdom of ends can instate freedom and equality only because it is separate from the tumult of the everyday. It is in fact necessary, suggests Rawls, to think of it as prior to political authority, or, in his terms, as an "original position." Rawls' indebtedness to Kant is explicit: "The description of the original position is an attempt to interpret this conception [i.e. the kingdom of ends]."[42] The Kantian strategy consists in positing ante-political equality as separate from particularity, independent of immanent interests, and thus it is opposed to Hobbes' state of nature. Further, it is linked not to a non-human transcendent authority, but to an authority derived from humanity itself, which now becomes an end in itself.

We can find in the *Ethics* a response to this position too. The starting point is the equation of virtue and power according to Definition 8 of Part IV. This equation evades the Kantian position according to which there is a moral law to which every human action is answerable. If virtue is power, then instead of a law outside causality, human actions follow the patterns of the unfolding of power relations. This entails that the other is part of the system of calculation of power dynamics. Thus, in the Corollary 1 to Proposition 35 Spinoza avers: "There is no singular thing in Nature which is more useful to man than a man who lives according to the guidance of reason." In other words, "man is a god to man" so long as men realize the fundamental inequality of power relations. And Spinoza takes this thought to its logical conclusion in Corollary 2 to the same Proposition: "When each man most seeks his own advantage for himself, then men are most useful to one another." Human relations are power relations. This entails the opposite of Kant's position, namely, men are means to each other. There is nothing more ethical for Spinoza than this "kingdom of means." The recognition of the inherent usefulness of man to man is a principle of Spinoza's democracy. According to Proposition 37—which, significantly, according to the

Scholium, concludes the discussion of "what the foundations of the state are"—it is this inherent usefulness that leads to a sense of community: "The good, which everyone who seeks virtue wants for himself, he also desires for other men." The inequality of power relations does not have to lead to the exploitation of one man by another. Instead, the recognition of the inequality of power as the fact that differential power relations are the basis of interaction is the condition of participating and cooperating in the struggles and contestations that form society. More emphatically, there is society so long as there are these contestations. We cannot exist with others in a virtuous way unless we realize that, just like us, their aim is to increase their power. Differently put, human relationality is premised on power inequality whereby man is a means to others. We can be with others only if we are attuned to this power differential—that is, so long as we are attuned to static equality.

* * *

We have seen, then, that the thinking of equality within the Western philosophical and political tradition goes back to Aristotle's conception of geometric equality. The important aspect of geometric equality is that it guarantees a sense of authority. But the difficulty is that it cannot account for the competing claims of different articulations of geometric equality to hold sway over this authority. There is a civil war in nuce within geometric equality. To bypass this difficulty and to establish sovereign authority, an ante-political space of absolute equality is posited. Spinoza stands opposed to this triple move of equality. He challenges the establishment of authority through the Axiom to Part IV, which is incommensurable with the possibility of absolute power and which delineates a space in common. The Spinozan position allows for a conceptualization of equality which is not dependent on authority, but consists rather in the equality of access to participation in the differential unfolding of power.

Notes

1 For an account of the reception of Spinoza's thought, see Christopher Norris, "Spinoza and the Conflict of Interpretations," in ed. by Dimitris Vardoulakis, *Spinoza Now* (Minneapolis: University of Minnesota Press, 2011), 3–37. I am using the qualification "almost" to indicate the wide variety of interpretations of what Spinoza's conception of democracy consist in. For instance, whereas

1. Leo Strauss is adamant that Spinoza "was the philosopher who founded liberal democracy," Negri on the contrary is equally adamant that Spinoza rejects liberal democracy in favor of what he calls "absolute democracy." See respectively *Spinoza's Critique of Religion* (New York: Schocken, 1965), 16; and, Antonio Negri, "*Reliqua desiderantur*: A Conjecture for a Definition of the Concept of Democracy in the final Spinoza," in *Subversive Spinoza: (Un)contemporary Variations*, trans. Timothy S. Murphy et al. (Manchester: Manchester University Press, 2004), 9–27.

2. This is not the case with the other important concept for democracy, namely, freedom. Spinoza thematizes freedom explicitly: for instance, the entire *Tractatus Theologico-Politicus* is, as the subtitle says, a defense of the "freedom to philosophize." And, there are numerous articles and monographs on Spinoza's conception of freedom—which are in fact so well-known that I will not list them here.

3. I know of only two articles which attempt to deal systematically with Spinoza's theory of equality: Michael Hoffheimer, "The Four Equals: Analyzing Spinoza's Idea of Equality," *Philosophia*, 15.3 (1985), 237–49, and, Beth Lord, "Spinoza, Equality, and Hierarchy," *History of Philosophy Quarterly*, 31.1 (2014), 59–78. They attempt to synthesize scattered remarks about equality in Spinoza's works. However none of them attempts to situate these remarks in relation the position that Spinoza rejects. I argue in this paper that it is crucial to understand Spinoza's engagement with the conception of equality, going back to Aristotle, which has dominated the Western philosophical tradition.

4. Aristotle, *Athenian Constitution*, in *The Athenian Constitution; The Eudemian Ethics; On Virtues and Vices*, trans. H. Rackham (Cambridge, MA: Harvard University Press, 1935), V.2.

5. Jacques Rancière discusses the Athenian election to office by lot with reference to Plato's *Laws* in *Hatred of Democracy*, trans. Steve Corcoran (London: Verso, 2006), 40–41. Opposing the Platonic critique, Rancière describes election by lot as the "scandal [which] lies in the disjoining of entitlements to govern from any analogy to those that order social relations" (41). Thus Rancière presents election by lot to accord with his own conception of democracy as based on the contingent and on the erasure of all hierarchies or "entitlements." But the Solonian innovation to elect officers of the state by lot is far less radical than Rancière wants it to be. In fact, according to *The Athenian Constitution*, election by lot is simply an expression of Solon's assertion of the virtue of every citizen, which is wholly in accord with the conception of geometric equality that Rancière is critical of.

6. See especially Jacques Rancière, *Disagreement: Politics and Philosophy*, trans. Julie Rose (Minneapolis: University of Minnesota Press, 1999); and, *The Ignorant Schoolmaster Schoolmaster: Five Lessons in Intellectual Emancipation*, trans. Kristin Ross (Stanford, CA: Stanford University Press, 1991).

7   The important point is that, despite their similarities, Rancière retains a notion of the free will, while Spinoza does not. I develop this comparison in detail in my *Democracy and Violence* (forthcoming).

8   Antonio Negri, *The Savage Anomaly: The Power of Spinoza's Metaphysics and Politics*, trans. Michael Hardt (Minneapolis: University of Minnesota Press, 1991), 158. Filippo del Lucchese also says: "It would be difficult to exaggerate the importance of this axiom. … [T]his startling axiom … can in any case serve as a backdrop to the entire *Ethics*." *Conflict, Power, and Multitude in Machiavelli and Spinoza* (London: Continuum, 2009), 52.

9   This also can be understood in a rather prosaic way: we are all subject to death to the extent that sooner or later there will be an external cause that is so much more powerful that it will end our life.

10 As a species of justice, equality is connected to the pursuit of virtue. Even though the link with virtue provides an initial point of contact with Spinoza, Aristotle qualifies equality in a specific, limited sense. See Aristotle, *Nicomachean Ethics*, trans. H. Rackham (Cambridge, MA: Harvard University Press, 2003), 1130b, 6–10.

11 Aristotle, *Nicomachean Ethics*, 1131b, 25.

12 Aristotle, *Nicomachean Ethics*, 1131b, 38.

13 The distinction between arithmetic and geometric equality can also be found in Plato. For instance, see *Laws*, trans. E.G. Burry (Cambridge, MA: Harvard University Press, 1961), 757, B-C. However, Aristotle's discussion in *Nicomachean Ethics* Book V is the most detailed one that has been preserved from ancient Greek philosophy.

14 I retain here the term "distributive justice" to describe geometrical equality because it has been the traditional translation of the expression τὸ ἐνδιανομῇ δίκαιον. This is a misleading translation, given that distributive justice in English denotes the distribution of goods and wealth in a social or economic context. The word "διανομή" in Greek is closely related to νόμος, the law. This should be read in conjunction with Aristotle's assertion that "the actions that spring from virtue in general [i.e. the actions that are just] are in the main identical with the actions that are according to law" (Aristotle, *Nicomachean Ethics*, 1130b, 23–25). From this perspective, a more cumbersome but nevertheless more accurate rendering of "διανομή" would be "a justice that performs or enacts a legal or legitimate action." There is of course a lot more to say about the use of this word to denote justice from the perspective of geometrical equality, but I simply wanted to point out here the infelicitous translation of "distributive justice" into English.

15 Aristotle, *Nicomachean Ethics*, 1131b, 25–26. The strength of geometric equality—namely, that it avoids the reductionism of measuring human relations by being based on a metier of equality—is also its greatest weakness, since such a metier is never self-evident. For a succinct presentation of this criticism, see Harry Frankfurt, "The Moral Irrelevance of Equality," *Public Affairs Quarterly*, 14.2 (2000), 87–103.

16 Aristotle, *Nicomachean Ethics*, 1131b, 26–29.
17 I am saying "almost" so as to include the possibility that a sense of equality can exist which does not depend on geometric equality, such as Rancière's mentioned earlier.
18 John Rawls, *A Theory of Justice* (Cambridge, MA: Belknap Press, 1999, 2nd revised edition), see, for example, 104 and 122.
19 "Tautotita" [Identity], http://www.xryshaygh.com/index.php/kinima, my translation (accessed January 2014).
20 Lucchese, *Conflict, Power, and Multitude*, 52.
21 See my *Sovereignty and Its Other: Toward the Dejustification of Violence* (New York: Fordham University Press, 2013) and in *Democracy and Violence* (forthcoming).
22 Lucchese, *Conflict, Power, and Multitude*, 17.
23 Lucchese, *Conflict, Power, and Multitude*, 37.
24 Lucchese, *Conflict, Power, and Multitude*, 42.
25 I should note another terminological difficulty with the English translation of Aristotle at this point. At the opening of Book V, Aristotle introduces the issue of the *metabole* of constitutions. This does not mean revolution in the modern senses, whereby revolution denotes a break from the past—the establishment of a new authority and a new era. Instead, *metabole* means change or transformation from one state to another. This idea resonates with Aristotle's classification of the three possible constitutions, namely, democracy, oligarchy and aristocracy. *Metabole* denotes the transition from one of the constitutions to one of the other two. Book V is about revolution in the sense of *metabole*.
26 Aristotle, *Politics*, trans. H. Rackham (Cambridge, MA.: Harvard University Press, 1998), 1301a, 29–30, 31–32. Cf. *Nicomachean Ethics*, 1131b, 26–29.
27 Aristotle, *Politics*, 1302a, 23–24.
28 Aristotle, *Politics*, 1301a, 39–40.
29 Lucchese, *Conflict, Power, and Multitude*, 135.
30 Augustine, *The City of God Against the Pagans*, ed. and trans. by R.W. Dyson (New York: Cambridge University Press, 1998), XIV.10.
31 Augustine, *City of God*, XIV.26.
32 Augustine, *City of God*, XIII.21.
33 Augustine, *City of God*, XIV.13.
34 John Hick, *Evil and the God of Love* (New York: Palgrave Macmillan, 2010 [1st ed. 1966]), 212.
35 The opposite has been argued by various scholars. For instance, under the influence of Hobbes' own interpretation in his introduction to his translation of Thucydides, scholars have argued that the Greeks already had a conception of the state of nature understood as such an ante-political space. I think that this is a mistaken interpretation. I cannot take this issue up here, but I discuss it in detail in Chapter 2 of *Sovereignty and Its Other*.

36 For the most detailed comparison between Spinoza and Augustine see Milad Doueihi, *Augustine and Spinoza*, trans. Jane Marie Todd (Cambridge, MA: Harvard University Press, 2010).
37 Thomas Hobbes, *Leviathan*, ed. by Richard Tuck (Cambridge: Cambridge University Press, 1999), 86–87.
38 Hobbes, *De Cive*, in ed. by H. Warrender, *The Clarendon Edition of the Philosophical Works of Thomas Hobbes*, vol. III (Oxford: Clarendon, 1983), §1.
39 Hobbes' translation of Thucydides can be found in volume 8 of *The English Works of Thomas Hobbes of Malmesbury*, ed. by William Molesworth (London: John Bohn, 1839), volume 8.
40 Immanuel Kant, *Groundwork of the Metaphysics of Morals*, trans. Mary Gregor (Cambridge: Cambridge University Press, 2002), 41.
41 On the correlation between biopolitics and liberalism, see Michel Foucault's lectures *The Birth of Biopolitics: Lectures at the Collège de France, 1978–79*, ed. by Michel Senellart, trans. Graham Burchell (New York: Palgrave Macmillan, 2008).
42 Rawls, *A Theory of Justice*, 221.

Bibliography

Acampora, Christa Davis. *Contenting Nietzsche*. Chicago: University of Chicago Press, 2013.
Aristotle. *Athenian Constitution*, in trans. by Harris Rackham, *The Athenian Constitution: The Eudemian Ethics: On Virtues and Vices*. Cambridge: Harvard University Press, 1935.
Aristotle. *Nicomachean Ethics*, trans. by Harris Rackham. Cambridge: Harvard University Press, 2013.
Aristotle. *Politics*, trans. by Harris Rackham. Cambridge: Harvard University Press, 1998.
Augustine. *The City of God against the Pagans*, trans. and ed. by R.W. Dyson. New York: Cambridge University Press, 1998.
Del Lucchese, Filippo. *Conflict, Power, and Multitude in Machiavelli and Spinoza*. London: Continuum, 2009.
Doueihi, Milad. *Augustine and Spinoza*. Translated by Jane Marie Todd. Cambridge, Mass.: Harvard University Press, 2010.
Foucault, Michel. *The Birth of Biopolitics: Lectures at the Collège de France, 1978–79*. Edited by Michel Senellart, translated by Graham Burchell. New York: Palgrave Macmillan, 2008.
Frankfurt, Harry. "The Moral Irrelevance of Equality", *Public Affairs Quarterly*, 14.2 (2000), 87–103.
Golden Dawn. "Tautotita" [Identity]. Translated by the author. Accessed January, 2014. http://www.xryshaygh.com/kinima

Hick, John. *Evil and the God of Love*. New York: Palgrave Macmillan, 2010.
Hobbes, Thomas. *De Cive*, in ed. by H. Warrender, *The Clarendon Edition of the Philosophical Works of Thomas Hobbes*, vol. III. Oxford: Clarendon, 1983.
Hobbes, Thomas. *Leviathan*, ed. by Richard Tuck. Cambridge: Cambridge University Press, 1999.
Hobbes, Thomas. *The English Works of Thomas Hobbes of Malmesbury*, vol. VIII, ed. by William Molesworth. London: John Bohn, 1839.
Hoffheimer, Michael. "The Four Equals: Analyzing Spinoza's Idea of Equality", *Philosphia*, 15.3 (1985), 237–49.
Kant, Immanuel. *Groundwork for the Metaphysics of Morals*, trans. by Mary Gregor. Cambridge: Cambridge University Press, 2002.
Lord, Beth. "Spinoza, Equality, and Hierarchy", *History of Philosophy Quarterly*, 31.1 (2014), 59–78.
Negri, Antonio. *The Savage Anomaly: The Power of Spinoza's Metaphysics and Politics*. Translated by Michael Hardt. Minneapolis: University of Minnesota Press, 1991.
Negri, Antonio. "*Reliqua desiderantur*: A Conjecture for a Definition of the Concept of Democracy in the final Spinoza", in *Subversive Spinoza: (Un)contemporary Variations*. Translated by Timothy S. Murphy et al. Manchester: Manchester U. P., 2004, 9–27.
Nietzsche, Friedrich. *On the Genealogy of Morality and Other Writings*. trans. by Carol Diethe and ed. by Keith Ansell-Pearson. Cambridge: Cambridge University Press, 2006.
Norris, Christopher. "Spinoza and the Conflict of Interpretations," in ed. Dimitris Vardoulakis, *Spinoza Now*. Minneapolis: University of Minnesota Press, 2011, 3–37.
Plato. *Laws*. Translated by E.G. Burry. Cambridge, Mass.: Harvard University Press, 1961.
Rancière, Jacques. *The Ignorant Schoolmaster Schoolmaster: Five Lessons in Intellectual Emancipation*. Translated by Kristin Ross. Stanford: Stanford University Press, 1991.
Rancière, Jacques. *Disagreement: Politics and Philosophy*. Translated by Julie Rose. Minneapolis: University of Minnesota Press, 1999.
Rancière, Jacques. *Hatred of Democracy*, trans. by Steve Corcoran. London: Verso, 2006.
Rawls, John. *A Theory of Justice*, 2nd revised edition. Cambridge: Belknap Press, 1999.
Strauss, Leo. *Spinoza's Critique of Religion*. New York: Schocken, 1965.
Vardoulakis, Dimitris. *Sovereignty and its Other: Toward the Dejustification of Violence*. New York: Fordham University Press, 2013.
Vardoulakis, Dimitris. *Democracy and Violence* (forthcoming).

2

Spinoza's Ethics and Politics of Freedom: Active and Passive Power

Aurelia Armstrong

Orientation: Ethical freedom and politics

In "Two Concepts of Liberty," Isaiah Berlin identifies two problems with the ideal of rational autonomy constructed within the tradition of positive liberty. His overarching concern is that this ideal represents freedom as a function of retreating into the inner citadel, and thus encourages an attitude of indifference toward our social and political circumstances. The other danger of the doctrine of liberation by reason is that, in identifying a single form of the rational life as an ideal of human perfection, it enables a "monstrous impersonation" whereby coercion comes to be seen as the very means to freedom. For Berlin, any perfectionist political program that pursues rational freedom as a normative goal risks becoming tyrannical.[1]

Recent work on Spinoza within the tradition of liberal political theory may be fruitfully understood as implicitly addressing Berlin's concerns about the dangers of positive liberty as a normative goal for politics. According to Douglas Den Uyl and Steven Smith, Spinoza avoids the dangers of perfectionism in politics because his conception of human perfectibility consists not in the transformation of an individual in accordance with a specific ideal, but rather in the realization of possibilities inherent in that individual, which she, crucially, develops autonomously. Spinozistic freedom, thus construed, belongs to a self-perfectionist tradition of autonomy, which is easily dissociated from politics since it includes as a constitutive condition of the freedom at which it aims that it is achievable only by the individual's own intellectual activity.[2] This interpretation of Spinozistic freedom as a form of "autonomous autonomy" rescues Spinoza from Berlin's worries about political perfectionism and paternalism, but only by confirming Berlin's suspicion that the ethical ideal of freedom as rational self-direction insulates the self from social and political realities.

This paper critically examines the grounds for the claim that Spinoza's *Ethics* is concerned with a type of freedom that politics is ill-suited to promote and questions the assumption that Spinoza's conception of freedom or activity is best understood in "profoundly individualistic" terms as the private pursuit of ethical perfection, or the self-realization of rational autonomy. I suggest that the hyper-individualistic conception of freedom attributed to Spinoza by some recent liberal theorists involves a distortion of Spinoza's account of ethical liberation, which has its source in a failure to adequately think through the complex relations between essential power, the internal causal activity of things, and external causes. To construe ethical liberation as the autonomous realization and expression of the rational self is, I suggest, to treat the individual as an ideally, or potentially, self-contained whole capable of acting and producing effects that follow from her nature by virtue of internal causal power alone. This view of the individual, and of the kind of activity of which she is capable, reflects a particular interpretation of Spinoza's conceptions of activity and freedom.

In the *Ethics*, Spinoza identifies freedom with activity and defines both in terms of causality. An individual who is active or free is described by Spinoza as the adequate cause of certain effects that follow from her nature, in the sense that these effects can be understood through her nature or essence alone rather than reflecting the influence of external things upon her (*E* III, D8).[3] If being an adequate cause is taken to mean that individual essences are, or could be, the sole, exclusive cause of the effects they produce, then Spinoza's ideal of active self-determination would indeed have to be described as a form of "autonomous autonomy," and nothing external to the individual could contribute to promoting it. It is, I suggest, this privileging of the perspective of essence in the account of individual freedom and activity that furnishes the metaphysical foundations for Spinoza's alleged political liberalism, and underpins the claim that Spinoza's ethical goal of freedom is a kind of activity that cannot be promoted by political means.

But is Spinozistic freedom best understood in terms of a power of acting that depends on internal resources alone? To imagine freedom in these terms conflicts with Spinoza's determinism, according to which, as finite existing modes, individuals are necessarily acted upon and affected by things in the world around them, without which, Spinoza tells us, they could "neither exist nor be determined to act" and to produce effects (*E* I, P28). To exist, for Spinoza, means to be a part of nature actively expressing the power of God in a determinate way through interaction with others. In order to account for the freedom and rational activity of *actually existing* individuals, then, one would have to adjust the interpretation of activity as adequate causation, or causal self-sufficiency, so as to allow for a co-production of effects; that is, a production of internal effects that both follows from and expresses the nature of the individual, so that it can be understood through her essence, while at the same time arising from external causes. I suggest that Spinoza offers just such a double view of activity in his theory of the affects, where he allows for passively produced transitions to states of greater activity, power and perfection. While passive joys indicate the beneficial influence of external causes acting on us, Spinoza suggests that at least some of these joys—those that involve an overall, sustained increase in an individual's power of acting—count as activities. For Spinoza, such reliably empowering joys are typically the product of relations with others who agree in nature with us.

We can understand the importance Spinoza accords to the notion of agreement (*convenientia*) in Part IV of the *Ethics* in light of his concern to outline the concrete conditions of empowerment and liberation for actually existing individuals. Agreement denotes a form of interaction in which the striving of each individual to preserve and develop his or her nature and power is supported, rather than thwarted, by the similar striving of others. A relation of agreement obtains when individuals are able to act together in the construction of a more powerful, common nature as a condition for the active self-development of each (*E* IV, P18S; *Ep.* 32). The more we manage to agree in nature, the less subject we are to the arbitrary power of external things and, consequently, the greater our power to act from the necessity of our own natures. If the process of producing agreements in nature is the very means by which debilitating compulsion by external things may become instead a form of liberating cooperation, then even constraints—insofar as they enable individuals to maximize agreements and minimize disagreements—contribute to increasing each individual's autonomy.

I understand autonomy here to entail both increasing power to act in reliably self-enhancing ways and decreasing subjection to the arbitrary power of external forces. In this sense, dependence on the power of the state, insofar as it promotes both these outcomes, increases our autonomy. In this light, contra the liberal interpretation, I suggest that if we are, as Spinoza contends, freer in a state this is not just because the state protects us from relationships that threaten our power, but also because a state constitutionally constrained to take the welfare and interests of all citizens into account acts positively as a vector for building relationships of agreement and cooperation, which enhance individual and collective power (*E* IV, P73).

The liberal interpretation and beyond

While there are different versions of the liberal interpretation, they share a commitment to the view that Spinoza's *Ethics* is concerned with a type of freedom that politics is ill-suited to promote. The rationale behind this judgment is relatively simple: the freedom that the *Ethics* exhorts us to pursue consists in intellectual liberation from the bondage of the passions through the formation of adequate ideas, that is, in rational self-determination, and it would be unrealistic to imagine that the state could act upon us to bring about this result. The claim here is not that the state is powerless to promote more rational forms of conduct, but rather that there is a crucial difference for Spinoza between being made to behave in a way that is consistent with reason, and genuinely rational activity or freedom. As Douglas Den Uyl explains, while the state may, through the external regulation of conduct, be able to encourage "as if" rational behavior in citizens, such behavior is not equivalent to freedom in Spinoza's sense because it is not a direct, active expression of our rational nature.[4]

The distinction between acting *in accordance with* reason and acting *from* reason serves to articulate the difference between those states in which the individual is passively directed by external forces, and those states in which she is internally self-directed, necessitated by her own power or, in other words, autonomous. For Den Uyl, it is Spinoza's conception of ethical freedom as active self-determination, the *autonomous* and *endogenous* development and perfection of the individual's essential nature, which renders it unsuitable as a normative goal for politics. As Den Uyl explains:

> to foster autonomy would mean we would have some clear conception of how to bring activity about through political means; but that would be odd, since activity is something that comes from within and not from without. Politics is always concerned with what is "outside" of us, in the ordinary sense of always operating in the public forum and in the technical Spinozistic sense that is connected to passivity.[5]

In this passage, Den Uyl appeals to the foundational distinctions of Spinoza's thought between activity and passivity, and interiority and exteriority in support of the claim that Spinoza's conception of ethical freedom is "deeply anti-political."[6] It is, he says, because Spinozistic activity "comes from within" that it cannot be fostered by "what is outside of us." Since Spinoza offers numerous examples of the ways in which our power of acting may be augmented by "what is outside of us," we must understand this appeal to the criterion of internality as an attempt to restrict what will count as genuine activity and freedom to those effects of which we are the adequate cause.[7] But while it is true that Spinoza identifies freedom with a power of producing effects that follow from and express one's nature, it does not follow from this definition that the power to produce self-preserving, internal effects is a function of internal causal power alone and, thus, that it cannot be fostered by what is outside us.

To generate *this* conclusion, it would be necessary to add the further qualification that, for Spinoza, freedom is a type of activity that is achievable only by the individual's own efforts. It is this understanding of Spinozistic freedom as the autonomous production of endogenous effects, and therefore as an essentially private project of "self-perfection through the adequacy of our ideas," that serves to justify the liberal view, according to which Spinoza regards politics as having only a very limited function, which is that of securing the negative conditions—freedom from violence and social discord—that would allow individuals to pursue the personal project of freedom unhindered.[8] On this view, Spinoza's conception of the relation between politics and freedom is best captured by his claim that "a man can be free in any kind of state" (*TTP* 580–81, note 33). The democratic state might be preferable for a whole host of reasons, but with regard to the pursuit of rational autonomy, "the best we could say is that 'democracy' does not contradict autonomy ... and not that it fosters it."[9]

Steven Smith offers a particularly clear statement of the liberal interpretation:

> Unlike Plato or Maimonides, Spinoza does not advocate the rule of a philosopher-king or prophet who might educate his subjects to a lofty vision of human perfection. Spinoza's politics are, by contrast, starkly anti-perfectibilian. He is not bereft of an idea of human perfection, but he does doubt that politics or law is the most appropriate means by which to achieve it.[10]

Smith's contention that Spinoza combines a non-perfectionist politics with a lofty, neo-Stoic vision of ethical perfection implies that one cannot equate the ethical notion of freedom as rational activity which the *Ethics* exhorts us to pursue with the term "freedom" as it used in Spinoza's political writings. But if there are two different senses of freedom at issue in Spinoza's *Ethics* and in his political writings, how should we understand Spinoza's claim in the *Theological-Political Treatise* that the true purpose of the state is freedom? Den Uyl responds to this problem by arguing that, in his political thought, Spinoza uses the term "freedom" as a synonym for peace, that is, co-operative and obedient conduct. Citizens may thus be free in a political sense when the laws of the commonwealth work to guarantee their physical security and peaceful co-existence, and yet "be completely passive (hence, unfree) from an ethical perspective."[11] In other words, while the provision of peace and stability might create a suitable environment for the private pursuit of rational autonomy, Den Uyl argues that the most that can be said about such political supports is that they *reduce obstacles* to the self-realization of endogenous power and not that they directly contribute to promoting freedom.[12] Still, one might think that if, as Den Uyl admits, supported striving accords with rational autonomy because it minimizes the forces that oppose active *conatus*, then it could be argued that the state has an indirect role to play in fostering freedom. Perhaps, as Michael Rosenthal argues, "participation in political life helps create conditions (i.e., stability) under which the higher goods, such as philosophy, can be realized" and, presumably, without which such goods would be unlikely to flourish.[13] But, for Den Uyl at least, even this much perfectionism would be too much for Spinoza since, as he points out, a peaceful and secure democratic polity might leave those who are active free to be active, but it also leaves them free to be passive, and could be "fully functional and successful in the absence of *any* active participants. Therefore ... we would be equally entitled to say that democracy encourages passivity; but if it encourages both activity and passivity, it is either trivial or contradictory."[14]

In an important critical response to this view, Justin Steinberg has argued that it is possible to build a case for the state's liberating potential, thereby making sense of Spinoza's claim in Chapter 20 of the *Theological-Political Treatise* that "the aim of the state is, in reality, freedom," if we relate Spinoza's account of the kind of causal self-sufficiency or independence we enjoy by virtue of having adequate ideas to his general account of freedom as a thing's power of acting (*TTP* 567). Steinberg suggests that once causal self-sufficiency is understood as the maximally active expression of one's power of acting, it becomes possible to argue that anything that reliably augments one's power and promotes one's overall joy serves to make one more causally independent, that is, less subject to the power of external causes and more capable of producing self-preserving effects.[15] Building on the claim that, for Spinoza, one's degree of freedom is co-extensive with one's power of acting, Steinberg argues that, "insofar as the state is able to aid the power of acting of its subjects *in any way,* it may be said to be directly liberating."[16] Steinberg draws on this general account of freedom and empowerment to demonstrate how the state can positively and directly liberate citizen-subjects by influencing their behavioral patterns, affective dispositions and cognitive powers.[17] Although Steinberg concedes that the state cannot act directly to make citizens fully rational, he argues that a well-organized state can do a great deal to foster prudential activity, to curb destructive passions and to encourage joyful, social affects that agree with reason even if they do not follow from rational understanding. Thus, it can bring it about that citizens within the state are led to behave in a reliably empowering and joyful manner, which is to say, as if they were guided by reason.

I noted above that Den Uyl, like Steinberg, draws a distinction between acting *from* reason and acting *in accordance with* reason as a way of marking the difference between fully rational activity based on the possession of adequate ideas and states in which conformity to the dictates of reason is achieved more passively, by means of the regulation of the passions. This familiar distinction, however, functions quite differently in each account. In Den Uyl's case, it serves to support his claim that Spinoza regards politics as having "a simple, limited function that, in itself, has nothing to do with perfection, activity, or blessedness."[18] That simple, limited function consists in establishing stability and security by inducing citizens to obey the laws of the state. Since it is rational to obey the law, citizens who are made to do so may be said to behave as if they were rational. For Den Uyl, however, to be induced to behave in a way that is consistent with reason is a form of passive empowerment that contributes nothing to promoting genuine freedom and activity. While citizens in a well-ordered and harmonious state enjoy many advantages, these advantages do not include any gains in their levels of activity, or degree of freedom. Indeed, a striking feature of Den Uyl's treatment of Spinozistic freedom is the almost complete absence of any analysis of the relation between active self-development and passive empowerment. Although Den Uyl acknowledges that, for Spinoza, passivity is not necessarily opposed to activity and that certain passive experiences (of pleasure) may contribute to human wellbeing, he understands the nature of this contribution to be indirect: passive pleasures "give us increased motivation," but only by virtue of rendering us "less passive," so that in this case we are *less impeded* by our emotions than we would be if subject to painful emotions.[19]

The decision to describe passive empowerment as a transition to a state of lesser passivity rather than to a condition of greater activity reveals Den Uyl's commitment to a radically dichotomous understanding of activity and passivity. According to this (standard) view, which will be examined more closely in the next section, Spinoza regards activity and passivity as mutually exclusive categories. Thus, one is either active or passive, either actively self-determining or passively affected by external causes, either a free man or a slave. As long as activity and passivity are opposed in this fashion, it is impossible to attribute any directly liberating role to agencies external to the individual, since to be subject to external influences, no matter how empowering, is to passively undergo change rather than to be the adequate cause of one's own actions and thoughts.

It is not surprising, therefore, to find that Steinberg's alternative analysis of the state's directly liberating function depends on rejecting the "inadequacy" of the free man/slave dichotomy in order to make conceptual space for a mediating third term: "the citizen-subject."[20] While the free man and the slave are exemplars of free activity and passionate bondage, respectively, and thus ideal models of human perfection and imperfection, the "citizen-subject" occupies an intermediary position between these extremes. Unlike the slave whose actions benefit only "him who commands," the citizen-subject of a state in which "the welfare of the whole people, not the ruler is the supreme law" acts in his own interests in obeying the laws that uphold the common good (*TTP* 16/531). Because the citizen-subject's own interests are served by his compliance to the law, he will be more powerful and joyful than the slave whose obedience to the law is motivated only by fear of the consequences of his disobedience. As Steinberg notes, Spinoza exploits the distinction between the citizen-subject and the slave in order to explain the difference between a flourishing civil condition marked by "genuine peace," and a condition of mere stability.[21] While fearful, slavish conformity to the law is all that is required in order to establish a stable and enduring state, the genuinely peaceful state "consists not in the absence of war but in the union or harmony of minds" (*TP* 6.4). Spinoza contends, moreover, that a condition of genuine peace and harmony is achieved when citizens come to act from strength of mind (*fortitudo*) (*TP* 5.4).[22] A state that seeks to promote peace is, therefore, committed to a great deal more than merely protecting citizens from the politically destabilizing effects of anti-social, destructive passions. Since peace is a positive condition of civic harmony that consists in the agreement of minds/bodies, the state that strives to foster peace must work to promote sociable, joyful, power-enhancing affects. Steinberg contends that a well-governed state, which, through the effectiveness of its laws and institutions, manages to replace destructive, anti-social passions with sociable, power-promoting affects, brings it about that citizens are reliably empowered and joyful, that is, that they live in a more fully rational manner. In doing so, it ensures that only a small gap remains between the degree of freedom enjoyed by citizen-subjects and the rational autonomy of the free man.[23]

Each of these accounts of freedom foregrounds a different aspect of Spinoza's ontology of power and individuality. For liberal interpreters, Spinozistic freedom is understood in relation to primary power, as the self-assertion of each individual's singular essence in the production of those effects that follow necessarily from it. Freedom thus construed amounts to individualized self-determination, the striving for personal empowerment through the cultivation of reason. In the alternative view proposed by Steinberg, freedom is interpreted as a collective, socially and politically instituted power of acting that individuals become increasingly capable of developing and exercising as their relations with external things become co-operative and mutually beneficial. This difference is reflected in the different ways in which politics figures in each account. While the liberal interpretation conceives of the state as a mechanism for aggregating atomic individuals, so that conflicts among them can be avoided, thus leaving them free to pursue the project of rational autonomy unhindered, Steinberg's reading emphasizes the role the state plays in transforming the quality of the relationships through which individual striving is enacted as integral to the development of each individual's power of acting. Finally, and relatedly, it is significant that each view also differs over the issue of how reason should be understood. Rationality figures in the liberal interpretation primarily as an intellectual capacity for adequate understanding and, derivatively, in its instrumental orientation in politics, as a form of prudential reasoning whereby individuals agree to cooperate with others as a means to satisfy their own interests. Although these aspects of reason are not ignored in the view developed by Steinberg, it is clear that, in this view, rationality denotes, in addition, that quality of a way of life characterized by a high degree of civic harmony and agreement among citizens. It is over the question of the role that is played by this way of life in liberating the individual that the contrast between the two interpretations we have been examining comes into clearest view. Whereas liberal interpreters construe "cooperation by mutual agreement" as a surrogate for rational autonomy, or, at best, a precondition for the private pursuit of ethical perfection, Steinberg's reading suggests that the harmonious agreement of minds/bodies produced by the good state is a necessary (though not sufficient) condition for the active realization of each individual's nature and freedom.

Since each of these interpretations develops different aspects of Spinoza's account of action and passion, we need to consider this account more closely in order to clarify Spinoza's position. In considering this account, I argue that Spinoza's investigations into the conditions of liberation leads to a questioning of the dichotomy between (internally caused) activity and (externally conditioned) passive empowerment, which is pursued especially through the consideration of a class of relation between things which "agree in nature."

Two schemas of activity and passivity

The opposition of actions and passions should not conceal the other opposition that constitutes the second principle of Spinozism: that of joyful passive affections and sad passive affections. One increases our power, the other diminishes it. We come closer to our power of action insofar as we are affected by joy. The ethical question falls then, in Spinoza, into two parts: How can we come to produce active affections? *But first of all:* How can we come to experience a maximum of joyful passions?[24]

This passage from *Expressionism in Philosophy* provide a condensed summary of two key distinctions—between action and passion, and passive augmentation and diminution of the power to act—that Gilles Deleuze identifies as central to understanding Spinoza's account of ethical liberation. Drawing on Spinoza's claim that joyful passions are an increase in power occasioned by external things, Deleuze claims that "the increase may proceed indefinitely, but we will never come into full possession of our power of action until we have active affections."[25] There is, in other words, a logical gap between a passive increase in our power of acting, and action proper. The necessity of that gap follows from Spinoza's definition of action: "we act when something happens, in us or outside us, of which we are the adequate cause, that is (by D1), when something in us or outside us follows from our nature, which can be understood clearly through it alone" (*E* III, D2). Although all actions have prior causes, it is only when what we do follows from and reflects our inherent power that we can properly be said to act or be active. Spinoza contrasts action—acting on the basis of adequate ideas and active affects—with passion. In passion, we are acted on by external forces, so that what we do is not explicable solely with reference to our essential power but must also be referred to the power of external things and the way they affect us.

Deleuze argues that while we must acknowledge the absolute character of the opposition between action and passion, this should not blind us to "the other opposition that constitutes the second principle of Spinozism: that of joyful passive affections and sad passive affections." This second principle refers to a distinction, internal to the category of passion, between joyful passive affects, which are cognitive correlates of an increase in the body's power of acting under the influence of external things, and sad passive affects, which indicate a decrease in this power. In the definitions that are the starting point of Part III of the *Ethics*, Spinoza explains that if we could be the adequate cause of any of these passively produced affections, the resulting affect would have to be understood as an action (*actionem*) rather than a passion (*passionem*) (*E* III, D3). Building on the possibility opened up by the idea of passive increases in our power of acting that may be understood as activities, Deleuze claims that, though they are passively produced, joyful affects express our power of acting in a way that brings us closer to "our power of action." According to the reading proposed by Deleuze, Spinoza presents "reason's initial endeavour" as the striving to increase our power of acting through experiencing a maximum of joyful passions.

Deleuze's reading alerts us to the fact that Spinoza deploys two distinct schemas of activity and passivity in his metaphysics and ethics, which obey different logics. On the one hand, in the distinction between action and passion, activity and passivity are opposed. Action refers to that state of activity in which the individual is determined by her nature alone. Spinoza evokes this conception of activity in his definition of freedom in Part I of the *Ethics*. That thing is called free, he says, "which exists from the necessity of its nature alone, and is determined to act [*ad agendum*] by itself alone" (*E* I, D7; *E* 58). Although human beings, as finite modes, can never be the cause of their own existence, Spinoza suggest that they may be more or less self-determining depending on the extent to which their actions and thoughts follow from internal rather than external causes. When an individual manages to form adequate ideas of the causes of her passive affects, she ceases to merely passively undergo the effects— affections and affects—produced in her by the impact of external things. In adequately understanding these causes she acts through her own nature or power, and therefore, according to a principle internal to her, of which she is the adequate cause. If action is the elimination of passion through the formation of adequate ideas of one's passions, then becoming more active is simply the process of becoming less passive, less subject to passive affects. Thus, according to this schema, action and passion are mutually exclusive categories, and vary in inverse proportion to each other.

On the other hand, in the idea of joyful passions that increase our power of acting, passivity and activity are more complexly related. Spinoza defines affects as modifications (affections) of the body's power of acting, together with the ideas of these modifications. An individual's "power of acting" is her essence, or perfection, which is expressed in existence as a striving (*conatus*) to persevere in being (*E* III, P7). The power that defines each individual undergoes modification under the impact of external things so that she becomes more or less capable of doing those things that promote her preservation (*E* III, P9S). The transition from lesser to greater power is experienced as joy, which is both an increase in the body's power of acting, and "that passion by which the mind passes to a greater perfection" (*E* III, P11S). In allowing that our essential power is subject to variation, and may be passively augmented, Spinoza seems to unsettle the opposition between action and passion.

Although the difficulties posed by the existence of these two schemas of activity and passivity in Spinoza's thought has been discussed surprisingly little in the scholarly literature, commentators within the Anglo-American tradition who have addressed these difficulties generally argue that the two accounts are incompatible, and that the idea of passive activities outlined in Spinoza's theory of the affects in Part III of the *Ethics* is incoherent.[26] These interpretations typically make the coherence of Spinoza's account of activity turn on rejecting or deflating the idea of joyful passions as passively produced activities. The key feature of these readings is the restriction of action proper in Spinoza to activity that follows from the guidance of reason, that is, from adequate ideas, which express the innate power of the mind to understand and order its thoughts according to the true order of nature. From this perspective, all passions, whether joyful or sad, reflect the impact of external forces of which we can only have inadequate ideas, and thus represent forms of passivity, of external determination that alienate us from our power of action.

Following Spinoza's claim in Part I of the *Ethics* that each finite thing expresses the power of God in a certain and determinate way, this standard view considers activity purely as a function of the unfolding and expression of each thing's essential nature, which is just the immanent, causal power of God or Substance which acts "in" each thing and determines it to produce its effects (*E* I, P34 and P36). According to this view, activity consists in the internal realization of a thing's eternal essence or power. Each individual would fully express this active power were it not for the fact that, in existence, individuals are exposed to external forces that counter or block their striving. Considered from the perspective of the individual striving to actively realize her power of acting, external things figure merely as sources of self-alienation, smaller or greater impediments to the full unfolding and expression of endogenous power. Thus, we might say that, to be active according to this view is to act in oneself or to remain in oneself as far as one can by achieving the greatest degree of causal self-sufficiency possible for a finite existing mode. In practice, in existence, this effort to remain in oneself—the striving for causal self-sufficiency—will entail endeavoring to resist or overcome the self-alienating influences of external things, experienced as passions, through the formation of adequate ideas which directly express the innate rational power of the mind. It is clearly this standard view of activity upon which the liberal interpretation depends.

In critical dialogue with the basic commitments of this view, Lee Rice offers an alternative solution to "the puzzle of passive activities," which seeks to dissolve the appearance of a paradox by challenging the assumptions made about the nature of Spinozistic action itself within the standard account. According to Rice, the judgment that no "affect that was passively produced could result in an activity" is based on the mistaken view that what Spinoza means by activity is behavior that originates within us, and of which we are the sole or total cause.[27] Rice argues that Spinoza's determinism makes this view of activity untenable— "Spinoza simply denies that *any* finite mode can ever be the originating cause of *any* activity"—but that it does so without thereby depriving individuals of agency.[28] Rather, Spinoza's version of determinism requires us to rethink activity as the effect of a double causality: the activity of each individual must be explained in terms of the *interaction* between an interior aspect—an essential power of acting, and of producing effects that can be understood through the individual's own nature—and an exterior aspect—the power of the environment acting on her. It is the reciprocal determination of these two aspects—the internal causal force and external causes in their interactions—that will determine whether a particular encounter results in increased or decreased activity for the affected/affecting individuals. Rice argues that certain passions represent external modifications of an individual that result in the enhancement of that individual's power to do those things that follow from her nature. Although these changes arise from a passive affect, and the affected individual is only their partial cause, because they are such that the individual could be their adequate cause, they may be understood as activities.[29] Michael Schrijvers argues along similar lines: "There are certain external influences on the body that favor or diminish its capacity to interact with other bodies, so that it is more or less easy to do what it does autonomously."[30]

The adjustment that Rice and Schrijvers make to the standard view is to insist on the difference that concrete forms of existence make to essence. Rice points out that because Spinoza's metaphysics locates individuality within an interactive, interdependent network of causes, the active realization of essential power can never be entirely up to the individual. Conative striving occurs within an environment that impacts on our striving, and we experience these modifications in our power affectively. Rice's contention that, for Spinoza, interaction with external things can play a positive role in enabling individuals to do that of which they are the adequate cause reminds us that Spinoza defines the existing individual, not only in terms of a power of acting, or doing those things that can be explained by her nature, but also in terms of a power of being acted upon and affected by external things. Only existing beings—which are determined to exist and to produce effects by other existing things—possess this power to affect and be affected, and therefore to undergo changes which may either enhance or diminish their striving. The whole point of Spinoza's theory of the affects in Part III of the *Ethics* is to show that human essence *in existence* is inseparable from a capacity to affect and be affected and, therefore, that essences cannot be considered in abstraction from the relations through which they are actualized.[31] It is because we are parts of nature in constant interaction with other parts that our essential power is determined, in existence, as a variable power of acting, which may be enhanced or diminished depending on the nature of the relations into which we enter. As Spinoza explains:

> It is impossible for a man not to be a part of nature and not to follow the common order of Nature. But if he lives among such individuals as agree with his nature, his power of acting will thereby be aided and encouraged. On the other hand, if he is among men who do not agree at all with his nature, he will hardly be able to accommodate himself to them without greatly changing himself. (*E* IV, Ap. 7)

Spinoza's appeal to the notions of agreement and disagreement in this passage reveals the centrality of relational interaction to the constitution of an individual's essential power of acting. The claim that our power of acting is aided and encouraged when we are related to others with whom we agree in nature and, conversely, restrained by relations of disagreement, contains a series of important insights regarding the nature of our power.[32]

It reveals, firstly, that the power that defines us is not fixed, but variable, subject to influences that render us more or less capable of doing those things that follow from our nature. Spinoza exploits this idea of a variable power of acting in his discussion of bodily and mental capacity in Part II of the *Ethics*, where he tells us that "in proportion as a body is more capable than others of doing many things at once, or being acted on in many ways at once, so its mind is more capable than others of perceiving many things at once" (*E* II, P13S; see also *E* II, P14). In reiterating this claim in Part IV of the *Ethics*, Spinoza expands this perspective to include "whatever so disposes the human body that it can be affected in a great many ways, or renders it capable of affecting external bodies in a great many ways" (*E* IV, P38). Such things, says Spinoza, are useful to us, and the more they render us capable of affecting and being affected, the more useful they are. Here, then, we see that in addition to defining the power of existing things as a flexible capacity to affect and be affected, Spinoza is also concerned to show that this capacity may be passively augmented, that is, that we may be *rendered* more capable of acting and thinking by virtue of the action of external things upon us. In making this claim, Spinoza is admitting that there is a difference between the power that constitutes our nature as an eternal essence, and the way in which that power is enacted in existence.[33] In existence, the active production of those effects that follow from our nature is never a matter of the unimpeded self-expression of essential power, but is instead always a co-production, the result of a special cooperation with external things. But how are we to understand this process of co-production, which requires us to accept the idea that passive changes in our power may also constitute active states of our being? What kinds of relation aid our striving, enabling us to become more active and to realize our powers of acting and thinking? Spinoza's answer to these questions can be found in his account of the different ways in which we may be related to others, either through relations of agreement or disagreement.

In foregrounding the notion of agreement, and signaling its importance to understanding Spinoza's efforts to explain how passive transitions in power might engender active states of being, my interpretation differs from the readings offered by Rice and Schrijvers. Their interpretations tend to focus on the idea of a conditional stimulation of innate powers, whereas I am concerned to show how Spinoza's discussion of acting with others to produce a common nature contains the resources for explaining how compulsion by external forces may become instead a form of liberating cooperation that frees us from the arbitrary power of external things.

Spinoza defines the notions of agreement and disagreement in terms of the degree to which things share a common nature (*E* IV, P29–P31). Things that have much in common agree with one another, while things that share little or nothing disagree. What Spinoza means by sharing a common nature can be grasped by reflecting on his description of how parts can come together to form greater wholes in Nature:

> By coherence of parts I mean simply this, that the laws of nature of one part adapts itself to the laws or nature of another part in such wise that there is the least possible opposition between them. On the question of whole and parts, I consider things as parts of a whole to the extent that their natures adapt themselves to one another so that they are in the closest possible agreement. Insofar as they are different from one another, to that extent each one forms in our mind a separate idea and is therefore considered as a whole and not a part. (*Ep.* 32)

Spinoza thus regards things as parts of a greater whole to the extent that they are compelled to "adapt themselves to one another" according to common laws. This process of mutual adaptation, or "reciprocal modification" produces a shared nature, that is, a high degree of agreement and commonality, while still preserving the singular nature of the parts. Here, then, we see that parts are defined both by their capacity to affect and be affected by other parts, which is what allows them to be adapted to one another without losing their singular natures, and also by the way they fit together, or agree with other parts, so as to form together a common nature, a larger whole. To be a part of a larger whole rather than a distinct, self-sufficient whole is to be co-defined by one's relations with others, in the sense that the effects one becomes capable of producing as a result of coordinating one's actions with others are not produced by oneself alone but in concert with others.

When individuals act together in this way to construct a shared nature, they cease to act as compelling external forces in relation to one another and become instead co-actors in a common enterprise from which all benefit, since they are now supported, rather than thwarted, in their striving, by the combined power of others. Spinoza surely has this process in mind in the *Treatise on the Emendation of the Intellect* when he links the process of perfecting his own nature to the formation of a civil society. In this context, he writes:

> This, then, is the end for which I strive, to acquire the nature I have described and to endeavour that many should acquire it along with me. That is to say, my own happiness involves my making an effort to persuade many others to think as I do, so that their understanding and their desire should entirely accord with my understanding and my desire. To bring this about, it is necessary (1) to understand as much about Nature as suffices for acquiring such a nature, and (2) to establish such a social order as will enable as many as possible to reach this goal with the greatest possible ease and assurance. (*TIE* 15)

When in Part IV of the *Ethics*, Spinoza turns from a consideration of the causes of man's lack of power to consider "which affects agree with the laws of human reason," he focuses especially on our relations with those whose nature agrees entirely with our own. In this context, Spinoza tells us that:

> Man can wish for nothing more helpful to the preservation of his being than that all should so agree in all things that the minds of bodies of all would compose, as it were, one mind and one body; that all should strive together, as far as they can, to preserve their being; and that all, together, should seek for themselves the common advantage of all. (*E* IV, P18S)

We learn from the following propositions that nothing can be good for us except insofar as it agrees with our nature and that the more a thing agrees with our nature, the more useful or power-enhancing it is for us (*E* IV, P31C). Spinoza also tells us that only that which leads to understanding is most useful to us (*E* IV, P27). It is clear from these propositions that the process of maximizing agreements in nature is integrally related to the striving for understanding, and thus that both harmonious interaction and understanding are essential to the rational life. But how should the relation between these two features be understood?

Spinoza offers us a two-stage response to this question, which begins with the identification of reason as the source of empowering agreements (*E* IV, P35). Those who live according to the guidance of reason will naturally agree in nature with one another, and this is so because rational desire is the striving for understanding, and understanding is a common (non-competitive) good that can be enjoyed equally by all (*E* IV, P36). Thus, those who are rational will be engaged in the pursuit of a joint enterprise from which all equally benefit. However, since all of us are subject to passions to varying degrees and, insofar as we are, "cannot be said to agree in nature," something other than reason is required in order to bring about agreements in nature; namely, the civil state, which has "the power to prescribe a common rule of life, to make laws, and to maintain them—not by reason, which cannot restrain the affects (by P17S), but by threats" (*E* IV, P37S). Although this is an enforced form of agreement that does not arise from reason, Spinoza suggests that it can engender reason. For, he says, "those things which bring it about that men live harmoniously at the same time bring it about that they live according to the guidance of reason" (*E* IV, P40D). Here it is no longer reason that is presented as the source of empowering agreements, but rather the state that constrains us to live together harmoniously according to common laws that is presented as the formative condition for the development of a maximally empowering, increasingly rational way of life. Thus, while it is, as Spinoza notes, "the rational principle of seeking our own advantage ... [that] teaches us to establish a bond with men," the relative weakness of rational desires as compared with passionate ones imposes the necessity of supplementing reason with an external, agreement-generating power, which is able to bring about that which reason recommends but which, unaided, reason is powerless to achieve (*E* IV, P37S). If the passive production of agreements effected by the state is a necessary supplement to reason's endeavor, in the sense that it empowers me to do that which I would do if I were rational, this is because it modifies the way I interact with others. By minimizing the degree of disagreement between individuals, the (good) state reduces opposition to each individual's striving, and by maximizing the possibilities for agreement, for joyful, mutually beneficial interaction among citizens, it acts as a vector for empowering forms of cooperation that make each individual more capable of producing effects that follow from their own natures than they would be if alone, and opposed or unsupported in their striving. In fact, in general terms, we might say that what the good state does is to compel individuals to operate as parts "so that they harmonize with one another" rather than as distinct wholes, which are "out of harmony with one another" (*Ep.* 32).

While it is clearly a good thing from Spinoza's point of view to live as reason recommends in accordance with the principle of common life and common advantage in a state, it is still not clear in what sense the political construction of agreements may be related to the striving for understanding. How might the enjoyment of a shared way of life, characterized by a high degree of unity and agreement, actually contribute to making us more capable of understanding *and* acting? How we respond to this question will depend on what we take reasoning or understanding to be.

Spinoza presents an account of understanding in the *Ethics* that casts it as a project of acquiring adequate ideas and extending adequate knowledge of the properties of things, culminating in the knowledge of God or Nature (*E* IV, P28).[34] Our minds, he suggests, are most active, and we attain our highest state of virtue, perfection and blessedness, when we engage in the loving contemplative comprehension of God or Nature, and grasp our own natures as parts of Nature as a whole (*E* IV, P27). The fruits of such understanding are ethical and practical, expressed as much in our powers of acting, or doing those things that conduce to our own and others' joy and empowerment, as in our powers of thinking, or understanding things adequately. Spinoza includes, among the signs of wisdom, knowing how to take pleasure in things, refreshing and restoring the body and mind "with pleasant food and drink, with scents, with the beauty of green plants, with decoration, music, sports, the theater," seeking to strengthen the bonds of rational friendship, and actively obeying the laws of the state (*E* IV, P45S; Ap. 12; P73D). As these and other qualities of the wise attest to, genuine understanding has a practical dimension, which is manifest in the way we relate to ourselves and interact with others within the broader social and political environments that constitute our collective milieu.

It might be tempting to interpret Spinoza's claims about the practical implications of understanding as implying the priority of understanding over acting. According to this view, I would have to cultivate my powers of understanding in the first instance in order to be able to grasp how best to live, and then apply that understanding in my practical dealings with the world. Spinoza's project in the *Ethics* can be interpreted in just this way, as seeking to equip us with the knowledge necessary in order to be able to live a flourishing life. However, as Spinoza is well aware, this cannot be the whole story. If understanding is necessarily enacted, if it is practical or practiced knowledge, then in addition to certain intellectual powers, we will need to cultivate a range of other kinds of powers or capabilities that enable us to put our understanding into practice so as to be able to live in the most joyful, empowering way possible. Moreover, cultivating these powers and abilities is unlikely to be up to us alone. For example, if I suffer from a failure of self-respect, which prevents me from imagining myself capable of pursuing my ideas of the good life, I may be able to employ the remedial measures outlined in Spinoza's version of cognitive therapy to transform this disabling affective self-appraisal into more adequate, joyful self-understanding, but the success of this endeavor will surely *also* depend on the presence of supportive relationships through which I learn through experience how it feels to be treated as worthy of respect, taken seriously as an equal, listened to, and so on. Without such confirming, formative experiences I am unlikely to be able to develop or exercise the powers and affective dispositions that I need in order to be able to think, feel and act differently in the world, and so unable to put my more adequate self-understanding into practice. If genuine understanding is incomplete without the skills and abilities that enable us to enact it in our ways of living and being, and if cultivating these physical and intellectual aptitudes and powers requires both the right kinds of support for our bodies and minds and an environment in which we are able to develop and exercise these powers, then understanding is neither a purely intellectual, nor an essentially individualistic achievement.

It is because practical understanding requires the cultivation of powers and dispositions that enable us to enact it that its passive genesis is both possible and necessary for Spinoza. To be habituated by good social and political institutions to act in a way that accords with reason—that is, to be required to consider and to adapt responsively to the needs and interests of others, so that their wellbeing may come to be included in one's own—is to acquire the embodied skills, affective dispositions and discriminating receptive powers that enable us to put our understanding into practice in the constitution of ways of life most conducive to collective joy and empowerment. The practical understanding that perfects our nature, and through which we realize the greatest degree of joy, power and freedom possible for us, is thus co-extensive with the construction of harmonious political communities that sustain, develop and extend our powers of acting and thinking together. Finally, in addition to fostering capacities that enable us to enact our understanding, Spinoza's account of reasoning as a matter of forming adequate ideas of those properties that are common to "the human body and certain external bodies by which the human body is usually affected" suggests that political arrangements that produce real agreements between bodies and minds, and so enable us to share a common nature, may actually aid the mind's power to understand (*E* II, P39C).[35] In short, if we are to conserve, develop and perfect our own natures Spinoza suggests that we must strive, with the support of just social and political institutions, to agree with others so as to form with them a more powerful, common nature as a condition for the self-development of each. It is by striving to cooperate, by learning to operate as parts of the partial wholes that we construct with others, that we are freed from the overwhelming power of external forces, and so empowered to develop and perfect our singular natures. Thus, while the path to freedom and perfection envisaged by Spinoza may indeed, as liberal interpreters remind us, be a matter of cultivating the power to act from reason, the reading proposed here suggests that we cannot cultivate this power alone, or for ourselves as private individuals, but only insofar as we participate in the collective project of striving together, as far as we can, to preserve our being, and together seek the common advantage of all (*E* IV, P18S).

Notes

1   Isaiah Berlin, "Two Concepts of Liberty," in *Four Essays on Liberty* (Oxford: Oxford University Press, 1969), 118–72.
2   For the purposes of this chapter, I understand the liberal interpretation of Spinoza to entail a commitment to the view that the state's primary function is the protection of negative liberties rather than the promotion of positive liberty, virtue or the good. The liberal interpretation of Spinoza was first developed by Lewis Feuer in *Spinoza and the Rise of Liberalism* (Boston, MA: Beacon Press, 1958). Here I draw primarily on recent influential work in this tradition: Steven B. Smith, *Spinoza, Liberalism, and the Question of Jewish Identity* (New Haven: Yale University Press, 1997); Douglas Den Uyl, *Power, State and Freedom: An Interpretation of Spinoza's Political Thought* (Assen, The Netherlands: Van Gorcum, 1983); and Den Uyl, "Autonomous Autonomy: Spinoza on Autonomy, Perfectionism and Politics," *Social Philosophy and Policy* 20.2 (2003), 30–69.
3   All references to the Ethics are to *A Spinoza Reader: The Ethics and Other Works*, trans. by E. Curley (Princeton, NJ: Princeton University Press, 1994). All other references to Spinoza's works are to *Complete Works*, trans. by Samuel Shirley (Indianapolis, IN: Hackett, 2002). All references to the Latin are to *Opera*, ed. Carl Gebhardt (Heidelberg: Carl Windters Universitätsbuchhandlung, 1924).

4   Den Uyl, "Autonomous Autonomy," 55.
5   Den Uyl, "Autonomous Autonomy," 55.
6   Den Uyl, "Autonomous Autonomy," 55.
7   Spinoza offers numerous examples of being acted upon and affected by "what is outside of us" in ways that augment our power to persevere and thrive. Apart from the material supports necessary for the preservation of life, he points to the value of rational friendships and close relationships with men more generally and also to the advantages of living under the protection of the law in a state (*E* IV, P39; P35; P37; P73). Indeed, in a general formula, Spinoza claims that whatever acts upon us to make our bodies more capable of affecting and being affected by external bodies in many ways is advantageous to us, that is, increases our powers of acting and thinking (*E* IV, P38; *E* V, P38).
8   Den Uyl, "Autonomous Autonomy," 49.
9   Den Uyl, "Autonomous Autonomy," 55.
10 Smith, *Liberalism*, 137.
11 Den Uyl, "Autonomous Autonomy," 59.
12 This is reminiscent of Wartofsky's solution to the problem posed by Spinoza's claim that joyful passions increase our power of acting only insofar as they counteract those passions that decrease it; see note 26.
13 Michael A. Rosenthal, "Tolerance as a virtue in Spinoza's *Ethics*," *Journal of the History of Philosophy* 39.4 (2001), 549.
14 Den Uyl, "Autonomous Autonomy," 55–56.
15 Justin Steinberg, "Spinoza on Civil Liberation," *Journal of the History of Philosophy* 47.1 (2009), 41.
16 Steinberg, "Civil Liberation," 42.
17 Steinberg, "Civil Liberation," 36.
18 Den Uyl, "Autonomous Autonomy," 55.
19 Den Uyl, "Autonomous Autonomy," 42.
20 Steinberg, "Civil Liberation," 44. Steinberg's use of the term "citizen-subject" is intended to capture the terminological changes and continuities from the *Theological-Political Treatise* and the *Political Treatise*. I follow Steinberg's (and Spinoza's) use of the masculine personal pronoun in this passage.
21 Steinberg, "Civil Liberation," 47.
22 As Steinberg notes, Spinoza's use of the term "*fortitudo*" to describe the affective state that supports peace is puzzling since *fortitudo* is an active, rational affect and most people, Spinoza contends, cannot be expected to act primarily from reason. This observation leads Steinberg to suggest that, while complete peace may be an unattainable ideal, a close approximation of perfect peace is possible "if citizens are motivated by stable, sociable affects, that is, only if they are generally joyful or powerful" ("Civil Liberation," 49).
23 Steinberg, "Civil Liberation," 54.

24 Gilles Deleuze, *Expressionism in Philosophy: Spinoza*, trans. by M. Joughin (New York: Zone Books, 1992), 246.

25 Deleuze, *Expressionism*, 246.

26 For an example of the incoherence claim, see Jonathan Bennett, *A Study of Spinoza's Ethics* (Indianapolis, IN: Hackett, 1984), 258. For an example of the deflationary reading, see Marx Wartofsky, "Action and Passion: Spinoza's Construction of a Scientific Psychology," in ed. by Marjorie Grene, *Spinoza: A Collection of Critical Essays* (New York: Doubleday, 1973). Wartofsky asks: "But how can passions increase our power of acting? Obviously they cannot, on Spinoza's theory." His solution to this dilemma is to propose that the only sense in which passions can be said to increase our power "is the sense in which they are counterposed to other passions which *decrease* our power of acting; and the resultant effect of this composition of forces is a *lesser decrease* (by virtue of that, a relative increment) in our power of acting" (348).

27 Lee Rice, "Action in Spinoza's Account of Affectivity," in ed. by Y. Yovel, *Desire and Affect: Spinoza as Psychologist* (New York: Little Room Press, 1999), 161. Although Rice, following Spinoza, does not use the phrase "total cause" to describe adequate causation, his appeal to the notion of origination in this context seems to entail the idea of being the sole or total cause of one's effects. The fact that Spinoza refers to inadequate causes as partial causes might be taken to support this view of adequate causation, but Rice argues that this interpretation is incorrect.

28 Rice, "Action," 161.

29 Rice, "Action," 159.

30 Michael Schrijvers, "The *Conatus* and the Mutual Relationship between Active and Passive Affects in Spinoza," in ed. by Y. Yovel, *Desire and Affect: Spinoza as Psychologist* (New York: Little Room Press, 1999), 74–75.

31 See Aurelia Armstrong, "Autonomy and the Relational Individual: Spinoza and Feminism," in ed. by Moira Gatens, *Feminist Interpretations of Benedict Spinoza* (Pennsylvania: The Pennsylvania University Press, 2009), 50–52, for a discussion of the relational nature of the Spinozist individual.

32 Spinoza introduces the notion of agreement in his discussion of the nature of bodies in *Ethics* II (P13, L2) and draws out the social and political implications of the notion in *Ethics* IV (P29–P35).

33 For a thoughtful discussion of the relation between eternal essence and existing essence, which offers an account of Spinoza's view of the difference that concrete conditions of existence make to the way essences exist, see Andrea Sangiacomo, "What Are Human Beings? Essences and Aptitudes in Spinoza's Anthropology," *Journal of Early Modern Studies* 2.2 (2013), 78–100.

34 The following discussion is indebted to Susan James' argument that, for Spinoza, understanding is a matter of knowing how to bring something about, and thus, a practical skill that is enacted in the project of empowering our bodies and minds.

James develops this account in "Spinoza, the Body, and the Good Life," in ed. by Matthew Kisner and Andrew Youpa, *Essays on Spinoza's Ethical Theory* (Oxford: Oxford University Press, 2014), 143–59.

35 For an alternative account of how participating in political communities fosters adequate understanding, see Matthew J. Kisner's *Spinoza on Human Freedom: Reason, Autonomy and the Good Life* (Cambridge: Cambridge University Press, 2011), ch. 11.

Bibliography

Armstrong, Aurelia. "Autonomy and the Relational Individual: Spinoza and Feminism," in ed. by M. Gatens, *Feminist Interpretations of Benedict Spinoza*. Pennsylvania: Pennsylvania University Press, 2009, 43–63.

Balibar, Etienne. "Spinoza: From Individuality to Transindividuality," in *Mededelingen vanwege het Spinozahuis*. Delft: Eburon, 1997.

Bennett, Jonathan. *A Study of Spinoza's Ethics*. Indianapolis: Hackett, 1984.

Berlin, Isaiah. "Two Concepts of Liberty," in *Four Essays on Liberty*. Oxford: Oxford University Press, 1969, 118–72.

Deleuze, Gilles. *Expressionism in Philosophy: Spinoza*, trans. by M. Joughin. New York: Zone Books, 1992.

Den Uyl, Douglas. "Autonomous Autonomy: Spinoza on Autonomy, Perfectionism and Politics," *Social Philosophy and Policy* 20.2 (2003), 30–69.

Den Uyl, Douglas. *Power, State and Freedom: An Interpretation of Spinoza's Political Thought*. Assen, The Netherlands: Van Gorcum, 1983.

Feuer, Lewis. *Spinoza and the Rise of Liberalism*. Boston: Beacon Press, 1958.

James, Susan. "Spinoza, the Body, and the Good Life," in ed. by Matthew Kisner and Andrew Youpa, *Essays on Spinoza's Ethical Theory*. Oxford: Oxford University Press, 2014, 143–59.

Kisner, Matthew J. *Spinoza on Human Freedom: Reason, Autonomy and the Good Life*. Cambridge: Cambridge University Press, 2011.

Rice, Lee. "Action in Spinoza's Account of Affectivity," in ed. by Y. Yovel, *Desire and Affect: Spinoza as Psychologist*. New York: Little Room Press, 1999, 155–68.

Rosenthal, Michael A. "'Tolerance as a Virtue in Spinoza's *Ethics*," *Journal of the History of Philosophy* 39.4 (2001), 535–57.

Sangiacomo, Andrea. "What Are Human Beings? Essences and Aptitudes in Spinoza's Anthropology," *Journal of Early Modern Studies* 2.2 (2013), 78–100.

Schrijvers, Michael. "The *Conatus* and the Mutual Relationship between Active and Passive Affects in Spinoza," in ed. by Y. Yovel, *Desire and Affect: Spinoza as Psychologist*. New York: Little Room Press, 1999, 63–78.

Smith, Steven B. *Spinoza, Liberalism, and the Question of Jewish Identity*. New Haven: Yale University Press, 1997.

Spinoza. *Complete Works*, trans. by Samuel Shirley. Indianapolis, IN: Hackett, 2002.

Spinoza. *Ethics*, in *A Spinoza Reader: The Ethics and Other Works*, trans. by E. Curley. Princeton, NJ: Princeton University Press, 1994.

Spinoza. *Opera*, ed. Carl Gebhardt. Heidelberg: Carl Windters Universitätsbuchhandlung, 1924.

Steinberg, Justin. "Spinoza on Civil Liberation," *Journal of the History of Philosophy* 47.1 (2009), 35–58.

Wartofsky, Marx. "Action and Passion: Spinoza's Construction of a Scientific Psychology," in ed. by Marjorie Grene, *Spinoza: A Collection of Critical Essays*. New York: Doubleday, 1973, 329–53.

3

Grammars of *Conatus*: Or, On the Primacy of Resistance in Spinoza, Foucault and Deleuze

Cesare Casarino

Three centuries ago certain fools were astonished because Spinoza wanted the liberation of man, even though he did not believe in his freedom or even in his particular existence. Today new fools, or even the same ones reincarnated, are astonished because the Foucault who had spoken of the death of man took part in political struggle.

Gilles Deleuze

A false problem; or, the dialectic of power and resistance

In his unparalleled study of Michel Foucault, Gilles Deleuze writes: "the final word on power is that *resistance comes first.*"[1] Deleuze's daring political and ontological wager circumvents entirely the sterile impasse reached by many a debate on the nature of power relations in the wake of the publication of *La volonté de savoir* in 1976. Moreover, Deleuze's wager in effect denounces this impasse as a false problem.

The impasse may be encapsulated thus: if, as Foucault claims, "where there is power, there is resistance" and "resistance is never in a position of exteriority with respect to power,"[2] it follows then that resistance is caught always already in networks of power, and that it enables and supports such networks to the extent to which it constitutes one of their permanent and necessary components; resistance, thus, is futile and even counter-productive in so far as it provides us with the illusion of fighting power when in actuality power needs and is fuelled by it.

Foucault had foreseen such objections. In this passage, for example, he both invokes the objections and offers a detailed counter-rebuttal to them:

> Should it be said that one is necessarily "inside" power, that there is no "escaping" it, that there is no relation of absolute exteriority with respect to it? ... This would be to misrecognize the strictly relational character of power relationships. Their existence depends on a multiplicity of points of resistance: these play the role of adversary, target, support, or handle in power relations. These points of resistance are present everywhere in the power network. ... But this does not mean that they are only a reaction or rebound, forming with respect to the basic domination an underside that is in the end always passive, doomed to perpetual defeat. ... [N]either are they a lure or promise that is of necessity betrayed. They are the odd term in relations of power; they are inscribed in the latter as an irreducible opposite.[3]

Such a nuanced counter-rebuttal nonetheless backfires in the end. In a way, Foucault reconfirms the legitimate concerns expressed in those objections: for all of his reassurance that resistance is not "only a reaction or rebound," is not "always passive" and "doomed to perpetual defeat," is not always necessarily "betrayed," in this passage "points of resistance" seem also to dig their claws deeper and deeper into the very logic of power, to the point that resistance becomes power's "odd term" and "irreducible opposite." Even though the adjective "irreducible" could be taken to mean "unassimilable" and hence refractory to the lure of the *Aufhebung*, Foucault is not able to dispel completely an interpretation of the relation between power and resistance as a dialectical, mutually determining, binary opposition. It is such a dialectical deadlock between power and resistance that Deleuze's wager aims to invalidate and to uncover as a false problem. To declare that "the final word on power is that *resistance comes first*," in fact, is tantamount to saying that the relation between power and resistance is not a dialectical one. And my own wager in this essay is that, whether or not Deleuze's wager constitutes a valid interpretation of Foucault, his wager is certainly most pertinent to Baruch Spinoza. It is of Spinoza's ontology that one can truly say: "*resistance comes first*." For Spinoza anticipated our present impasse, our false problem.[4]

A false problem is not a non-existent problem, is not nothing. It is instructive here to follow Spinoza's definition of falsity: "Falsity consists in the privation of knowledge which inadequate, i.e., mutilated and confused, ideas involve" (*E* II, P35).[5] In the Proof, Spinoza adds: "falsity cannot consist in absolute privation ... nor again can it consist in absolute ignorance." Confined strictly to the realm of the relative, the false can never be absolute, which means that it cannot be even nothing absolutely: the false is privation of knowledge and privation of knowledge cannot be absolute, which means that falsity is very limited, very confused, very inadequate knowledge, yet still knowledge. (Truth, on the other hand, belongs entirely to the realm of the absolute. It is in the wake of such a definition of falsity that Spinoza famously writes: "just as light manifests both itself and the darkness, so truth is the standard [*norma*] both of itself and of falsity," *E* II, P43S.) A false problem, thus, needs to be understood as an inadequate problem, namely, a problem that is inadequate to its solution as long as it is posed in a way that makes it insoluble. The question then becomes: if the problem of the dialectical deadlock between power and resistance is a poorly conceived, inadequately posed problem, how is one to pose the problem of the relation between power and resistance adequately?

We may find an answer to this question in the way in which Spinoza poses the problem of the relation between the true and the false. Were falsity to constitute the criterion of truth and truth to constitute the criterion of falsity, were the true and the false to be binary opposites, then we would be caught in an infinite dialectical relay without any possible resolution, we would be lost in a mirror-hall where the true and the false could no longer be distinguished from one another, in short, we would be trapped in the *mise-en-abyme* of the relative, which, as Spinoza warned, can only lead to skepticism (*E* I, Ap.). For Spinoza, however, the relation between the true and the false is not one of mutual inversion, opposition, reciprocity and determination because the true and the false are not on equal footing: the false is false relative to the true, yet the true is true only in relation to itself. In Spinoza, the relation between the true and the false involves at least two different types of relations: on the one hand, the self-positing and self-constituting relation of truth to itself, the self-relation of truth, and, on the other hand, the relation between the true and the false—and the former is logically prior to the latter. None of these relations can be dialectical: the relation between the true and the false may be imagined to be a dialectical relation of binary opposites only by foreclosing the prior self-relation of truth, which, when not foreclosed, displaces and forestalls the dialectic before it even emerges; and the self-relation of truth is not a dialectical relation because it is not a relation between binary opposites but a relation among multiple and heterogeneous parts—for the fact that truth is self-positing and absolute does not mean that it is not composite and complex. What is primary is the self-positing relation of truth, whereas the relation between the true and the false is secondary to and determined by the self-relation of truth. Or, *the final word on the false is that the true comes first*.

I am proposing, in other words, that Spinoza poses the problem of the relation between power and resistance in the same way in which he poses the problem of the relation between the true and the false: in Spinoza, *resistance is the standard of itself and of power*. And yet, how is one to demonstrate this proposition when only "truth" (i.e., *veritas*), "falsity" (i.e., *falsitas*) and "power" (i.e., *potestas* and *potentia*) are crucial words and concepts for Spinoza, whereas the word "resistance" does not occur anywhere in his works?[6] Clearly, the demonstration hinges on showing how the concept of "resistance" is present and crucial in Spinoza even in the absence of the word "resistance." For I believe it may be possible to find the primacy of the concept of resistance inscribed in the grammars of *conatus*.

A singular concept; or, *Conatus*

When it comes to *conatus*, word and concept do not coincide completely and much lies in that gap.[7] We encounter both concept and word first in a complex verbal construction in Proposition 6 of Part III of the *Ethics*: "*Unaquaeque res, quantùm in se est, in suo esse perseverare conatur*." "Each thing, in so far as it is in itself, strives to persevere in its being." Leaving the concept aside for the moment, let us note (a) that the word appears here not as a noun (i.e., *conatus*, a striving) but in a verbal form, (b) that the verb in question (i.e., *conor*, to strive) is a deponent verb exhibiting aspects of both active and passive voices (i.e., signifying an active meaning through a passive verbal form), and (c) that the voice of this verb, hence, may well be indistinguishable from the intensive middle voice in which the grammatical subject is at once subject of an action and subject of a passion, in which the subject is always subject *of* and subjected *to* the direct action of the verb, in which the subject acts and is acted upon, affects and is affected, at one and the same time. In short, the word is first encountered as a verb that marks a zone of indistinction between subject and object as well as between action and passion.[8] And yet—even though the specificity of this verb is important since it implies a self-relation already by itself—it would be misguided to mistake the word for the concept here or elsewhere: to do so would lead to an interpretation of the concept of *conatus* as something akin to the Lacanian drive. (After all, what does the drive do if not repeatedly strive?) As we shall see, however, *conatus* is not drive but desire or love—these two are the same.[9]

The concept of *conatus* is first articulated by Spinoza in the *entire* verbal construction—"*in suo esse perseverare conatur*," "striving to persevere in its being"—which is then repeated *verbatim* multiple times in rapid succession (e.g., after its first occurrence in Part III of the *Ethics* Proposition 6, we encounter it again in P6Pr., P7, P7Pr., P8, P9 and P9Pr.). It is only after the verbal construction has been repeated already twice that the noun with which we usually denote the concept—that is, *conatus*—makes its first appearances (in *E* III, P7Pr., P8 and so on). In each of the first three appearances, however, Spinoza qualifies the noun very precisely and always in the same way, namely, "[t]he striving by which each thing strives to persevere in its being" (*E* III, P7, P7Pr., P8). And later, after having stated in *E* III, P9, that the "mind ... strives to persevere in its being for an indefinite duration, and is conscious of this striving," the Scholium to this proposition, so as to make things perfectly clear, begins thus: "This striving, when it is related to the mind alone, is called 'will'"—as if to emphasize: *this* specific type of striving, and not others (*E* III, P9S). In short, Spinoza takes great care to explain that the meaning of the concept of *conatus* is not mere striving, is not just any striving, but is specifically *the striving to persevere in one's being*.

From here onwards—that is, from the moment in which the relation between word and concept has been established—Spinoza often will use the word *conatus* as a condensation of the entire verbal construction, omitting the construction itself altogether: eventually the word does denote and coincide with the concept, not because the word suddenly is able to signify the concept entirely by itself, but because, since at least Proposition 7 of Part III of the *Ethics*, the word *conatus* is no longer equal to itself and has been re-signified as to mean no longer mere striving but striving to persevere in one's being. For example, Spinoza writes: "We shall strive to do everything which we imagine men ... to view with pleasure" (*E* III, P29). And in the Scholium he adds: "This striving to do something [*Hic conatus aliquid agendi*] ... the sole cause of which is that we may please men, is called, 'ambition.'" Such a *conatus agendi* would be easily misconstrued without an understanding of *conatus* degree zero, that is, without previous knowledge of the fact that the concept of *conatus* means to strive to persevere in one's being. Why, after all, would we strive to do something that pleases others? We strive in this manner because we imagine such a striving to contribute to the striving to persevere in our being. This *conatus agendi* constitutes a redetermination of *conatus*: it indicates a power of acting that is put in motion and actualized by the striving to persevere in one's being. This is all to say (a) that, after Propositions 6–9 in Part III and their attendant Demonstrations and Scholia, the word *conatus* is most often found without the original verbal construction, and (b) that this fact may lead easily to misunderstandings unless one remembers that in such cases Spinoza uses *conatus* in effect as an abbreviation for *conatus quo unaquaeque res in suo esse perseverare conatur*. The latter is precisely the way in which I will use *conatus* from now onwards.

As soon as *conatus* emerges in the text of the *Ethics*, however, it begets a concatenation of equivalences. As early as Proposition 7 of Part III of the *Ethics*, Spinoza explains that *conatus* is "the actual essence of the thing," and in Proof he specifies: "So, the power [*potentia*], i.e., the striving [*conatus*], of each thing by which, either alone or with others, it either acts or strives to act—that is ... the power [*potentia*], i.e., the striving [*conatus*], by which it strives to persevere in its being—is nothing other than the given, i.e., the actual essence of the thing." *Conatus* = *essentia* in the sense that *conatus* = *potentia* = *essentia*. Modal essence consists of a certain degree of power that is the particular mode's striving to persevere in its being.[10] Shortly thereafter we learn that *conatus* is also "appetite" ["*appetitus*"] and "desire" ["*cupiditas*"]—the difference between the two being one of consciousness: "Desire is appetite together with a consciousness of the appetite" (*E* III, P9S). Moreover, we come full circle when we learn in *E* III, P56Pr., as well as in the first Definition of the Affects, that "[d]esire is the very essence of man," "*Cupiditas est ipsa hominis essentia*." Lastly, beyond Part III, *conatus* will undergo a significant metamorphosis in Part IV of the *Ethics*, where *conatus* = *virtus*—a metamorphosis to which I will return—and it will finally be linked to intuitive knowledge in Part V. Disentangling such a complex concatenation of concepts is a task that goes beyond the scope of this essay. Here, I will only highlight a feature of this concatenation that is most relevant to my arguments.

This concatenation of concepts is inflected in a particular way by Spinoza's singular understanding of essence. Thus: "I say that there belongs to the essence of a thing that which, being given, the thing is necessarily posited, and which, being taken away, the thing is necessarily negated; or that without which a thing can neither exist nor be conceived, and conversely that which can neither exist nor be conceived without the thing" (*E* II, D2). Had Spinoza not added this last and decisive caveat—that is, "and conversely that which can neither exist nor be conceived without the thing"—we would be dealing with an essentialist definition of essence that could exceed and transcend the mode in question and hence that could constitute the essence also of other modes or even of substance. That this is a particularly crucial matter for Spinoza is evident from how strongly he emphasizes this feature of essence in the last sentences of the following Scholium:

> For my intention here was simply to explain why I did not say that there belongs to the essence of a thing that without which the thing can neither exist nor be conceived ... Instead of this I said that there necessarily constitutes the essence

of a thing that which, being given, the thing is posited, and which, being taken away, the thing is negated; or that without which a thing can neither exist nor be conceived, and conversely that which can neither exist nor be conceived without the thing. (*E* II, P10S2)

The difference between what Spinoza did not say and what he stresses he did say instead is exactly the subordinate parallel clause which expresses the mutual immanence and mutual correspondence between a thing and its essence without any remainder: "and conversely that which can neither exist nor be conceived without the thing." For Spinoza, *essence is singularity*. (This is valid not only for modal essence but also for the essence of substance: only the latter, in fact, is existence; only when it comes to substance are essence and existence one and the same—see *E* I, D1 and *E* I, P20.) Further, Spinoza throws in a final clincher: "That which is common to all things ... and which is equally in the part and in the whole constitutes the essence of no singular thing" (*E* II, P37). The essence of each and every thing is singular and cannot be shared in common. But the essence of a thing is its *conatus*, that is, its power [*potentia*]. Moreover, when it comes to the human thing, that essence which is its *conatus* is also its desire. In short, the rule of singularity must apply transitively to all four concepts—essence, *conatus*, power and desire. The *conatus* of each and every thing can only be singular. Essence inflects conatus in the singular: to each its own *conatus*.

An ethical solution; or, a common life

The essence of any thing is the striving by which that thing strives to persevere in its being. But what does it mean to persevere and, moreover, to persevere in one's being? And what exactly is this being in question here? The time has come to focus on the other part of the verbal construction expressing the concept of *conatus*, namely, "*in suo esse perseverare.*" If the verb *conor* implies a self-relation already in its form and denotes a semantic field that is eminently dynamic, there seems to be something somewhat static about *persevero*. Indeed, there is a certain *gravitas* about this verb: *persevero*, in fact, derives from *per-severus*. The adjective *severus* means severe, stern; as a preposition, *per* may mean across, through—in spatial and/or temporal terms; and when it is used as a verbal prefix, as it is in this case, *per-* may retain one or more among the meanings of the preposition or may simply function as an intensive.

To persevere, thus, means either to be severe through time and space, or to be severe through and through, namely, to be particularly, completely, thoroughly severe. Either way, permanence, persistence and even defiance in the face of adverse circumstances are implied—all of which is soon made clear by Spinoza ("The striving by which each thing strives to persevere in its being involves, not a finite, but an indefinite time," *E* III, P8), as well as in the proof of the same proposition (in which it becomes evident that what is at stake in such a perseverance is nothing less than the deferral and avoidance of the thing being "destroyed by an external cause"). Isn't this the perilous condition in which each and every thing always finds itself, namely, to be constantly under threat of destruction by external causes? It is this threat that lends *gravitas* to such perseverance: to persevere here means to be severe in the face of danger. Far from being static (even in a homeostatic sense), *persevero* too is a highly dynamic verb that implies relations of force: stoic endurance rather than stoppage, suspension, paralysis, or immobility. In Spinoza, *persevero* is to insist in being against all odds.

What being is at stake in such a perseverance? Spinoza writes "*in suo esse perseverare*" rather than *in sua existentia perseverare* or simply *perseverare*. Had he written *in sua existentia perseverare*, it would have been legitimate to interpret the concept of *conatus* as some sort of survival instinct—an interpretation that is even more inadequate than the one that understands *conatus* as drive. For Spinoza, being—that is, *esse*—is not sheer existence. The being in question here is both existence *and* essence. Moreover, this being is the non-identity of essence and existence. And it is because there is a gap, a fissure, a relating non-relation between essence and existence that it is possible and indispensable to speak of ethics and of politics (rather than of mere survival). *Conatus* may be as good a name as any for such a relating non-relation that is constitutive of the ethical and of the political. Indeed, it is precisely because *conatus* is the striving to persevere *in the non-identity of essence and existence* that it invests and constitutes the realms of the ethical and of the political in and as its determinations of desire and of virtue. The essence of the thing is the striving by which each thing strives to persevere both in its essence and in its existence under adverse conditions: isn't this tantamount to saying that *conatus* qua essence is standard of itself and of existence? Doesn't this mean that the realms of the ethical and of the political that are opened up by the relating non-relation between essence and existence depend on the self-relation of essence for their articulations and resolutions? *Conatus* then ought to be understood as the incessant striving, struggle, negotiation and adjustment between these two different types of relations (i.e., the self-relation of essence and the relating non-relation between essence and existence) for an indefinite period of time. Such an incessant striving gives logical and ontological precedence to essence over existence, but only in a very specific way. The fact that essence is standard of itself and of existence does not mean that existence has to raise itself to the level of essence and has to live up to essence; on the contrary, the only ethical-political imperative here is that one find and produce that singular way to strive to persevere in one's being that is worthy of one's existence and its inevitable contingencies, accidents and wounds—which are inevitable because one exists in adverse, unpredictable, inconstant conditions by definition. It is essence that must strive incessantly to relate to itself in such a way that existence becomes worthy of being such as it is, that is, worthy of being lived such as it is here and now rather than such as one imagines it should be or will be in an always already deferred utopian future. Essence, after all, is power qua *potentia*, namely, potentiality to become different from what one is—a potentiality that starts from what is rather than from what ought to be. *Conatus* is not love of life and especially not love of life at all costs. *Conatus* is love of life worth living, namely, that love of life which actively makes this life worthy of being lived.

If it seems far-fetched to draw such conclusions from the linguistic and conceptual grammars of *conatus*, one need only turn to Part IV where *conatus* finally turns into *virtus*. While articulating the dicta of reason according to which human beings ought to live, Spinoza writes:

> Since reason demands nothing that is contrary to Nature, it therefore demands that each person should love himself, should look for what is useful to him (which is truly useful), should seek everything that truly leads a man to greater perfection, and, in absolute terms, that everyone, in so far as he is in himself, should strive to preserve his being [*suum esse ... conservare conetur*] ... Then, since virtue ... is simply acting from the laws of one's own nature, and since no one ... strives to preserve his being except from the laws of his own nature, from this it follows, first, that the basis of virtue is the striving to preserve one's own being and that happiness consists in the fact that a man is able to preserve his being. (*E* IV, P18S)

The fact that in this passage—and throughout much of Part IV—striving is no longer *striving to persevere in one's being* but *striving to preserve one's being* may seem to pose difficulties here. The substitution of *conservare* for *perseverare*, after all, may well represent a conservative turn in Spinoza's arguments: *conservo*, unlike *persevero*, does connote a certain stasis and does seem to tilt *conatus* toward notions such as instinct of self-preservation and the like.

And yet, first of all, we need to consider that *conatus* degree zero has been well established in Part III of the *Ethics* already and hence that in Part IV the meaning of this concept can be posited as a given and that "*suum esse ... conservare conetur*" here constitutes in effect a second-degree *conatus*. For example, Spinoza writes:

> Virtue is human power [*potentia*] itself, which is defined by the essence of man alone (by Def. 8, Part 4); that is (by Prop. 7, Part3), which is defined solely by the striving by which a man strives to persevere [*perseverare*] in his being. The more, therefore, each person strives to preserve [*conservare*] his being, and is able to do so, the more he is endowed with virtue; consequently (by Props. 4 and 6, Part 3), in so far as he neglects to preserve [*conservare*] his being, to that extent he is lacking in power [*impotens*]. Q.E.D. (*E* IV, P20Pr.)

As it is customary in a proof, Spinoza reminds us of the previous propositions constituting the condition of possibility for the emergence and adequacy of the proposition at hand: in this sense, a proof always outlines an ontogenesis of that which it demonstrates. Here, crucially, *conatus* degree zero—that is, striving to persevere in one's being—precedes and enables *conatus* qua striving to preserve one's being, almost as if to say that anything we might understand as self-preservation constitutes a secondary consequence and feature of a prior striving to persevere in being.

Secondly, even in this redetermination of *conatus* what is at stake is not simply existence but being, which, as we established earlier, includes both existence *and* essence. Spinoza here writes "*suum esse ... conservare conetur*" rather than *suam existentiam conservare conetur*. Spinoza is perfectly capable to specify when what is at stake is the perseverance and preservation of existence only, as he does, for example, in the last three sentences of the Preface to Part IV, in which the distinction between persevering in existence and persevering in essence is made very clear. The striving to preserve one's being, thus, is not only a conservative striving to preserve one's existence just as it is but also a projective striving to preserve one's essence, that is, one's potential for changing one's existence, one's capability for becoming different from what one is. Even in its second-order redetermination of striving to preserve one's being, *conatus* still constitutes the paradox of a striving to maintain a state of affairs such that an event may be able to take place in and transform that very state of affairs which is to be maintained.

Having shown how the shift from *persevero* to *conservo* in the grammar of *conatus* does *not* constitute a conservative turn in the articulation of this concept, let us further explore the *conatus* in Part IV:

> Since reason demands nothing that is contrary to Nature, it therefore demands that each person should love himself, should look for what is useful to him (which is truly useful), should seek everything that truly leads a man to greater perfection, and, in absolute terms, that everyone, in so far as he is in himself, should strive to preserve his being [*suum esse ... conservare conetur*]. ... Then, since virtue ... is simply acting from the laws of one's own nature, and since no one ... strives to preserve his being except from the laws of his own nature, from this it follows, first, that the basis of virtue is the striving to preserve one's own being and that happiness consists in the fact that a man is able to preserve his being. (*E* IV, P18S)

Conatus here reaches the level of the absolute that is proper of truth and of the ethical: it is "in absolute terms" "that everyone ... should strive to preserve his being;" further, such a striving is "the basis of virtue" and its goal constitutes happiness itself. It is not the imagination, it is reason itself—that is, the realm of the true—that "demands that each person should love himself, should look for what is useful to him ... should seek everything that truly leads a man to greater perfection," etc. *Conatus as self-love*. *Conatus* is indeed that love which produces one's life as worthy of being lived.

As the rest of this Scholium makes clear, such a form of self-love has nothing in common with utilitarianism, individualism, instrumental reason, or other variations on that theme which is the imagination and its specular, narcissistic and egocentric relations:

> It follows ... that we can never bring it about that we need nothing outside ourselves [*extra nos*] to preserve our being and that we live in such a way that we have no dealings [*nullum commercium*] with things which are outside us [*extra nos*]. ... Therefore, there exist many things outside us [*extra nos*] that are useful and which, consequently, are to be sought. Of these, none can be conceived as more excellent than those that agree [*conveniunt*] entirely with our nature. For if (for example) two individuals of the same nature are joined with each other, they constitute an individual that is twice as powerful [*potentius*] as either. Nothing ... is more useful to man than man. I mean by this that men can ask for nothing that is more efficacious for the preservation of their being than all men should agree [*conveniant*] in everything in such a way that the minds and bodies of all should, as it were, constitute one mind and one body, and that all, as far as they can, should simultaneously strive to

preserve their own being [*suum esse conservare conentur*], and that all should simultaneously look for the common benefit of all [*omnium commune utile*]. From this it follows that men who are governed by reason—that is, men who, under the guidance of reason, look for what is useful to them [*suum utile*]— seek for themselves nothing that they do not desire for the rest of human beings, and so they are just, faithful, and honorable. These are the dicta of reason, which I have decided to state here in a few words, before I begin to demonstrate them in an order that is more detailed. I did this so that I might, if possible, gain the attention of those who believe that the principle that each person is bound to look for what is useful to him [*suum utile*] is the basis of impiety, and not of virtue and piety. (*E* IV, P18S)

Here, *conatus* opens itself up to the outside and to the common. More precisely, *conatus* shows itself always to have included the outside and the common as its own condition of possibility: "we can never bring it about that we need nothing outside ourselves to preserve our being and that we live in such a way that we have no dealings with things which are outside us." And precisely because the outside and the common constitute the condition of possibility of *conatus* in the first place, then *conatus* finds its highest determination in and as that collective *conatus* in which "all ... should simultaneously strive to preserve their own being ... and look for the common benefit of all." *Conatus* constitutes the immanent mediation that brings us from the outside and the common back to the outside and to the common: it is the *dispositif* that at once finds its condition of possibility in the outside and in the common as well as potentiates the outside and the common by re-determining them with a higher degree of virtue, with a higher degree of ethical and political power.

There is no guarantee that *conatus* shall correctly identify what is "truly useful" for such a potentiation and redetermination of its own condition of possibility. The principle of utility articulated in this passage does not index an individualist utilitarianism essentially characterized by competition for the useful; it is a principle of utility, rather, that posits the "truly useful" as that which is at once the useful for one (*suum utile*) and the useful for all (*omnium commune utile*). But far from indicating some sort of utopian idealism, such a principle of utility bears witness instead to the difficulty of self-love, self-relation and self-constitution understood as collective process of co-operation: on the one hand, from the standpoint of reason, the self is always already open to the outside and to the common, and hence self-love can only be a collective process; on the other hand, from the standpoint of the imagination, the self is solipsistic interiority inimical and opposed to the outside and to the common (i.e., the self has a dialectical relation to the outside and to the common understood as imaginary and specular other), and hence self-love can only be narcissism and egotism of the worst varieties. (Incidentally, while the latter standpoint is succinctly encapsulated by that dictum which has dominated the modern history of political philosophy at least since Thomas Hobbes' *De Cive*—namely, "*homo homini lupus*"—the former standpoint is succinctly encapsulated by Spinoza in his own rather different dictum in the above passage, namely, "*Homini ... nihil homine utilius*," "Nothing ... is more useful to man than man." This is Spinoza's direct answer and corrective to Hobbes' dictum). The difficulty of the type of self-love advocated by Spinoza is manifested lexically in these two passages in parenthetical yet crucial clauses such as "in so far as he is in himself," "as it were," "as far as they can," etc. But even had such provisos been absent from this passage, it is well known that Spinoza had no illusions about the fact that human beings are seldom guided also by reason and are mostly guided only by the imagination. From that fact, however, Spinoza never draws the conclusion that there is something essentially competitive and antagonistic about human relations and that human conflict is destiny unless the human is saved from itself by that *deus ex machina* which is sovereign power. Spinoza, rather, uses that fact so as to produce instead a powerful demonstration and affirmation of the collective nature of *conatus*—a nature that the imagination may well distort or foreclose altogether but that does not simply cease to be even when distorted or foreclosed. *Conatus* is not only self-love and not only love that produces one's life as worthy of being lived. *Conatus* is love that turns the only life there is into life worth living, namely, life outside and in common.

Leaving aside the question of the outside for the moment, my insistence on the inseparability of *conatus* and the common may seem unwarranted given that the only lexical evidence I have adduced so far is the expression "*omnium commune utile*" in the passage quoted above. Moreover, did I not go to great lengths in the second section of this essay to explain how for Spinoza the *conatus* of each and every thing is singular? How then can *conatus* be both singular *and* common? My question in this essay, however, has been: how can it *not* be both? The solution to this conundrum lies in the specific way in which Spinoza conceives of the relation between essence and existence. As I explained earlier, the essence of the thing is singular and cannot be shared in common, *conatus* is the essence of the thing, and hence *conatus* qua essence of the thing is singular and cannot be shared in common. *The point is that if essence is singular and cannot be shared in common, existence can only be common.* Though Spinoza has given us many indications of the necessary commonality of existence already—e.g., "we can never bring it about that we need nothing outside ourselves to preserve our being and that we live in such a way that we have no dealings with things which are outside us …" and "Nothing … is more useful to man than man"—let us also return briefly to Proposition 37 of Part II of the *Ethics*, which I will now quote in full: "That which is common to all things [*omnibus commune*] (see Lemma 2 above) and which is equally in the part and in the whole constitutes the essence of no singular thing [*nullius rei singularis essentiam*]." In this passage, the common and the singular seem to be absolutely incompatible.

But what exactly is that "which is common to all things?" Within the parenthesis, Spinoza points laconically to "Lemma 2" for the answer to this question. This Lemma simply states: "All bodies agree in certain things [*Omnia corpora in quibusdam convenient*]" (*E* II, L2). Here, the verb *convenio* means also to come together, to join. (Incidentally, *convenio* is also the verb used by Lucretius when describing the collision and union of the atoms in *De Rerum Natura*.)[11] And it is once again to this lemma that Spinoza will turn in the corollary to the following proposition, in which those foundational building-blocks of reason, that is, the "common notions," are mentioned for the first time: "From this it follows that there are certain ideas, i.e., notions, which are common to all human beings [*notiones, omnibus hominibus communes*]. For (by Lem. 2) all bodies agree in some things, which (by the preceding Proposition) must be conceived adequately, i.e., clearly and distinctly by all" (*E* II, P38C). Besides irrefutably anchoring the *Ursprung* of reason in corporeality and tethering reason firmly to the imagination, this truly remarkable passage also goes a long way in providing a possible solution to the conundrum of the relation between the singular and the common. For if there is one thing in which all bodies certainly agree is in having an indeterminate yet finite existence: for Spinoza, "existence" cannot not be a notion "common to all human beings." In this sense, *conatus* needs to be understood as the thing's striving to persevere in the non-identity of its own singular essence and its own common existence—a relating non-relation of non-identity that makes essence and existence, the singular and the common, irreducible to yet inextricable, distinct yet indiscernible from one another.[12] *Conatus* is that singular process by which each one of us strives to be at once singular and common without either forfeiting one's singularity or abjuring the common. For Spinoza, there where essence and existence are not one and the same—namely, in modes—there being is singular common. *Conatus* is the exemplary manifestation of being singular common.[13]

A topologico-political conclusion; or, *Conatus extra nos*

We have traveled far from Foucault and Deleuze, from the false problem of the dialectic of power and resistance, from stating that in Spinoza resistance is the standard of itself and of power, and from attempting to show that such a conception of resistance is inscribed in the linguistic and conceptual grammars of *conatus*. And yet, we have been traveling through a topological space, in which what is far may also be near—we have been traveling always in the proximity of the set of all sets. ... "Topology" is the title of the second section of Deleuze's *Foucault*. It is undoubtedly the topological character of Spinoza's ontology that inspires and guides Deleuze in his own distinctly Spinozist readings of Foucault. Here, I would like to locate *conatus* also in this other grammar—a topologico-political grammar—by enlisting the help of Deleuze's Spinozist Foucault. From this standpoint, *conatus* is a point on the boundary of the set of all sets, a knot on what Deleuze, inspired by Herman Melville, calls "the twisting line of the outside."[14]

Earlier, I referred to *conatus* as always already open to the outside and including the outside—thereby also implying that *conatus* may be conceived of as an inside-outside complex, as an inside of the outside, as an enfolding of the outside in which the outside is contained inside. Unlike in Foucault and Deleuze, neither the word nor the concept of outside plays an explicit and important role in Spinoza—and yet the concept is there implicit throughout. It could be argued that Spinoza's ontology does not admit of any outside: being is the immanence of substance and modes without remainder (i.e., no mode is not in substance, and substance does not include anything that is not a mode). By the same token, however, the entire plane of immanence constituted by substance and modes can be considered infinite and absolute outside—an undoubtedly heterogeneous outside, yet the outside of no inside. Certainly, the latter is similar to what Foucault calls "outside" in his essay on Maurice Blanchot, "*La pensée du dehors*"—though Spinoza's absolute outside is a potentially more radical concept to the extent to which, unlike Foucault's outside, it does not privilege the attribute of thought and involves just as importantly the attribute of extension. Spinoza's absolute outside is more akin to Deleuze's re-elaboration of Foucault's outside as force field, as the field of force relations.

Absolute outside, however, is not the only kind of outside in Spinoza: there is also another outside, a relative or modal outside—and it is there that *conatus* is first located in Spinoza's text. In Part IV, we read:

> we can never bring it about that we need nothing outside ourselves [*extra nos*] to preserve our being and that we live in such a way that we have no dealings

> [*nullum commercium*] with things which are outside us [*extra nos*] ... Therefore, there exist many things outside us [*extra nos*] that are useful and which, consequently, are to be sought ... Nothing ... is more useful to man than man. (*E* IV, P18S)

The outside indexed by the construction "*extra nos*" is first of all relative rather than absolute: it applies to modes of thought and modes of extension, in short, to what Spinoza in this passage refers to as "things." We are things among things in a world of things in which each and every thing is outside relative to each and every other thing—and, willy-nilly, *conatus* brings the thing outside of itself and makes it interact with other things. *Conatus*—namely, the very essence of the thing—is *extra nos*, is outside ourselves, is between the thing and other things, and hence produces and constitutes the thing as open set relative to and interactive with other open sets.[15]

Deleuze captures well the difference between relative outside and absolute outside when distinguishing between "exteriority" and "the outside." Deleuze writes:

> We must distinguish between exteriority and the outside. Exteriority is still a form, as in *The Archeology of Knowledge*—even two forms which are exterior to one another, since knowledge is made of the two environments of light and language, seeing and speaking. But the outside concerns force: if force is always in relation with other forces, forces necessarily refer to an irreducible outside which no longer even has any form and is made up of distances that cannot be broken down through which one force acts upon another or is acted upon by another. It is always from the outside that a force confers on others or receives from others the variable position [*affectation*] to be found only at a particular distance or in a particular relation. There is therefore a becoming of forces which remains distinct from the history of forms, since it operates in a different dimension. It is *an outside which is farther away* than any external world and even any form of exteriority, which henceforth becomes infinitely closer ... [F]orces operate in a different space to that of forms, the space of the Outside, where the relation is precisely a "non-relation", the place a "non-place", and history a becoming.[16]

In earlier passages, Deleuze had already explained that forms, of course, are traversed by forces and their relations and indeed constitute their actualization and integration: even though forces always relate to other forces—that is, even though forces always affect and are affected by other forces—forms and forces, as well as power and knowledge, are nonetheless immanent and in a relation of "mutual presupposition and capture."[17] In this context, hence, the distinction between "exteriority" and "the outside" is a distinction *within* the heterogeneous plane of immanence: it describes the difference in nature between these two dimensions of the one and only plane. Exteriority is relative outside: it is the measurable and divisible distance at once separating and relating historical forms of knowledge, namely, modes. The "Outside," on the other hand, is Spinoza's absolute outside consisting of the entire plane of immanence of substance and modes, which is formless, immeasurable and indivisible, and *which appertains to forces*—namely, as Deleuze puts it, "which no longer even has any form and is made up of distances that cannot be broken down through which one force acts upon another or is acted upon by another." Repeatedly throughout the *Ethics*, Spinoza puts much emphasis on the apparent paradox of the measurability and divisibility of modes and the immeasurability and indivisibility of substance (such as, most famously, in *E* I, P15S). In his articulation of the "Outside," however, Deleuze explicitly recasts Spinoza's absolute outside or plane of immanence not only as immeasurable and indivisible but also as the field that is crisscrossed and interwoven by force relations.

As I stated earlier, the outside posited by "*extra nos*" is undoubtedly relative: *conatus* is *extra nos* in the sense that it opens and relates modes to each other, in the sense that it connects historical forms of knowledge that are exterior to one another. In this context, moreover, *conatus* is itself a form of exteriority, a form of relation, namely, it is the historical form that materializes and incorporates the relation between forms or modes that are exterior to one another. The historicity of *conatus* as form of relation is expressed lexically in and as the word *commercium*: "we can never bring it about that we need nothing outside ourselves [*extra nos*] to preserve our being and that we live in such a way that we have no dealings [*nullum commercium*] with things which are outside us [*extra nos*]" (*E* IV, P18S). This historicity is unmistakable: it is the historicity of mercantile capital. Spinoza's word choice for the "dealings" that are necessary for life—namely, *commercium*—is used to designate not only any type of dealing in general but also commerce and mercantile transactions in particular: *conatus* here is conceptualized as form of relation that implies and presupposes certain relations of force, namely, relations of exchange and, more specifically, capitalist exchange relations.

And yet the outside posited by "*extra nos*" is also absolute outside or plane of immanence: *conatus* is *extra nos* also in the sense that it is force that affects and that is affected by other forces—thereby always indexing the plane of immanence which is produced and reproduced as open force field by all such relations and affections, that very plane upon which all forces ceaselessly fold and unfold. For what is that striving to persevere in one's being if not force par excellence? And what did we discover earlier about the verbs of *conatus*—namely, *conor, persevero* and even *conservo*—if not that they all, in various ways, refer to relations of force? And what else is being envisioned in the culminating statement that nothing "is more useful to man than man" if not joining forces, if not the collective integration of all *conatus* as force relations? *Conatus* has two faces or two openings, one turned toward the relative outside that opens modes up to other modes, and the other turned toward the absolute outside or plane of immanence understood as open field of force relations, as open set of all sets. At once form of relation and relation of force, *conatus* is outside—both relatively and absolutely.

And it is precisely when it is outside absolutely, when it is a knot on the line of the absolute outside, that *conatus* is not only force but also resistance. Deleuze writes:

> It is still from the outside that a force affects, or is affected by, others. The power to affect or be affected is carried out in a variable way, depending on the forces involved in the relation. The diagram, understood as determination of a set of relations between forces, never exhausts force, which can enter into other relations and compositions. The diagram stems from the outside but the outside does not merge with any diagram, and continues instead to "draw" new ones. In this way the outside is always an opening on to a future [*avenir*]: nothing ends, since nothing has begun, but everything metamorphoses. In this sense force displays potentiality with respect to the diagram in which it is captured, or possesses a third power which presents itself as capacity for "resistance." In fact, alongside (or rather as counterpart of) singularities of power which correspond to its relations, a diagram of forces presents singularities of resistance, such as "points, knots or focuses" which act in turn on the strata [i.e., historical formations], but in such a way as to make change possible. Moreover, the final word on power is that *resistance comes first* [*la résistance est première*] to the extent that power relations operate completely within the diagram, while resistances necessarily operate in a direct relation with the outside from which the diagrams emerge. This means that a social field resists more than it strategizes, and that the thought of the outside is a thought of resistance.[18]

The word for "power" in this passage is *pouvoir* (approximately corresponding to the Latin word *potestas*) rather than *puissance* (approximately corresponding to the Latin word *potentia*, which is the word Spinoza uses in the description of *conatus* as the power of the thing). Throughout his *Foucault*, Deleuze uses *pouvoir* whenever re-elaborating Foucault's theory of power in *La volonté de savoir* and elsewhere (undoubtedly due to the fact that Foucault himself uses the word *pouvoir* in that book). Though the word *puissance* is nowhere to be found in Deleuze's *Foucault*, the concept of *puissance* is repeatedly expressed in the various articulations of the word and concept of force. In the above passage, for example, Deleuze writes that "force displays potentiality with respect to the diagram in which it is captured, or possesses a third power which presents itself as capacity for 'resistance.'" And earlier, Deleuze writes: "The statement integrates into language the intensity of the affects, the differential relation between forces, the singularities of power (potentialities)."[19] Here, (a) the materials of linguistic integration are not three different building blocks but three different ways of describing the same set of phenomena, three different points of view on the same *combinatoire*, and (b) the singularities of power constitute potentialities because they have not yet been integrated and actualized in and as language (or, put differently, because they have not yet been integrated and actualized in and as "diagram understood as determination of a set of relations between forces," such as, for example, Foucault's diagram par excellence, namely, "*le dispositif panoptique*").[20] Undoubtedly—as Deleuze explains—for Foucault "power is a relation between forces, or rather every relation between forces is a 'power relation,'" and, at the same time, "force essentially exists in relation with other forces, such that any force is already a relation, that is to say power."[21] The point, however, is that *conatus is first of all force not power*, that *conatus* qua *potentia* is logically and ontologically prior to whatever type of *potestas* may nonetheless instantiate it, capture it and be constituted by it.

Such a logical and ontological primacy, as well as such "mutual presupposition and capture," is evident in Definition 8 of Part IV of the *Ethics*: "By virtue and power [*potentiam*] I understand the same; that is … virtue, in so far as it is related to man, is the very essence, i.e., the nature, of man, in so far as he has the power [*potestatem*] of doing certain things which can be understood through the laws of his nature alone." According to the logic articulated in this passage, it is the case both (a) that *potentia* comes before *potestas* and that, indeed, the final word on *potestas* is that *potentia* comes first, and (b) that *conatus* qua *potentia* is the essence of the human thing to the extent to which it repeatedly actualizes and re-actualizes itself as *potestas* in human existence, namely, to the extent to which it realizes our indeterminate yet finite existence in and as acts of self-determination (i.e., acts of liberation or freedom). *Conatus* is at once (a) *potentia* logically and ontologically prior to *potestas*, as well as (b) *potentia* only to the extent to which it realizes itself as *potestas* qua self-determination.

Whence resistance? As we saw earlier, *conatus* is double: it is both historical form of relation as well as relation of force. *Conatus* as relation of force, however, is itself also double: with respect to existence, *conatus* qua force is force of power (*pouvoir, potestas*); with respect to essence, *conatus* qua force is force of resistance (*puissance, potentia*). Thence what we might call the triad of *conatus*: (1) form of relation, (2) relation of force expressed as power and (3) relation of force expressed as resistance. (This is perhaps why in the passage quoted above Deleuze refers to force as possessing "a *third* power which presents itself as capacity for 'resistance.'") *Conatus* operates on three different levels at once: as form of relation at the level of strata (namely, at the level of the historical formations or "social field," which in this case bear the name of mercantile capital); as relation of force expressed as power at the level of the diagram (namely, at the level of the historical arrangement, integration and determination of all force relations, which in this case bear the name of capitalist exchange relations, by definition unequal and asymmetrical); and as relation of force expressed as resistance at the level of the outside (namely, at the level of the absolute outside or plane of immanence, which is always becoming, and which Spinoza in the Appendix to Part I of the *Ethics* significantly calls *concatenatio rerum*, "the concatenation of all things.")[22] As Deleuze puts it in the passage above: "The diagram stems from the outside but the outside does not merge with any diagram." It is when led by the imagination that we mistake the outside for the diagram—in effect merging the two in the same image of the world—thereby believing that the only way to concatenate all things is through capitalist exchange relations. Deleuze also writes: "the final word on power is that *resistance comes first* [*la résistance est première*] to the extent that power relations operate completely within the diagram, while resistances necessarily operate in a direct relation with the outside from which the diagrams emerge." It is when we are unwilling and unable to distinguish between the diagram and the outside that we also mistake resistance for power—merging the two in the same image of force—thereby actualizing resistance at best futilely as the dialectical binary opposite of power rather than as that force of the outside which may change power and its diagram (for the better or for the worse or both).

But if the imagination shoves us into the arms of the dialectic of power and resistance, is then reason, which always gives us adequate knowledge of the world, sufficient for *conatus* to disengage power from resistance and *potestas* from *potentia*? Is reason sufficient for *conatus* to articulate the always chiasmic relations between power and resistance and between *potestas* and *potentia* in such a way that the latter may have not only logical and ontological but also *political* primacy—namely, capacity for historical change—over the former? Despite the fact that the dicta of reason posit that "nothing is more useful to man than man" and lead all *conatus* to transform the human community in such a way that to strive to persevere in one's being, to look for what is useful for oneself, and to look "for the common benefit of all" are one and the same, and despite the fact that Spinoza adds that "to act absolutely in accordance with virtue is simply to act, live, and preserve one's being (these three mean the same) in accordance with the guidance of reason" (*E* IV, P24)—despite all that, Spinoza's answer to this burning question ultimately is no. Reason does pave the way—thereby enabling us to conceptualize and even to desire such a human community—but it does not take us there. Had reason sufficed, after all, there would have been no need for Spinoza to conceive of a third kind of knowledge inclusive of yet beyond both the first (i.e., imagination) and the second (i.e., reason), namely, intuition.

So far, we have traveled through and confined ourselves to Parts III and IV—due to the fact that the word and the concept of *conatus* are first and most centrally articulated there—and we have not ventured into Part V and its primary concern, namely, the third kind of knowledge or intuition and the eternal intellectual love of God that arises from it.[23] Though there is neither time nor space for a prolonged adventure into EV, we do need to note at least that it is neither in imagination nor in reason but in intuition that *conatus* finds its fullest and most virtuous realization.

Let us start with Proposition 25: "The highest striving of the mind [*Summum Mentis conatus*], and its highest virtue, is to understand things by the third kind of knowledge" (*E* V, P25). A bit later he adds: "The striving or desire [*Conatus seu Cupiditas*] of knowing things by the third kind of knowledge cannot arise from the first kind of knowledge but can arise from the second" (*E* V, P28). (In case we be misled by the facts that here such a striving is referred to as a striving of the mind and that the love of God that arises from the third kind of knowledge is defined as "intellectual," we need to note that in Proposition 13 of Part II Spinoza defines the mind as the idea of the body and, further, that throughout Part V Spinoza repeatedly explains how the third kind of knowledge involves necessarily also the body, such as, for example, in *E* V, P29 and *E* V, P29Pr.) When *conatus* is no longer completely under the spell of the imagination and is primarily under the guidance of reason, it can at best metamorphose into the desire for extending and reaching beyond reason and for achieving the third kind of knowledge: in its final and highest redetermination, the striving to persevere in one's being is not only the rational striving to preserve one's being and to look for that which is truly useful—namely, useful at once for oneself and for all—but also the striving to know the world and to understand things according to intuition. The best possible way to strive to persevere in one's being is to intuit. But what exactly is to intuit?

Already in Part II Spinoza tells us that the third kind of knowledge "proceeds from an adequate idea of the formal essence of some of the attributes of God to an adequate knowledge of the essence of things" (*E* II, P40S2)—and this definition of the third kind of knowledge is repeated several times in Part V. To intuit is to achieve "adequate knowledge of the essence of things," and such a knowledge "proceeds," derives, is deduced from the essence of substance. To be known adequately, modal essence needs to be deduced from the essence of substance. Intuitive knowledge entails not only understanding that *aliquid* which makes each and every thing singularly what it is but also understanding such an *aliquid* by starting from that which necessarily exists in the thing, which is not its own essence but the essence of substance. Through a deductive procedure, such knowledge produces a link between the essence of substance and the essence of modes: it reaches and comprehends the singular essence of each and every thing by linking it to the essence of substance that is immanent yet irreducible to it. In short, it is at one stroke that intuitive knowledge understands modal essence and links it to the essence of substance. This is to say that intuitive knowledge conceives of modal essence in and as the link to the essence of substance: modal essence is the link between itself and that which causes all modes to exist as linked to one another. It turns out that that which is most singular about each and every thing derives from, and consists in its being a link to the link of all links, namely, a link to absolute outside or plane of immanence or concatenation of all things. That which is most singular in us all—namely, *conatus* qua essence—is the way in which we relate to our being embedded in and constituted by the concatenation of all things, is our singular manner of being-in-common, is our singular position in being-in-the-world and the potentiality of that position.

The fullest fulfillment of *conatus*, thus, is to know the essence of things, to know their *conatus*. *Conatus* fulfills itself in knowledge of *conatus* qua essence—a knowledge that can be achieved only at the point of tangency with the outside, namely, there where *conatus* becomes force of resistance. In its highest realization and redetermination, *conatus* is resistance. To intuit is to resist: intuition takes place on the line of the outside where the striving to persevere in one's being turns into the striving to resist. Moreover, intuition is radically transformative knowledge—which is why *conatus* qua *essentia* and qua *potentia* has not only logical and ontological but also political primacy. Spinoza writes:

[T]he knowledge of singular things, which I have called intuitive, or, of the third kind ... is more powerful than the universal knowledge that I have said to be of the second kind. For although I have shown generally in Part One that all things ... depend on God in respect of essence and existence, yet that demonstration—although legitimate and beyond doubt—does not so affect our mind as when it is inferred from the very essence of any singular thing which we declare to depend on God. (*E* V, P36S)

Knowing within the limits of reason alone does not change a thing. Such is the trouble with reason: it is too general, too "universal"—and hence it does not affect us enough. Reason lacks enough power to move us, to change us significantly. In particular, that which Spinoza demonstrates according to reason in Part I— namely, "that all things ... depend on God in respect of essence and existence," that all things are embedded in that which at once causes them and inheres in them, that all things are concatenated—is never so "powerful" as when *conatus* realizes itself in knowledge of *conatus* as that "very essence" which depends on absolute outside or plane of immanence or concatenation of all things, is never so "powerful" as when *conatus* realizes itself in knowledge of *conatus* as that "very essence" which is resistance. There where *conatus* is resistance— namely, on the line of the outside—there *conatus* is most powerful and stands to transform radically all *conatus*. Deleuze can say that the "diagram of forces presents singularities of resistance ... which act in turn on the strata ... in such a way as to make change possible" because "power relations operate completely within the diagram, while resistances necessarily operate in a direct relation with the outside from which the diagrams emerge"—thereby being capable of changing both historical strata and diagrams of power. Indeed, it is only because intuition re-determines *conatus* as resistance by relating and linking it to the absolute outside that radical politics is at all possible.

But if, as Spinoza cautions, the third kind of knowledge is not only not guaranteed but also difficult to achieve and rarely achieved, and if it is such a radically transformative knowledge that re-determines *conatus* as resistance, how can we say that the final word on power is that *resistance comes first*? It would make more sense to say that, if and when resistance does come, it certainly comes last! The point, however, is that *resistance always comes first and last*. As always in topological-political space-time, *conatus* as resistance comes first and last because it belongs to another space, to another time, to another dimension, namely, eternity. It might help here to remember that the third kind of knowledge is knowledge *sub quadam aeternitatis specie*, namely, under a certain species of eternity. Intuition is knowledge from the standpoint of eternity. This means that knowledge of modal essence as link to the essence of substance is not only knowledge of that which is eternal but also eternal knowledge: it itself takes place, operates and unfolds in eternity. Diagrams of power are constituted and integrated by reason and in history, while acts of resistance come into being by intuition and in eternity. Power lives in history, while the moment of resistance—much like the moment of love—is eternal. Spinoza writes: "The intellectual love of God that arises from the third kind of knowledge is eternal" (*E* V, P33). In the Scholium, he adds: "Although this love of God does not have a beginning ... yet it has all the perfections of love, just as if it had come into being. ... Nor there is any difference here, except that the mind will have had eternally these same perfections that we have just supposed to be added to it." Once in love or in resistance, it is *just as if* such love and such resistance had come into being—for when truly loving, when truly resisting, there was no beginning and there shall be no end, there is no before and no after, there is endurance without duration, and the first and the last are each the future anterior of the other. When in love and in resistance, above all, there is no fear of death—which condition Spinoza indicates as supreme freedom (see *E* V, P38; *E* V, P38S; *E* V, P39; and *E* V, P39S). Is there anything more politically explosive that striving to persevere in one's being without fear of death?

When discussing Definition 8 of Part IV, we saw that under the guidance of reason, on the one hand, *conatus* qua *potentia* is logically and ontologically prior to *potestas*, and, on the other hand, *conatus* qua *potentia* constitutes the essence of the human only to the extent to which it repeatedly actualizes itself as *potestas* in human existence, namely, only to the extent to which it realizes our indeterminate yet finite existence in and as acts of self-determination, in and as sovereign acts of freedom. But if reason leads *conatus* down the path of sovereignty, it does so only in order to pave the way for the third kind of knowledge and its superior self-determination and supreme freedom. Intuition turns *conatus* into resistance thereby delivering us from self-determination and freedom intended as sovereign *potestas* and delivering us instead up to the terrifying joy of the absence of the fear of death. *Potestas* is a necessary path, a necessary strategy and a necessary achievement—as long as one does not stop there. *Potestas* must be achieved only so as to be relinquished in an ultimate surrender to and affirmation of being-in-common. Such surrender and affirmation never completely erase the possibility of the re-constitution of *potestas*, which lies in abeyance even when relinquished and deactivated.[24] And yet such surrender and affirmation also beget another freedom, namely, not the freedom of sovereignty but the freedom and liberation from sovereignty:

only the latter is that freedom to which the title of Part V refers—"*De Potentia Intellectus, seu De Libertate Humana*"—a freedom that is all but synonymous with *potentia*.[25] *Potestas* derives from *potentia* and leads to *potentia*—which always comes first and last. This other freedom or liberation is achieved only when *conatus* is the striving to persevere in one's being not as sovereign but as being singular common *extra nos*.

Acknowledgment

I would like to thank Tony Brown, Anjali Ganapathy, Moira Gatens, Patricia Hayes, Joe Hughes, Qadri Ismail, Paolo Israel, Premesh Lalu, Ryan Nefdt, Sara Nelson, Fernanda Pinto de Almeida, Arun Saldanha, Michelle Smith, Jane Taylor, Ross Truscott, Maurits van Bever Donker, all members of the Spinoza Scholarship Group at the University of Minnesota, as well as particularly engaged audiences at Western Sydney University and at The Centre for Humanities Research at The University of the Western Cape, for their incisive questions and comments on earlier versions of this essay. I am grateful, above all, to Kiarina Kordela and Dimitris Vardoulakis: without their exceptional intellectual incitements and inducements, I would have never written this essay in the first place.

Notes

1   Gilles Deleuze, *Foucault*, trans. by Seán Hand (Minneapolis: University of Minnesota Press, 1988), 89. Gilles Deleuze, *Foucault* (Paris: Les Éditions de Minuit, 1986), 95.

2   Michel Foucault, *The History of Sexuality. Volume I: An Introduction*, trans. by Robert Hurley (New York: Vintage Books, 1990), 97. Translation modified. Michel Foucault, *Histoire de la sexualité 1. La volonté de savoir* (Paris: Gallimard, 1976), 125-26.

3   Foucault, *The History of Sexuality*, 95-96. Translation modified. Foucault, *Histoire de la sexualité 1*, 126-27.

4   For a different attempt to articulate the primacy of resistance—one that turns to Marx rather than to Spinoza—see Michael Hardt and Antonio Negri, *Multitude. War and Democracy in the Age of Empire* (New York: The Penguin Press, 2004), 64-69.

5   Spinoza, *Ethics*, trans. by G. H. R. Parkinson (Oxford: Oxford University Press, 2000)—on occasion, translations are modified. Spinoza, *Opera*, ed. by C. Gebhardt (Heidelberg: Carl Winters, 1925).

6   Neither *resistentia* nor *resisto* are listed in Emilia Giancotti Boscherini's *Lexicon Spinozanum* (The Hague: Martinus Nijhoff, 1970).
7   It could be argued that the concept is implicit in the intricate constellation consisting of the first eight definitions which opens the *Ethics* and in which the word is absent. In particular, the concept is already present in the way in which this whole effects one of its parts, that is, in the way in which this entire constellation of eight definitions determines the significance of *E* I, D7. It is the explicit emergence of *conatus* in the *Ethics*, however, that concerns me here.
8   On the importance of this zone of indistinction for Spinoza, see Giorgio Agamben, "Absolute Immanence," in *Potentialities: Collected Essays in Philosophy*, trans. by Daniel Heller-Roazen (Stanford, CA: Stanford University Press, 1999), 234–45.
9   On the relation between *conatus*, desire and love, see the mesmerizing last pages of Lacan's *Seminar XI*. Jacques Lacan, *The Seminar of Jacques Lacan. Book XI: The Four Fundamental Concepts of Psychoanalysis*, trans. by Alan Sheridan (New York: W.W. Norton, 1998), 275–76. But see also Agamben, "Absolute Immanence," 236, as well as Frédéric Lordon, *Willing Slaves of Capital: Spinoza and Marx on Desire*, trans. by Gabriel Ash (London: Verso, 2014), 72. Slavoj Zizek's purportedly Lacanian understanding of *conatus* seems to agree with my emphasis on the difference between *conatus* and drive. Zizek writes:

> What is unthinkable for [Spinoza] is what Freud called "death drive": the idea that *conatus* is based on a fundamental act of self-sabotaging. Spinoza, with his assertion of *conatus*, of every entity's striving to persist and strengthen its being and, in this way, striving for happiness, remains within the Aristotelian frame of what a good life is—what is outside his scope is what Kant calls 'categorical imperative,' an unconditional thrust that parasitizes upon a human subject without any regard for its well-being, 'beyond the pleasure-principle,' and that, for Lacan, is the name of desire at its purest.

Aside from the fact that to understand the death drive as "a fundamental act of self-sabotaging" is simplistic and misguided (e.g., by the same token, one could understand the death drive as a fundamental act of self-constitution), and aside from the fact that the conflation of "death drive" and "desire at its purest" in Lacan is a reductive and misleading rendition of Lacan's thought on these concepts, I will argue, contrary to Zizek, that *conatus* includes the possibility of self-destruction. Slavoj Zizek, "Spinoza, Kant, Hegel … and Badiou!" http://www.lacan.com/zizphilosophy1.htm. For a pointed and compelling rebuttal of Zizek's position that is far more faithful both to Lacan and to Spinoza, see A. Kiarina Kordela, "A Thought beyond Dualisms, Creationist and Evolutionist Alike," in ed. by Dimitris Vardoulakis, *Spinoza Now* (Minneapolis: University of Minnesota Press, 2011), 331–33.
10 On *conatus* as degree of power (*puissance*), see Gilles Deleuze, *Expressionism in Philosophy: Spinoza*, trans. by Martin Joughin (New York: Zone Books, 1992), 230–31,

but also 240. Gilles Deleuze, *Spinoza et le problème de l'expression* (Paris: Les Editions de Minuit, 1968), 209–10 and 219. But see also Gilles Deleuze, "Index of the Main Concepts of the *Ethics*," in *Spinoza: Practical Philosophy*, trans. by Robert Hurley (San Francisco, CA: City Lights Books, 1988), 98–99 and 102. Importantly, in his "Index" Deleuze does not have a separate entry for *conatus*; rather, he discusses *conatus* within the entry for "Power." On the relation between *conatus* and *potentia*, see also Antonio Negri, *The Savage Anomaly: The Power of Spinoza's Metaphysics and Politics*, trans. by Michael Hardt (Minneapolis: University of Minnesota Press, 1991), 146–47.

11 Titus Lucretius Carus, *De Rerum Natura*, Book V, Line 429. Lucretius, *On the Nature of Things*, trans. by W. H. D. Rouse (Cambridge: Harvard University Press, 1924), 416.

12 The essence of each and every thing is to strive to maintain its singularity and its commonality non-identical yet in symbiosis with one another: modes are essentially split in the sense that what fuels and sustains their being is precisely that which provides them with two irreducible, heterogeneous and asymmetrical aspects, one singular and one common. Far from constituting a lament mourning paradises lost of wholeness and bemoaning the irreparably fragmented and alienated nature of modal being and of the human condition, such a conception of the relation between singular essence and common existence posits their non-identity as the precondition for any project of liberation: for Spinoza, it is not in the fusion between the two that love and freedom lie; rather, it is in the constantly re-negotiated and re-determined mutual *adequacy* of the two that the potential for love, freedom and liberation lies.

13 I argue for the relating non-relation between singular and common in Spinoza also Cesare Casarino, "Marx before Spinoza: Notes toward an Investigation," in ed. by Vardoulakis, *Spinoza Now*, 213–14. On the relation between the singular and the common, see also Hardt and Negri's *Multitude*, 125, 198, 308, 348–49.

14 Deleuze, *Foucault*, 44. Deleuze, *Foucault*, 51.

15 Or, as Negri puts it, "*Conatus* extends itself toward the interindividual and intrahuman dynamic." Negri, *The Savage Anomaly*, 150. Translation modified. Antonio Negri, *Spinoza* (Rome: DeriveApprodi, 1998), 199.

16 Deleuze, *Foucault*, 86–87. Translation modified. Deleuze, *Foucault*, 92.

17 Deleuze, *Foucault*, 71–72, 74–75, 81–82. Deleuze, *Foucault*, 78–79, 81, 88–89.

18 Deleuze, *Foucault*, 90–91. Translation modified. Deleuze, *Foucault*, 95–96.

19 Deleuze, *Foucault*, 79. Deleuze, *Foucault*, 86.

20 Deleuze, *Foucault*, 36, but see also 31–39. Deleuze, *Foucault*, 44, 39–48.

21 Deleuze, *Foucault*, 70. Deleuze, *Foucault*, 77.

22 For a reading of the significance of *concatenatio rerum* in the *Ethics*, see Casarino, "Marx before Spinoza," 179–234; but see also Yves Citton, "ConcateNations: Globalization in a Spinozist Context," in ed. by Diane Morgan and Gary Bantham, *Cosmopolitics and the Emergence of a Future* (New York: Palgrave Macmillan, 2007), 91–117.

23 See *E* V, P32C. Spinoza writes that from "the third kind of knowledge there necessarily arises the intellectual love of God."
24 For an excellent argument regarding how Spinoza derails "the logic of sovereignty"—an argument which is based on the *Tractatus Theologico-Politicus* rather than on the *Ethics*, and which ultimately may be less hopeful than mine with respect to the possibility of relinquishing sovereignty—see Dimitris Vardoulakis, *Sovereignty and Its Other. Toward the Dejustification of Violence* (New York: Fordham University Press, 2013), 123, but see also 122–40.
25 On this matter, see also Lordon, *Willing Slaves of Capital*, 23.

Bibliography

Agamben, Giorgio. "Absolute Immanence," in *Potentialities: Collected Essays in Philosophy*, trans. by Daniel Heller-Roazen. Stanford, CA: Stanford University Press, 1999.

Casarino, Cesare. "Marx before Spinoza: Notes toward an Investigation," in ed. by Dimitris Vardoulakis, *Spinoza Now*. Minneapolis: University of Minnesota Press, 2011.

Citton, Yves. "ConcateNations: Globalization in a Spinozist Context," in ed. by Diane Morgan and Gary Bantham, *Cosmopolitics and the Emergence of a Future*. New York: Palgrave Macmillan, 2007.

Deleuze, Gilles. *Expressionism in Philosophy: Spinoza*, trans. by Martin Joughin. New York: Zone Books, 1992.

Deleuze, Gilles. *Foucault*. Paris: Les Éditions de Minuit, 1986.

Deleuze, Gilles. *Foucault*, trans. by Seán Hand. Minneapolis: University of Minnesota Press, 1988.

Deleuze, Gilles. "Index of the Main Concepts of the *Ethics*," in *Spinoza: Practical Philosophy*, trans. by Robert Hurley. San Francisco, CA: City Lights Books, 1988.

Deleuze, Gilles. *Spinoza et le problème de l'expression*. Paris: Les Éditions de Minuit, 1968.

Foucault, Michel. *Histoire de la sexualité 1. La volonté de savoir*. Paris: Gallimard, 1976.

Foucault, Michel. *The History of Sexuality. Volume I: An Introduction*, trans. by Robert Hurley. New York: Vintage Books, 1990.

Giancotti Boscherini, Emilia. *Lexicon Spinozanum*. The Hague: Martinus Nijhoff, 1970.

Hardt, Michael and Antonio Negri. *Multitude: War and Democracy in the Age of Empire*. New York: The Penguin Press, 2004.

Kordela, A. Kiarina. "A Thought beyond Dualisms, Creationist and Evolutionist Alike," in ed. by Dimitris Vardoulakis, *Spinoza Now*. Minneapolis: University of Minnesota Press, 2011.

Lacan, Jacques. *The Seminar of Jacques Lacan. Book XI: The Four Fundamental Concepts of Psychoanalysis*, trans. by Alan Sheridan. New York: W.W. Norton, 1998.

Lordon, Frédéric. *Willing Slaves of Capital: Spinoza and Marx on Desire*, trans. by Gabriel Ash. London: Verso, 2014.

Lucretius. *On the Nature of Things*, trans. by W. H. D. Rouse. Cambridge: Harvard University Press, 1924.

Negri, Antonio. *Spinoza: l'anomalia selvaggia; Spinoza sovversivo; Democrazia ed eternità in Spinoza*. Introductions by Gilles Deleuze, Pierre Macherey, and Alexandre Matheron. Rome: DeriveApprodi, 1998.

Negri, Antonio. *The Savage Anomaly: The Power of Spinoza's Metaphysics and Politics*, trans. by Michael Hardt. Minneapolis: University of Minnesota Press, 1991.

Spinoza. *Ethics*, ed. and trans. by G. H. R. Parkinson. Oxford: Oxford University Press, 2000.

Spinoza. *Opera*, v. 2, ed.by C. Gebhardt. Heidelberg: Carl Winters, 1925.

Vardoulakis, Dimitris. *Sovereignty and Its Other. Toward the Dejustification of Violence*. New York: Fordham University Press, 2013.

Zizek, Slavoj. "Spinoza, Kant, Hegel ... and Badiou!" http://www.lacan.com/zizphilosophy1.htm

4

Beyond Legitimacy: The State as an Imaginary Entity in Spinoza's Political Ontology

Juan Domingo Sánchez Estop

Introduction

When asked to write a contribution to a book on authority in Spinoza's philosophy, I felt somewhat perplexed: how could one discuss "authority" in Spinoza, since authority is in the mainstream tradition synonymous with legitimacy and Spinoza is, undoubtedly, a resolute opponent of any theory of legitimacy? Authority, at least in this meaning, is definitely not a Spinozist concept.

To explore this, I had first to discuss the occurrences of "authority" in Spinoza's works in order to define or to re-define authority in Spinozan terms. I see, then, authority redefined in Spinoza as the power to exact obedience. Authority would be a relation of obedience, but real authority, even in this context, has to be distinguished from mere obedience obtained by sheer violence, and more precisely it should be defined in terms of affects and subjectivation, that is, the production of the obedient subject. Accordingly, Part II of the *Ethics*, where Spinoza explores the dynamics of subjectivation, has been useful to examine the imaginary mechanisms behind obedience.

This whole redefinition of the concept of authority in Spinoza made me realize how anomalous Spinoza's position on this matter can be if compared to the mainstream tradition of political philosophy, which since antiquity has always viewed authority as the transcendent legitimacy of power. In describing this anomaly, I follow Antonio Negri's historiographical distinction of two lines in modern political philosophy: one that is "blessed" and another that is "accursed"; the former being based on a transcendent conception of legitimacy and the latter viewing legitimacy as an imaginary effect of real power. This leads me to an examination in terms of the Spinozan theory of imagination—as seen through Althusser's original views on Spinoza—of the political aspects of subjectivation, and as a necessary consequence, of the imaginary object of political obedience, the State, as a supposedly separate reality beyond social relations. The State could consequently be seen as an imaginary entity, as an "ens imaginationis" in Spinoza's own terms. This finally allows me to confirm the "two lines" hypothesis, through one of the few texts on the State written by Marx.

"Authority" in the tradition and in Spinoza

What is authority for Spinoza? Answering this question is no simple matter, since from the outset, when we look for the closest term to "authority" in the original Latin text of Spinoza, we realize that the English "authority" stands for two slightly different terms with different meanings: *auctoritas* and *authoritas*.

Auctoritas is a classical political term, meaning a kind of political command as distinct from mere power (*TP* 8.17, 8.44, 10.3-4).[1] What specifies *auctoritas* is that political command is sustained by a particular principle, related to the kind of obedience it inspires. Authority is thus not mere power, but something added to it.

Auctoritas comes from the Latin word *auctor*, and *auctor* from the verb *augere* (to augment, to sustain) in which what is sustained or augmented by authority is the political community through a regular reference to its foundation.[2] Authority in ancient Rome was the ground of legitimate power since it recalled, beyond the differences between the successive actors of power, the founding act of the *auctores*, the founders of the polity. Hence authority does not command obedience through violence nor through persuasion, but by the mere reference to the memory of this particular moment as a permanent source of legitimacy. As Paul Ricoeur summarizes this matter:

> Authority does border on violence as the power to impose obedience, that is, as domination. But what distinguishes it from violence is precisely the creditability attached to its character of legitimacy, at least, its claimed legitimacy, and, over against it, the credit or credence attached to its recognition or non-recognition or the right of my superior—as an institution or an individual—to impose obedience on me.[3]

Authority is the supplement to power that gives it legitimacy.

The other authority, written *authoritas*, has the same meaning as *auctoritas* in most occurrences in the works of Spinoza, mainly in the *Theologico-Political Treatise*, but also a specialized meaning related to philosophical or religious matters.⁴ In this second case, authority belongs to the "author," that is the classical universally recognized writer, in such instances as "Saint Paul's authority" (*TTP* 205) or "the authority of the 'doctors'" (*TTP* 234). In this meaning, it relates to the "argument of authority," which in scholastic philosophy took the opinions of some "authors" for valid truths one could readily use in sound argumentation.

Both *auctoritas* and *authoritas* were criticized by Spinoza from an ethical and epistemological point of view, since both are grounded in ethico-political or intellectual passiveness as opposed to the ethical and intellectual freedom and activity the *Ethics* promotes. However, *auctoritas* and *authoritas* remain perfectly relevant in political contexts as actual grounds of the polity. Accordingly, despite this nuance in its meaning, authority in Spinoza is, above all, an ethical and political fact, as it is intimately related to obedience, whether political or intellectual. *Authoritas,* in this second meaning, is then a special case of *auctoritas*, and *auctoritas* should be interpreted almost as a synonym of *potestas,* political power in general, always conceived by Spinoza in political contexts as power over power, as distinct to simple power (the ability to act) which Spinoza names *potentia*.

This approximation of *auctoritas* and *potestas* in Spinoza signals the end of a historical process in which both started out as separate. In ancient Rome, *auctoritas* and *potestas* were split into two different institutions: respectively the Senate and the magistrates. The Senate was composed of members of the aristocracy and the magistrates were elected by the people. In *De Legibus,* Cicero proposes to subject *potestas* to *auctoritas* within a moderate constitution in which the decrees of the Senate limit the "uncontrollable" power of the people through an appeal to the *status* (the constitution) of the City, but even doing this, he will attribute *potestas* and *auctoritas* to different institutions:

> Its [The Senate's] decrees shall be binding. For the fact is that if the Senate is recognized as the leader of public policy, and all the other orders defend its decrees, and are willing to allow the highest order to conduct the government by its wisdom, then this compromise, by which supreme power [*potestas*] is granted to the people and actual authority to the Senate [*auctoritas*], will make possible the maintenance of that balanced and harmonious constitution [*moderatus et concors civitatis status*] which I have described.⁵

Thus the power (*potestas*) of the people and the authority (*auctoritas*) of the Senate fuse into a legitimate power, that is, a popular power subject to the Senate's authority as its principle of legitimacy. Spinoza will entirely reverse and subvert this order since, as we will see, for him authority is not the basis for legitimate *potestas*, but an effect and a means of the actual exercise of *potestas*, that is, of the production of obedience. That is why many translations of Spinoza's works to modern languages rightly take *potestas* and *authoritas-auctoritas* in many contexts as almost synonyms. Nevertheless, at a theoretical level, a distinction must be kept between *potestas* and *auctoritas*, since, as we have seen, two different relations—summarizing two conceptions of power—can exist between them.

In order to make apparent Spinoza's innovation in this context, I will first present the ethical and physical roots of obedience as the *Ethics* analyze them in its second part, underlining its relation to imagination, which is not our "false consciousness," but "our lived world." Based on this, I will proceed to a discussion of the ways in which legitimacy and authority are represented, through a brief comparison of Spinoza's theory with theories that preceded it.

A short epistemology of obedience

In Spinoza, power and command immediately imply another term: obedience. Power only exists as one of the terms in the pair power-obedience (*potestas-obedientia*). This immediately transforms the question of authority into the question of (political) obedience. *Potestas* is for Spinoza the kind of power producing obedience, whatever the means to produce it, rational persuasion or imaginary intimidation:

> One man has another in his power if he holds him in bonds, or has deprived him of the arms and means of self-defence or escape, or has terrorised him, or has so attached the other to himself by benefit conferred that the man would rather please his benefactor than himself and live as the other would wish rather than at his own choosing. He who holds another in his power in the first or second way holds only the other's body, not his mind; in the third or fourth way he has made the other's body and his mind subject to his own right, but only as long as fear or hope endures. When one or the other is removed, the man remains in control of his own right. (*TP* 2.10)

Thus, even though *potestas* can be exerted through different means, the fact remains that every *potestas* produces obedience—be it passive or active. There is, however, an important difference between the physical means of *potestas* in the first two cases and the means used in the two other where it is no question of physical pressure, but of gaining the hearts and minds of the subject through fear and hope. As Spinoza has it: "Obedience is less a question of an external than internal action of the mind. Hence he is most under the dominion of another who resolves to obey every order of another wholeheartedly. Consequently, those exert the greatest power who reign in the hearts and minds of their subjects" (*TTP* 209).

Despite the fact that any kind of means used by *potestas* can produce obedience, since "it is not the reason for being obedient that makes a subject, but obedience as such" (*TTP* 209), the most effective power is the one founded on the subjects' inner obedience. This power capable of mobilizing inner obedience is maybe the one which most deserves to be named "authority," since it really involves the whole capacity of the subject and is much less the object of resistance than the violent one.

However, obedience is not a merely political concept, since like every other reality, it depends on a common ontological ground, be it called Nature or God. Consequently, more than in his political works, the roots of obedience should be explored in Spinoza's *Ethics*, the most political of his texts according to Antonio Negri, since "Spinoza's true politics is his metaphysics."[6] It is indeed his absolute refusal of any hierarchy or transcendence in Being that allows Spinoza to depart from the mainstream problematic of modern political philosophy, stressing the continuity between human society and nature. The *Ethics* takes its departure not, as Descartes' *Meditations*, in a free human subject discovering its transcendence to the world (as would later do Husserl's phenomenology following Descartes' steps) but in an already given worldly complexity, an infinite network of relations called God (or Nature), of which both the polity and the human individual are immanent parts and effects. According to this, we will follow Spinoza's analysis of imagination and then will discuss the representation of authority according to the theory of imagination, and the way subjects are manufactured through obedience.

Imagination as our "Lived World"

In Part II of the *Ethics*, Spinoza makes knowledge dependent on a dynamics of the individual, in which one can distinguish several degrees of activity. Mind is the idea of the body (*E* II, P13), and knowledge is an activity of the Mind (*mens*). Body and mind are the expression of the same thing in two attributes of God (*E* II, P7C). Hence, the dynamics of the body give us an exact indication about what happens in the mind (*E* II, P12). According to the relative passivity or activity of the mind (and the body) of a given individual, the mind of this individual can know things under three kinds of knowledge (*E* II, P40S2).

Spinoza calls the first kind of knowledge imagination, which is the correlative of the relative passiveness of our body when confronting other bodies. When affected several times by another body, our body keeps a trace of this body called *imago*: "When a liquid part of the human body is determined by an external body to impinge frequently on another part which is soft, it changes the surface of that part and impresses on it certain traces of the external body acting upon it" (*E* II, P12, Postulate 5). This image, which is not a representation of the other body, causes a deviation of the movements of our body at a physical level. Consequently, our body will act as if the other body were present, even when it is not. The correlate of this process in thought is "imagination" (*E* II, P17S). Imagination, determined as it is by the influence of the other body, represents this body as present, even when it is absent: "The mind is able to regard as present external bodies by which the human body has been once affected, even if they do not exist and are not present" (*E* II, P17C). We can see already in this text (unconnected to any political matter) how representation (the presence of an absence) is rooted for Spinoza in imagination and its physical dynamics, and not on the subject and the free will.

Thus, imagination is completely unable to determine the limits of my body and those of the other (*E* II, P16). In imagination, one has no direct access to the knowledge of things, but one knows them only through the affections they produce in me: "The human mind has no knowledge of the body, nor does it know it to exist, except through ideas of the affections by which the body is affected" (*E* II, P19). Hence, I do not know the world as it is, nor do I know myself as a distinct individual. Imagination produces this representation of the individual as an "inside"—as opposed to an outer world—we usually call consciousness. The limits of my imagination, as long as I stay in this first kind of knowledge are the limits of my world, of the world as I "live" it, or, in the terms of a philosophy of consciousness like Husserl's phenomenology, of my "*Lebenswelt*."

The series of propositions in Part II of the *Ethics* establishing the doctrine of imagination describe imagination as a state of relative passivity and its results as a closure of the individual inside its own representations. The closure of the individual in its consciousness makes the "outer world" problematic. This is why the main theories of knowledge have always put the problem of truth as the problem of either the correspondence or the adequation between the inner representations of our consciousness and the outer reality of the world. Many solutions were proposed to remedy this problem. For instance, in order to bridge the gap between inner representations and external realities, knowledge was conceived as the cause of external reality in idealism or as the appropriation of the core of knowledge (the essence) present in external reality in empiricism; or even, adequation between ideas and things was given a divine guarantee as in Descartes.

Spinoza will propose a completely different approach to knowledge since he considers consciousness not as the absolute and necessary ground for any real knowledge, but only as the effect of the external world on me as a psychic and physical individual. What had been the intimacy of consciousness is relocated in nature where, like all other finite realities, it is the effect of external causes. This will allow knowledge to free itself of imaginary consciousness and to recognize under some circumstances the existence of some common properties in my body and the other bodies, which will become the basis for activity and true knowledge. This will constitute the second kind of knowledge derived "from the fact that we have common notions and adequate ideas of the properties of things" (*E* II, P40S2). Knowing, for instance, that there is extension, distance, movement and rest, allows me to know some general relations determining my body and the other bodies, and this knowledge allows me to begin knowing those bodies and mine as they are, and no longer only as they affect me. Common notions based on these common properties are the point of departure of reason. Reason allows me to know the world through common properties and relations, but it allows me as well to proceed to a third kind of knowledge by which I know the singular essence of things as directly derived from God's attributes: "A third kind of knowledge […] proceeds from an adequate idea of the formal essence of certain attributes of God to an adequate knowledge of the essence of things" (*E* II, P40S2).

Imagination can indeed be overcome in some of its effects, but it never disappears as the background of human life. Imagination is not an error, but our "lived world," our "human condition" based on our finiteness. Spinoza gives us an example taken from the philosophical tradition to illustrate this permanence of the imagination:

> When we gaze at the sun, we see it as some two hundred feet distant from us. The error does not consist in simply seeing the sun in this way but in the fact that while we do so we are not aware of the true distance and the cause of our seeing it so. For although we may later become aware that the sun is more than six hundred times the diameter of the earth distant from us, we shall nevertheless continue to see it as close at hand. For it is not our ignorance of its true distance that causes us to see the sun to be so near; it is that the affection of our body involves the essence of the sun only to the extent that the body is affected by it. (*E* II, P35S)

To be sure, we can never get rid of what is a necessary illusion created by our finiteness and consequently by our relative passiveness in the world. Nevertheless, even if we continue to see the sun as a small and not too distant object in the sky, we can know through common notions the real distance and the real size of the sun and even the cause why we necessarily see the sun as we do. All this applies too, as we will see, to the representation of legitimacy and authority.

The representation of legitimacy and authority

The theory of imagination, or better, the theory of consciousness as imagination, will be the basis for Spinoza's *Ethics*, but also for his political theory. Just as our vision of the sun is produced as a necessary illusion by the real physical relations of natural bodies, other relations, namely the ones constituting the polity, will have similar effects on the perception of political realities. First of all, we have to describe these relations as they are in the order of nature, as analyzed in Spinoza's *Ethics*, and then we shall see how this order of nature produces as a necessary illusion the whole complex by which an individual sees himself as freely obeying to a legitimate power possessing "authority."

The political commonweal is, like any other reality, a part of nature. Moreover, it is an individual, but we should note that for Spinoza an individual far from being a simple reality, is a complex one:

> When a number of bodies of the same or different magnitude form close contact with one another through the pressure of other bodies upon them, or if they are moving at the same or different rates of speed so as to preserve an unvarying relation of movement among themselves, these bodies are said to be united with one another and all together to form one body or individual thing, which is distinguished from other things through this union of bodies. (*E* II, P13, L3D)

As for Hobbes, the political individual in Spinoza is composed of other individuals, that is, individual human beings. Individuals are combinations of smaller parts, but they are also the environments in which their constituent parts reproduce their existence.[7] Men need to reproduce different bodily parts through a constant metabolism with the rest of nature, and, for this, they have to cooperate (*E* IV, Ap. 27 and 28). Cooperation is affirmed, not as a mere possibility, but as the only framework where human life can be maintained and reproduced. For cooperation, society (*societas*), that is, the union of the different individuals under a common law, is needed. This is what the *Political Treatise* explicitly affirms:

> Now [...] every man in the state of Nature is in control of his own right just as long as he can guard himself from being subjugated by an other, and it is vain for one man alone to try to guard himself against all others. Hence it follows that as long as human natural right is determined by the power of each single individual and is possessed by each alone, it is of no account and is notional rather than factual, since there is no assurance that it can be made good. And there is no doubt that the more cause for fear a man has, the less power, and consequently the less right, he possesses. Furthermore, it is scarcely possible for men to support life and cultivate their minds without mutual assistance. We therefore conclude that the natural right specific to human beings can scarcely be conceived except where men have their rights in common and can together successfully defend the territories which they can inhabit and cultivate, protect themselves, repel all force, and live in accordance with the judgment of the entire community. (*TP* 2.15; cf. *TTP* 72)

Consequently, any natural right outside the relations of cooperation constituting society is simply abstract and void.

Cooperation, however, can be conceived in two different ways. If all men were rational and knew their true interest through common notions, a kind of anarchical cooperation would prevail in which men would help each other under no other laws than those deriving from nature and imposing cooperation: "Now if human beings were so constituted by nature that they desired nothing but what true reason points them to, society would surely need no laws; men would only need to learn true moral doctrine, in order to do what is truly useful of their own accord with upright and free mind" (*TTP* 72). This, however, is not the case for the majority of human beings who are prey to passions (*passionibus obnoxii*). Men should not be deemed to act according to reason, since our actions are much more often determined by our passions rooted in imagination than in reason. As the *Ethics* shows us, there is a huge difference between the regime of passions and the regime of reason. Passions, like imagination, are individually determined and separate individuals from one another. As Spinoza puts it: "In so far as men are prey to passion, they cannot, in that respect, be said to be naturally in harmony" (*E* IV, P32). Contrary to passions, reason, rooted as it is in the common qualities of nature, or, more precisely, in "common notions," creates convergence and harmony (*convenientia*) between human beings: "Only in so far as men live in obedience to reason, do they always necessarily agree in nature" (*E* IV, P35).

Since all human beings are subjected to passions, absolute harmony cannot exist, and a common civil law with a commonly recognized command is necessary. Law, power and obedience are then needed in order to correct the effect of human passions. Power acts accordingly as a source of fear and hope substituting the true ends of the common law with prizes and punishments, that is, with other ends that everyone, even the ignorant and passionate, can understand:

> Hence legislators have wisely contrived (in order to constrain all men equally) another purpose very different from the one which necessarily follows from the nature of laws. They promise to those who keep the laws things that the common people most desire, and threaten those who violate them with what they most fear. In this way they have tried to restrain the common people like a horse with a bridle, so far as it can be done. This is why the essence of law is taken to be a rule of life prescribed to men by the command of another; and consequently those who obey the laws are said to live under law and are regarded as subjects of it. (*TTP* 58)

There are two mechanisms of cooperation, respectively the free interaction of individuals and obedience to a common authority (*potestas*) under a common law. Since most people are subjected to passions, the main mechanism will be obedience. However, obedience, like everything in nature, has its own causes and produces a particular effect called the subject.

Manufacturing subjects through obedience

The function of *potestas* is defined in Spinoza, as we already have seen, by the effective production of obedience through a diverse range of mechanisms. However, this production of obedience entirely contrasts with the dominant theories of authority and legitimacy in that it does not suppose the existence of a subject prior to obedience, but, instead, of an individual who only becomes a subject through the operation of the very mechanisms producing obedience. In other words, power generates its legitimacy not by means of its action on subjects but through the production of subjects. The constitution of the subjects subjected to power, the subjects of obedience, is for Spinoza the same as the production of the subject as an agent. The subject (agent) is not a primary original reality, but an effect of a set of social relations, in this case, of power relations. One obeys authority, not because he is a free subject who judges and assesses the value inherent in a form of power facing him, but because he is constituted as a subject by a discourse and a set of material devices reproducing the relations of power.

Louis Althusser—the most Spinozist of the Marxist thinkers—named these devices Ideological State Apparatuses. Such apparatuses as the school, the family, the churches or many others concur in making individuals the subjects of social relations, including power. Subjects, according to Althusser, are produced by interpellation, by the recognition of the subject in the call of another subject in the framework of these apparatuses:

> I shall then suggest that ideology "acts" or "functions" in such a way that it "recruits" subjects among the individuals (it recruits them all), or "transforms" the individuals into subjects (it transforms them all) by that very precise operation which I have called interpellation or hailing, and which can be imagined along the lines of the most commonplace everyday police (or other) hailing: "Hey, you there!"[8]

Long before Althusser, Spinoza called "*imitatio affectuum*" (imitation of affects) this recognition through which I consider myself as any other individual interpellated as "you there": "By the very fact that we conceive a thing, which is like ourselves, and which we have not regarded with any emotion, to be affected with some emotion, we are ourselves affected with a like emotion [*affectus*]" (*E* III, P27). In "Ideology and Ideological State Apparatuses," Althusser makes an extensive use of the Spinozan doctrine of imagination and of the mechanisms of specular recognition based on imaginary knowledge, we could say—using Althusser's terminology—that the individuals constituted as such by recognizing themselves in these specular relations, "work by themselves" and act by themselves as "free subjects," "they recognize what they are and behave accordingly."[9] By this, they see themselves as free actors freely deciding their course of action from inside their consciousness, unaware of the causes determining their behavior: "They are, as I have often said already, conscious of their own actions and appetites, but ignorant of the causes whereby they are determined to any particular desire" (*E* IV, Pref). In this particular framework, what in reality is the completely exterior affection of an individual by a set of outer relations and institutions is lived as an inner experience.

Spinoza is no doubt a precursor of this Althusserian theory, which is strongly reminiscent of the criticism of the free will of the subject in the Appendix to Part I and in the Preface to Part IV of the *Ethics*. Criticism of free will is essential in Spinozism, but until very recently the mechanisms of subject production in Spinoza had not been paid sufficient attention by Spinoza scholars. Althusser was perhaps the first to raise awareness of the importance of Spinoza for a theory of ideology. Unsurprisingly, Althusser declared not Marx but Spinoza his main source of inspiration for his theory of the ideology:

> As is well known, the accusation of being in ideology only applies to others, never to oneself (unless one is really a Spinozist or a Marxist, which, in this matter, is to be exactly the same thing). This amounts to saying that ideology has no outside (for itself), but at the same time that it is nothing but outside (for science and reality). Spinoza explained this completely two centuries before Marx, who practised it but without explaining it in detail.[10]

Althusser's statement is justified, since Spinoza—as we saw—developed a theory of consciousness as an imaginary "lived world," but even more precisely in that he prefigures Althusser's theory of the Ideological State Apparatusses in the chapter of the *Theological-Political Treatise* where he discusses the utility of religious rituals prescribed by Moses and defines them as means to achieve obedience by producing subjects who always had in mind their own submission to a master governing their whole lives:

> And finally, in order that a people which could not run its own affairs should depend upon the words of its ruler, he did not permit them, accustomed as they were to slavery, to do anything at their own pleasure. They could do nothing without being obliged at the same time to bring to mind a law and follow commands that depended upon the will of the ruler alone. They were not permitted to plough or sow or reap as they pleased, nor could they eat or dress or shave their heads or beards as they pleased, but all in accordance with a fixed and specific ordinance of the law. They could not rejoice or do anything at all except in obedience to orders and commands prescribed by the law. Not only that, but they were obliged to have certain symbols on their doorposts, in their hands and between their eyes, to remind them continually of their obedience. (*TTP* 74–75)

One could hardly find before Foucault or Althusser a more explicit text on the production of obedience through techniques of discipline.

Legitimacy is thus not the cause of obedience, but its result. Just as Spinoza says that we do not desire a thing because it is good, but we declare it good because we desire it (*E* III, P9S), one can sustain that one does not obey a power because this power has authority, but, that, inversely, this power has authority as long as we obey to it. Since a covenant's validity depends entirely on the ability of the sovereign to enforce it through the obedience of the subject, no covenant is valid after its terms cannot be enforced any more by its parties (*TP* 2.12). As is the case with any other imaginary representation, the representation of authority and legitimacy—or of the State as a transcendent normative reality—is based on the (relative) passivity of the individual under social relations based on domination and the consequent inversion of causes and effects this kind of representations necessarily produces. We can safely apply to the part of nature that is the polity the same diagnosis about imaginary knowledge Spinoza already made in the Appendix to Part I of the *Ethics*: "this doctrine of Final Causes turns Nature completely upside down, for it regards as an effect that which is in fact a cause, and vice versa. Again, it makes that which is by nature first to be last; and finally, that which is highest and most perfect is held to be the most imperfect."

Thus, obedience produces the subjects and the subjects cooperate through obedience, but social cooperation has to be inscribed in a larger ontological framework. In determining this framework it is time to look again into the Spinozist "anomaly" at work.

Authority and obedience

Spinoza as an anomaly

To highlight Spinoza's originality, it is useful to contrast his theses with Thomas Hobbes'. Referring to the origin of law, Hobbes affirms—as Carl Schmitt reminds us—that authority, not truth, makes law: "*Auctoritas, non veritas, facit legem.*"[11] This means that *auctoritas*, a principle of political decision beyond any rational justification, but not equivalent to violence, is the base for the legal order, the order that should be obeyed by the citizens as legitimate. In other words, legal order depends on a decision by the sovereign based on his own authority. We could find a Spinozist paraphrase and perhaps an answer to this Hobbesian dictum in the statement of the *Theological-Political Treatise* quoted above, according to which: "It is not the reason for being obedient that makes a subject, but obedience as such" (*TTP* 209). The Hobbesian theory of political legitimacy is thus replaced by a materialist thesis on the efficacy of power. This materialist thesis is also a relational one, since power cannot but be a relation. Moreover, since only the relation of power defines who commands and who obeys, power is a relation producing its own terms, not a thing, nor an external relation between already existing things.

Through this thesis, Spinoza participates in a very definite trend of European political philosophy. According to Antonio Negri, there are two main trends in Western political philosophy: whereas the mainstream tradition of Western political philosophy, from Hobbes to Hegel, through Locke and Rousseau, sought to produce a consistent theory of legitimate power and legitimate obedience based on the concepts of consent, legal power, authority and legitimacy, Spinoza departs from this goal and thinks of obedience, and hence legitimacy, law and authority, in terms of mere efficacy.[12] Real authority is not based on the legitimacy of command, but on its ability to generate obedience. Spinoza, defining *potestas*, power or authority in these terms, is, as in so many other respects, the heir of Machiavelli, since for Machiavelli authority has no normative value, but should be thought instead in the terms of "the effectual truth of a matter [*la verità effettuale della cosa*]"[13] outside any transcendent or transcendental foundation. It is a fact of nature, submitted to the same laws applying to the rest of nature and not of a "moral" sphere distinct from nature. And as such fact of nature, it has to be considered as an effect (*E* I, P28), but also as the cause of effects of its own since "There is nothing [*nihil*] from whose nature some effect does not follow" (*E* I, P36).

We have seen that authority, once determined as a natural reality and conceived as the production of obedience, is a relation between two terms: the sovereign and the subject. This places Spinoza in sharp contrast to the mainstream theory of the state and, in fact, to any possible theory of the state. To be sure, the question of authority is intimately related to the question of the state. The state is defined by the mainstream current of Western political philosophy as the "actor" personifying and unifying the whole of society and transcendent to it (Hobbes), or, in other terms, as the moral personality of society. This can have such extreme expressions as Bossuet's dictum that "all the State is in the Prince's personality," but also more nuanced ones, as we see, for instance in Carré de Malberg's doctrine of "national sovereignty," the fact remaining that the state exists as a unity and as a person above the multitude.[14]

Nevertheless, the conception of the state as a transcendent, normative reality above the multitude of real society, which transforms the multitude into a people by means of representation, has no counterpart in antiquity nor in any political thought before the modern age and capitalism. Antiquity only knew theories of government, but not theories of the state. Government and state are indeed completely different things. While the State is based on the unity of the many, government is always based on an irreducible plurality. For the ancients, governing is managing plurality and creating harmony out of diversity. Since Plato, the need for a government of the *polis* is related to the need for the intellective soul, the superior part of the soul, to exert a rule over the other parts. In Plato, the intellective soul governs the two others, thus creating a harmony out of plurality. Both in the City and in human soul, the better part must govern the others. As Socrates says in the Republic:

> "To produce health is to establish the parts of the body in a relation of mastering, and being mastered by, one another that is according to nature, while to produce sickness is to establish a relation of ruling, and being ruled by, one another that is contrary to nature.[…]" "Then, in its turn," I said, "isn't to produce justice to establish the parts of the soul in a relation of mastering, and being mastered by, one another that is according to nature, while to produce injustice is to establish a relation of ruling, and being ruled by, one another that is contrary to nature?"[15]

What Plato describes here is precisely the kind of relation Cicero wished to establish between the Senate and the magistrates, a relation based in the harmony of the different parts of the polity under the rule of the better one.

Christianity created the conditions to think of authority as a transcendent reality, but the Christian doctrine of "regimen," despite the distance it took from the ancient theory of government, was not an autonomous theory of the State. One could find already in pre-medieval Christian thought a criticism of the ancient conception of political community as a harmonious whole in which a plurality is governed according to a common law. According to Augustine, justice would be necessary for the Roman Empire to become a real imperium or a legitimate political power:

> Justice being taken away, then, what are kingdoms but great robberies? For what are robberies themselves, but little kingdoms? The band itself is made up of men; it is ruled by the authority of a prince, it is knit together by the pact of the confederacy; the booty is divided by the law agreed on. If, by the admittance of abandoned men, this evil increases to such a degree that it holds places, fixes abodes, takes possession of cities, and subdues peoples, it assumes the more plainly the name of a kingdom, because the reality is now manifestly conferred on it, not by the removal of covetousness, but by the addition of impunity.[16]

But justice only comes from God. A gang of bandits exerts power through violence, which means that their power is only transitory, precarious and not guaranteed by any kind of legitimacy. According to the Christian view on politics, something not present in political power *per se*, but brought upon it from outside like "justice" as defined by God, gives the political command legitimacy and transforms mere force into authority. Criticizing ancient politics, Augustine introduces in political philosophy the need for a supplementary principle coming from outside the polity itself: a transcendent legitimacy, unknown to the ancient polities, coming from God or at least not immanent in the simple interaction of the different parts and agencies of society, nor given in its foundation like Roman *auctoritas*. Following this, in medieval Christian thought, actual power and the principle of legitimacy (justice or charity proceeding from God) that could transform power into the basis of a legitimate political community remain split and cannot be the elements of a consistent theory of authority.[17]

The horizon of war

In modern Western political thought, the two elements of "legitimate" political command identified by Augustine are still present, but they are diversely articulated according to each one of the two main antagonistic lines we presented above following Negri's historiographic suggestion:

There is a mainstream line that tries to combine power and justice. This one, by the means of different versions of the social contract, constructs legitimacy from inside the multitude as the result of the free will and the rational choice of the individuals who decide to transfer their power to a sovereign. The state, a reality beyond the multitude created by this transfer, simultaneously represents and unifies the multitude, as is the case in Hobbes, Locke, Kant, Rousseau or Hegel. Legitimacy is then based on accepted representation and power is based on justice since it is grounded on the free exercise of the rights of the contractors.

There is nevertheless another line, outside the mainstream and contrary to it, represented by Machiavelli and Spinoza and continued by Marx, for which the reality of political power is a correlation of forces, and power is, therefore, not transcendent to the multitude, but a result of its inner interactions. According to this line, no will or contract creates the society or the polity. Rather, different forms of polity develop from inside an always-already existing society.

The first line of legitimate power is, according to the second line, nothing but the temporary result of a balance between antagonistic forces in a permanent situation of war recalling Hobbes' "state of nature." Spinoza will explicitly inscribe himself in this second line in a famous statement of Letter 50. Asked about the difference between Hobbes' political philosophy and his own, Spinoza states:

> With regard to political theory, the difference between Hobbes and myself, which is the subject of your inquiry, consists in this, that I always preserve the natural right in its entirety, and I hold that the sovereign power in a State has right over a subject only in proportion to the excess of its power over that of a subject. This is always the case in a state of nature. (*Ep.* 50)

Political ontology, according to Spinoza, is thus a part of nature and follows the same rules as the rest of nature. In these non-exceptional circumstances, the sovereign only prevails over his subjects to the extent that he exceeds them in power. Only a stronger power can thus determine the action of a weaker one. Correlation of forces and antagonism are thus the only base of political authority.

This "state of nature," which Spinoza preserves "intact," was according to Hobbes a state of perpetual war.[18] Spinoza will assume this perpetual war as the perpetual framework for politics. This kind of war is not a vice of nature or of mankind, but a permanent horizon of reality, ontologically, not morally grounded. The state of nature is, according to Spinoza, the one ruled by the law of nature. The law of nature is but the expression through different finite realities of God's infinite and absolute power—a power not submitted to any rule, moral nor legal:

> So from the fact that the power of natural things by which they exist and act is the very power of God, we can readily understand what is the right of Nature. Since God has right over all things, and God's right is nothing other than God's power insofar as that is considered as absolutely free, it follows that every natural thing has as much right from Nature as it has power to exist and to act. For the power of every natural thing by which it exists and acts is nothing but the power of God, which is absolutely free. (*TP* 2.3).

Hence, the rights of natural things—man included—have no limits imposed upon them by transcendent values. Their only limits are the ones determined by their own power (potentia): "the natural right of Nature as a whole, and consequently the natural right of every individual, is coextensive with its power. Consequently, whatever each man does from the laws of his own nature, he does by the sovereign right of Nature, and he has as much right over Nature as his power extends" (*TP* 2.4). From this derives a correlation of forces between the different individuals—human and otherwise—determining a natural order in the absence of any transcendent rule or norm. This order, which cannot be separated from a perpetual war, is vividly described in Chapter 15 of the *Theological-Political Treatise*:

> By the right and order of nature I merely mean the rules determining the nature of each individual thing by which we conceive it as determined naturally to exist and to behave in a certain way. For example fish are determined by nature to swim and big fish to eat little ones, and therefore it is by sovereign natural right that fish have possession of the water and that big fish eat small fish. For it is certain that nature, considered wholly in itself, has a sovereign right to do

everything that it can do, i.e., the right of nature extends as far as its power extends. For the power of nature is the very power of God who has supreme right to [do] all things. (*TTP* 189)

To be sure, this ontological state of war is not the other of peace. Peace is not a norm and war is not an anomaly or a sin, but the very dimension of individual and collective action in a universe deprived of any moral or theological finality. This state of nature will be the horizon of human life even under the civil state and the common laws by which it is ruled. In this context, civil state is a particular aspect of the state of nature, the one in which men join their forces and cooperate with each other. In Chapter 16 of the *Theological-Political Treatise* the origin of the civil state is still—ambiguously—seen as the result of a transfer of power from the individuals to the sovereign, but this transfer is completely omitted in the *Political Treatise*. Spinoza argues there that the natural right of an isolated human being is almost void when he has to face alone the dangers of nature and to provide for his livelihood only by his own means. Therefore, cooperation and social life (*societas*) are inseparable from human life (*TP* 2.15).

Hence, the very context of natural perpetual war produces two effects in human society: on the one hand, it gives birth to society because individual men would never have survived without cooperation with other men, but, on the other hand, even inside human society, this perpetual war is not abolished, since power is based on it. In this common life, which is a natural fact inside a nature ruled by perpetual war, legitimacy, or what Saint Augustine named "*iustitia*," no longer exists as a transcendent end or a principle of legitimacy.

But it does still exist as the result of a practice of power. Legitimacy exists in this context as a product of imagination, as a necessary illusion produced by political power, as a means to reproduce its constitutive relations of force. In nature, neither legitimacy nor justice exist as normative values, but simply as the result of encounters and relations of cooperation among men. These relations can be more or less horizontal or hierarchical, but they remain grounded on a basic need for cooperation. Only the ignorant see these relations as an order (in both meanings of the term) imposed upon him "from above" by a power invested with "authority" (*TTP* 58).

One could summarize the difference between the two trends of political philosophy we have been discussing as follows: for the mainstream, the central question of political theory is: "why *should* one obey to power?"; for the other one: "Why *does* one actually obey to power?" These positions are based on two different and opposed scenarios representing two political ontologies: for the theories of legitimacy, authority—the basis of any legitimate power—is thought of as a value that a pre-existing subject could or should recognize in some forms of exercise of power, the "legitimate" ones being those that are based not on violence but on authority. For the theories based on the correlations of force, legitimacy and authority appear as the result of the correlation of forces constituting both the subject and the sovereign.

In the first case, authority is the reason why one should obey a given power, or conversely the reason why this power is a legitimate one. This implies a three-term relation between a subject, the holder of power and authority, in which the subject recognizes the authority—inherent in a holder of power—as the reason for his obedience, for his being a subject. This makes of the holder of power an exceptional kind of man, one who possesses something unique which justifies his domination on others and which the others recognize as the reason for their obedience. The sovereign has authority and because of this authority he and his government should be obeyed and are legitimate. As in so many other cases in ideological discourse, here reality is given an imaginary structure reflecting men's practices: just as knowledge recognizes truth inside its objects, desire recognizes goodness inside the objects of desire, and obedience recognizes its cause in a property of the holder of power—always reflecting Spinoza's principle in the Appendix to Part I of the *Ethics*, that, according to the ignorant, all things in the world serve human utility and desire.

On the inexistence of the State

Just as the ignorant see nature as governed by a rector or a legislator, the multitude sees social order as imposed by governors. Why does this happen? The explanation for this does not escape the common rule according to which images and imagination are produced. To be sure, the power of the commonwealth is based on relations, on the cooperation of the individuals in the creation and reproduction of their conditions of existence. The commonwealth is not a substance, but an individual—and an individual is always, for Spinoza, a complex and articulated reality. The existence and the actions of an individual are determined by a double complexity: the internal complexity of the relations composing the individual out of other simpler realities and the external complexity of all that determines the existence of such an individual. In a society, every human individual is part of a larger individual linked to others through relations.

In these conditions, the single individual experiences the power of society, not as a relation in which he takes part, but as a huge power overwhelming him. Just as in the example of the sun, it is a question of optics. Besides, this way to see common power as a substance opposed to individuals, as in modern mainstream theories of the State, which present States as big men (*magni homines*) or as persons, often incarnates power in one man. This man is then presented as possessing something exceptional, be it authority or charisma. However, he is only a man: nothing particular distinguishes him from the rest except his ability to be located at the center of a network of relations of obedience. This is particularly visible in the chapters of the *Theological-Political Treatise* on "Prophecy" and "The Prophets," in which the supposed exceptionality of the prophets is reduced to the intensity of their imagination and to the matching of their imagination and the imagination of the multitude. Despite this, the relations of cooperation easily appear to the multitude as relations of authority in which one individual is set apart as possessing a unique character entitling him to command and to be obeyed.

The human community based on cooperation sees itself as a substance independent of individuals and their actual relations, which are merely its "accidents," a substance which can take the shape of a single man through a relation of representation. This, however, is an illusion created by the imaginary and passion-based attitude of the many toward the community. To be sure, it is a necessary illusion shared by all human beings, including the rational few. The power of imagination is not abolished by the ability to rationally know the social relations of cooperation and the utility of cooperation and even the utility of obeying a single law and a single command.

Since it is the result of the imaginary transformation of a social relation into a substance through the common mechanisms of imagination, the State has no proper existence. As we have seen, power invested by authority does not belong as its property to any possible subject of attribution, since its only reality is the relation of obedience linking two—or more—persons. Obedience, to be sure, is not the result of authority, but the effect of a correlation of force. Since this correlation of force, like any effect implying an affected and an affecting body, creates an image made of words, of movements and not referring to the form of a given object (*E* II, P17S) and an imagination in the mind, the State is not a non-entity, but a mere appearance, what, in the Appendix to Part I of the *Ethics*, Spinoza calls "*ens imaginationis*," "an imaginary entity":

> We see therefore that all the notions whereby the common people are wont to explain Nature are merely modes of imagining, and denote not the nature of anything but only the constitution of the imagination. And because these notions have names as if they were the names of entities existing independently

of the imagination I call them "entities of imagination" [*entia imaginationis*] rather than "entities of reason" [*entia rationis*]. (*E* I, Ap.)

As in so many aspects, Spinoza's position in political philosophy is completely anomalous, since he is the only modern political philosopher who bases the commonwealth not on representation but on social cooperation, and who refuses to recognize representation as constitutive of the political community. This is not to say that representation does not have any place in Spinoza's conception of the polity, but he considers representation and its products as merely imaginary. Representation and command do not make the polity, as is the case in Hobbes who does not hesitate to state that "in a monarchy, the King is the people."[19] Representation of power as a transcendent substance or a person is but the necessary result of passivity and imagination. Spinoza in many respects was, as Althusser used to say, "Marx's only direct ancestor, from the philosophical standpoint."[20]

Conclusion

We could conclude, regarding the criticism of the very grounds of any theory of the State, that Spinoza agrees with Marx but perhaps less so with many Marxists. If Marx never developed a theory of the State, it was not due to a lack of time, but to the inconsistency of its presumed object. We can see Marx's project of a "critique of political economy" not as an improvement of political economy, but as the destruction of any pretention of scientific economy, in the same way as Kant's *Critique of Pure Reason* destroys all the claims to a scientific metaphysics. Perhaps not only economy as a self-regulated sphere falls under Marx's "critique," but also most probably, even if he never completed the volume of *Capital* on the State, the classical theories of the State.

We can conjecture from Marx's silence on the theory of the State, but also from some of his statements in the *Grundrisse* and other texts, that for Marx the State was not a reality beyond social relations or class struggle, but a necessary appearance (*Erscheinung*) produced by them. In the *Ethnological Notebooks*, Marx discussed a passage in Henry Sumner Maine's *Lectures on the Early History of Institutions*. Maine, one of the main historians of ancient law, criticized the "absolutist" and positivist theory of sovereignty proposed by the "analytical jurists," because it maintained that "the Sovereign person or group actually wields the stored-up force of society by an uncontrolled exercise of will."[21] Maine considers that this position is contradicted by the facts, since every sovereign power is actually limited by "moral" and "historical" factors.[22] This abstract and absolutist conception of sovereignty "is arrived at by throwing aside all the characteristics and attributes of Government and Society except one, and by connecting all forms of political superiority together through their common possession of force."[23] In other words, it is arrived at by ignoring authority (or "*auctoritas*" in the Roman sense) as a political reality, since what this abstraction of sovereignty leaves aside is "the history, the whole historical antecedents, of each society by which it has been determined where, in what person or group, the power of using the social force is to reside."[24]

The object of Marx's criticism is Maine's attempt to limit power through authority, his appeal to the founding moment of power and the ensuing tradition. This is, according to Marx, a limited and shallow criticism of power and should be replaced by the assumption that the sovereign power of the State is merely apparent and historically determined:

> Maine ignores this which is much deeper: that the apparent supreme and self-standing existence of the State is only apparent and that it, in all its forms is but an excrescence of society; in the same way as its appearance came with a given phase of social development, it will disappear again, once society has reached a phase to which it has not yet arrived by now.[25]

Spinoza's theory of imagination, which considers imagination as the product of given external circumstances and not as mere error or non-being, could possibly be a key to this theory of the imaginary nature of the State Marx is defending here. Spinoza, following Machiavelli, and followed by Marx in the "accursed line" of modern political philosophy, showed the way to a historical theory of the State which places it in the order of nature, not as a solid reality, but as an imaginary entity, an "*ens imaginationis*."

Notes

1. Except for the *Theological-Political Treatise*, all references to Spinoza's texts are to the Shirley edition of Spinoza, *Complete Works*. References to the *Theological-Political Treatise* are to the Jonathan Israel edition. For the Latin original text of Spinoza, I refer to the Gebhardt edition.

2. Cf. Hannah Arendt, *Between Past and Future*, ed. by Jerome Kohn (London: Penguin, 2006), 102.

   > The word *auctoritas* derives from the verb *augere*, "augment," and what authority or those in authority constantly augment is the foundation. Those endowed with authority were the elders, the Senate or the *patres*, who had

obtained it by descent and by transmission (tradition) from those who had laid the foundations for all things to come, the ancestors, whom the Romans therefore called the *maiores*.

3   Paul Ricoeur, *Reflections on the Just*, trans. by David Pellauer (Chicago: University of Chicago Press, 2007), 93.
4   For the terms authoritas/auctoritas, see Emilia Giancotti-Boscherini, *Lexicon Spinozanum* (The Hague: Nijhoff, 1971), 95–96.
5   Cicero, *De Legibus*, trans. by Clinton W. Keyes (Cambridge, MA: Harvard University Press, 1928), 492.
6   Antonio Negri, *The Savage Anomaly, the Power of Spinoza's Metaphysics and Politics*, trans. by Michael Hardt (Minneapolis: University of Minnesota Press, 1981), 114.
7

Now let us imagine, if you please, a tiny worm living in the blood, capable of distinguishing by sight the particles of the blood—lymph, etc.—and of intelligently observing how each particle, on colliding with another, either rebounds or communicates some degree of its motion, and so forth. That worm would be living in the blood as we are living in our part of the universe, and it would regard each individual particle of the blood as a whole, not a part, and it could have no idea as to how all the parts are controlled by the overall nature of the blood and compelled to mutual adaptation as the overall nature of the blood requires, so as to agree with one another in a definite way. (*Ep.* 32, 848)

8   Louis Althusser, "Ideology and Ideological State Apparatuses (Notes toward an Investigation)," in *Lenin and Philosophy and Other Essays*, trans. by Louis and Ben Brewster (New York: Monthly Review Press, 1971), 174.
9   Althusser, "Ideology," 181.
10 Althusser, "Ideology," 176.
11 "The classical representative of the decisionist type (if I may be permitted to coin this word) is Thomas Hobbes. The peculiar nature of this type explains why it, and not the other type, discovered the classic formulation of the antithesis: autoritas (sic), non veritas facit legem." Carl Schmitt, *Political Theology, Four Chapters on the Concept of Sovereignty*, trans. by George Schwabb (Cambridge, MA: MIT, 1985), 33. This classical formula can be found in the Latin version of *Leviathan*, ed. by William Molesworth (London, 1839–1845), ch. 26, 202.
12 Antonio Negri, *The Savage Anomaly: The Power of Spinoza's Metaphysics and Politics*, trans. by Michael Hardt (Minnesota: University of Minnesota Press, 1999).
13 Niccolò Machiavelli, *The Prince*, trans. by W. K. Marriott (London: J.M. Dent and Sons, New York: E.P. Dutton and Co., 1908), 121. Cf. Vittorio Morfino, *Il tempo e l'occasione: L'incontro Spinoza-Machiavelli* (Milano: Edizioni universitarie di lettere, economia, diritto, 2002).

14 Jacques-Bénigne Bossuet, *Politique tirée des propres paroles de l'Ecriture sainte à Monseigneur le Dauphin* (Paris: Pierre Cot, 1709), 248. Raymond Carré de Malberg, *Contribution à la théorie générale de l'État* (Paris: Sirey, 1920), 19. Carré de Malberg defends in this chapter his own theory of the personality of the State based on the doctrine of the national sovereignty, against the "German" theory of the sovereignty of the State. The State is for Carré de Malberg identical to the Nation, but distinct from the individuals who constitute the Nation. Even if the State is identified with the Nation (and is not entirely abstract as in the German *Staatslehre*), the State or the Nation as a historical social totality has a personality of its own.

15 Plato, *The Republic of Plato*, trans. by Allan Bloom (New York: Basic Books, 1991), 444a. This view has been developed by the Italian philosopher of law Giuseppe Duso in, for example, *Oltre la democrazia* (Rome: Carocci, 2004), 19.

16 Augustine, *The City of God*, in *The Works of Aurelius Augustine, Bishop of Hippo*, Vol. I., ed. and trans. by Marcus Dod (Edinburgh: T. & T. Clark, 1871), 140.

17 Less radical than Augustine in his rejection of the immanent order of the ancient polity, Aquinas will recognize the possibility of a polity based on natural law, but this polity is far from perfect and can only be perfected through charity, which only comes from God. See Paul J. Weithman, "Augustine and Aquinas on Original Sin and the Function of Political Authority," *Journal of the History of Philosophy*, 30.3 (1992), 353–76.

18 Thomas Hobbes, *Leviathan*, ed. by C. B. Macpherson (New York: Penguin, 1979), 185.

19 Thomas Hobbes, *De Cive or the Citizen*, ed. by Sterling P. Lamprecht (New York: Appleton-Century-Crofts, 1949), 135.

20 Louis Althusser and Etienne Balibar, *Reading Capital* (London: Verso, 1983), 102.

21 Henry Sumner Maine, *Lectures on the Early History of Institutions* (New York: Henry Holt and Company, 1875), 359.

22 Maine, *Lectures*, 359.

23 Maine, *Lectures*, 359.

24 Maine, *Lectures*, 360.

25 Karl Marx, *The Ethnological Notebooks*, trans. by L. Krader (Assen: Van Gorcum, 1974), 329.

Bibliography

Althusser, Louis. "Ideology and Ideological State Apparatuses. Notes toward an Investigation," in *Lenin and Philosophy and Other Essays*, trans. by Louis and Ben Brewster. New York: Monthly Review Press, 1971, 85–126.

Althusser, Louis and Etienne Balibar. *Reading Capital*. London: Verso, 1983.

Arendt, Hannah. *Between Past and Future*, ed. by Jerome Kohn. London: Penguin, 2006.

Augustine. *The City of God*, in ed. and trans. by Marcus Dod, *The Works of Aurelius Augustine, Bishop of Hippo*, Vol. I. Edinburgh: T. & T. Clark, 1871.

Cicero, *De Legibus*, trans. by Clinton W. Keyes. Cambridge, MA: Harvard University Press, 1928.

de Malberg, Raymond Carré. *Contribution à la théorie générale de l'État*. Paris: Sirey, 1920.

Duso, Giuseppe. *Oltre la democrazia*. Rome: Carocci, 2004.

Giancotti-Boscherini, Emilia. *Lexicon Spinozanum*. The Hague: Nijhoff, 1971.

Hobbes, Thomas. *De Cive or the Citizen*, ed. by Sterling P. Lamprecht. New York: Appleton-Century-Crofts, 1949.

Hobbes, Thomas. *Leviathan*, ed. by William Molesworth. London, 1839–1845.

Hobbes, Thomas. *Leviathan*, ed. by C. B. Macpherson. New York: Penguin, 1979.

Machiavelli, Niccolò. *The Prince*, trans. by W. K. Marriott. London: J.M. Dent and Sons, 1908.

Maine, Henry Sumner. *Lectures on the Early History of Institutions*. New York: Henry Holt and Company, 1875.

Marx, Karl. *The Ethnological Notebooks*, trans. by L. Krader. Assen: Van Gorcum, 1974.

Morfino, Vittorio. *Il tempo e l'occasione. L'incontro Spinoza-Machiavelli*. Milano: Edizioni universitarie di lettere, economia, diritto, 2002.

Negri, Antonio. *Savage Anomaly: The Power of Spinoza's Metaphysics and Politics*, trans. by Michael Hardt. Minneapolis: University of Minnesota Press, 1999.

Plato, *The Republic of Plato*, trans. by Allan Bloom, New York: Basic Books, 1991.

Ricoeur, Paul. *Reflections on the Just*, trans. by David Pellauer. Chicago: University of Chicago Press, 2007.

Schmitt, Carl. *Political Theology: Four Chapters on the Concept of Sovereignty*, trans. by George Schwabb. Cambridge, MA: MIT, 1985.

Spinoza, Baruch. *Complete Works*, trans. by Samuel Shirley. Indianapolis, IN: Hackett, 2002.

Spinoza, Baruch. *Spinoza Opera*, ed. by Carl Gebhardt. Heidelberg: Carl Winter-Verlag, 1925.

Spinoza, Baruch. *Theological-Political Treatise*, ed. by Jonathan Israel, trans. by Michael Silverthorne and Jonathan Israel. Cambridge: Cambridge University Press, 2007.

Weithman, Paul J. "Augustine and Aquinas on Original Sin and the Function of Political Authority," *Journal of the History of Philosophy* 30.3 (1992), 353–76.

The Cold Quietness of the Stars: Proof, Rhetoric and the Authority of Reason in the *Ethics*

Joe Hughes

1

This is an essay about the difficulty of reading Spinoza, and the ways in which an affirmation of that difficulty folds back on the image of thought we create in our encounter with his work. The way I want to work through this problem is by engaging with an argument developed by Alain Badiou in a short essay: "What is a Proof in Spinoza's *Ethics*?" which introduces a novel way of reading Spinoza: one that distances itself from the text and reads its patterns instead. The basic, implausible, thesis of Badiou's essay is just that nobody has yet asked what a proof in Spinoza's ethics is. If you do ask it—if you read, as he says, all the details of the proofs—you end up in a position with an uncanny similarity to his own. "My approach," he writes, is

> to take seriously in consideration the "geometrical order." I intend to read all the details of the proofs, to accept without restriction the fundamental idea of Spinoza himself: we can go mathematically from a mathematics of being to a mathematics of eternal love and intellectual blessedness. The secret of freedom lies in the full understanding of the logical necessity, and the political consequences are that the secret of victory of weakness and poverty over power and wealth does not lie in a negative revolt but in a positive discipline, or that the force of equality does not resemble the natural force of a storm but the mental inflexibility of a proof. With Spinoza's *more geometrico*, we learn that we have to act, not within the violent disorder of the chaos, but within the cold quietness of the stars.[1]

This approach has an equally important negative dimension. It is ultimately bound up in a polemic against two of the dominant readings of Spinoza on the continental scene, Deleuze's and Negri's. If we insist on the importance of the proof, Badiou says, we will ultimately have to reject

> all interpretations of Spinoza based on potency in terms of virtuality, on action in terms of actualization, or on desire in terms of creativity of life. In the geometrical order, which expresses the divine geometry or the mathematics of Being, nothing is virtual, and everything is actual. Nothing is a creation, and everything except God is a consequence. Even the act of thinking has no relation with a virtual disposition.[2]

The *Ethics*, here, become a kind of field on which contemporary positions in continental thought can play themselves out. It is as if you could read Deleuze or Negri or Badiou through their respective readings of Spinoza. Forget, for the moment, that Deleuze's reading of Spinoza on the question of the finite modes is explicitly inventive in a way that anticipates the claim of *Difference and Repetition* that a philosophy of immanence requires an inversion of Spinozism by making "substance turn around the modes."[3] And forget that Badiou means something quite different by "mathematics" than Spinoza.[4] It is as if, by focusing narrowly on the text of the *Ethics*, one could operate an implicit argument that a better reading of Spinoza leads to a better philosophy in the present.

This rhetorical flourish of polemic operates another implicit gesture worth making explicit—this time in the relation it establishes to the past. It is as if the field of philosophy past were a perpetual *terra nullius*, the prehistory of truth, awaiting the work of the philosopher who can return to its textures, find the details available to cultivation and set to work maximizing their productive powers in the name of post-historical truth. Such a position seems to be at odds with the letter of Badiou's other texts. Ontology, as mathematics, has a history, he writes in *Being and Event*. It is "presented exclusively in time as a situation, and new propositions are what periodize this presentation."[5] In a sense, Badiou immediately explains, this is a non-history. Mathematics is the immediate erasure of the historicity of this proposition-event: "propositions are true or false, demonstrated or refuted."[6] But—to anticipate a point to which I will return at the end of this essay—that the succession of events is immediately recaptured by an act of fidelity into a grand narrative (which is not a narrative) is only one way to think history, one that misses the strange historicity of truth itself implied in Spinoza's method.

In short, there are three questions Badiou's text poses and which I want to work through in the following pages: (1) what does it mean to read a proof, (2) how does this question determine a relation to the present, and (3) what kind of relation to the past is at stake here. Ultimately these will all fold back on a fourth—that immediate conjunction of the logical authority of reason and the political authority which Badiou calls the "secret of freedom."

2

All of these questions can be brought into sharper focus by considering what it means, in the context of Badiou's essay, to "read all the details of the proofs." He selects one proof—that of Proposition 28 in Part I of the *Ethics*—and draws up the skeleton for the proof.

Table 7.1 Alain Badiou's Skeleton of Proof of *Ethics* I, P28[7]

I	II	III	IV	V	VI	VII	VIII
						A1 D3 D5	
				D8	P20	C2.20	
			D4	P19			
					D2	P21–P22	
				A7	P11		
			D1	P7			
D3	P2–*P5	P6	C6				
A4 A5	P3						
				D1	P4	C24	
				D6	P14		P28
			D3 D6	P5–*P11			
		A1 A4	P4				
		D3 D5	P1				
					D5		
				A4	P25	C25	
				*P15			
				D3 D5 A1	P15		
				*P14			
					*P25	P26	
				Obvious	P16		
I	II	III	IV	V	VI	VII	VIII

Proposition 28 is to the far right, alone in column eight. Column seven lists the various statements P28 directly cites. Column six then tracks the citations implied in column seven, and so on. In this way, as it moves from right to left, the skeleton makes visible the ideal structure of the demonstrative process in the *Ethics* by making visible the system of implications. The table demonstrates, for Badiou, what it means to think "mathematically." Each proposition recuperates those that came before it and is explained only in terms of its predecessors. And, indeed, it is striking to see, at a glance, the way in which the propositions implicate and reproduce one another. In contrast to Deleuze's distinction between the three *Ethics*, which reintroduces a subterranean rhetorical and pedagogical element into the argument, Badiou suggests that by attending to the coherent circuit of demonstrative implication we discover in Spinoza a quite different sense of method, philosophy and the organization of life, both individual and collective.

There have been numerous attempts to formalize parts of the *Ethics* before. George Boole formalized parts of Part I in *An Investigation into the Laws of Thought* in 1854—the same year George Eliot began working on the first English translation of the *Ethics*. More recently, Charles Jarrett and Joel Friedman developed formal models of Part I of the *Ethics*. All end by acknowledging that it is impossible to formalize Spinoza without breaking radically from the letter of the text. Depending on the approach, it becomes necessary to introduce new distinctions and non-logical operators or to exclude other propositions. This led Boole to remark that too many people have attributed to Spinoza's text a "formal cogency, to which in reality it possesses no just claim."[8] Jarrett, for his part, includes a list of twenty-six non-logical operators he had to introduce and discusses the decisive interpretive decision he had to make (the subjectivist interpretation of the attributes).[9] Friedman notes that he had to add 165 extra premises, 32 of which were "not logically necessary."[10] But perhaps even more to the point: Boole stops at the seventh proposition of book one; Jarrett only presented his formalization of the first eleven propositions; Friedman has not yet published his, which he cites on at least two separate occasions as completed and forthcoming.

What is striking about Badiou's skeleton, in this context, is that it does not try to translate Spinoza into a logic that was not his own. The skeleton leaves intact the demonstrative structure of the *Ethics*, and indeed, takes it on its own terms claiming only to make visible what is hidden in the prosaic labyrinths of the proofs. At the same time though, like Boole or Jarret or Friedman, it bears witness to a desire for a form, one that is always forthcoming in its totality, always fragmented in its presentation. This is partly because such an approach attempts to bypass Spinoza's explicit commitment to speak according to "the power of understanding of ordinary people," which means: to speak prosaically, with words, which themselves are always "part of the imagination" (*TIE* 88–89).[11] One of the central claims of this essay is that to attend to the details of Spinoza's proofs is to attend to the vagaries of the imagination. More importantly, though, this desire for form always implicitly operates a distinction Spinoza's ontology cannot legitimate. It separates logical necessity from ontological necessity, and installs itself at the end of the ethical and pedagogical process. Spinoza frequently cautioned against such a leap: the performance of the laws of thought are not the thinking itself he writes (*TIE* 37), and it remains the case for Spinoza that the things we have been able to know according to the highest perfection of knowledge "have been very few" (*TIE* 22).[12]

This is, in any case, what I take to be the fantasy, in the psychoanalytic sense, of this skeleton: the wish that the succession of demonstrations can be formalized, that propositions can be converted to symbols and clarified by virtue of deductive relations between them. It is the fantasy that the movement of thought passes through a closed circuit of definitions, axioms, proofs and corollaries. Once you have the skeleton, you have all that really matters. Indeed, from this perspective, one begins to suspect that what is at stake here is not a close attention to the details of the proof, but rather, as I'll suggest in a moment, a radical excision of most of them. I would like to insist, though, that my aim in this essay is not to abandon the fantasy of demonstrative coherence, but to inhabit it and try to push it further, to attend to some of its unexpected detours and thus to introduce into the monochromatic formalism of its reconstruction the accidents and adventures of the prosaic—to restore to the skeleton not its meat, but its flesh. To do so, it is necessary to read Proposition 28 and its proof, which, curiously, Badiou does not quote.

Here is what Spinoza has written:

> P28: Every singular thing, or any thing which is finite and has a determinate existence, can neither exist nor be determined to produce an effect unless it is determined to exist and produce an effect by another cause, which is also finite and has a determinate existence; and again, this cause also can neither exist nor be determined to produce an effect unless it is determined to exist and produce an effect by another, which is also finite and has a determinate existence, and so on, to infinity.

And the demonstration:

> Dem.: Whatever has been determined to exist and produce an effect has been so determined by God (by I.P26 and I.P24C). But what is finite and has a determinate existence could not have been produced by the absolute nature of an attribute of God; for whatever follows from the absolute nature of an attribute of God is eternal and infinite (by I.P21). It had, therefore, to follow either from God or from an attribute of God insofar as it is considered to be affected by some mode. For there is nothing except substance and its modes (by I.A1, I.D3 and I.D5) and modes (by I.P25C) are nothing but affections of God's attributes. But it also could not follow from God, or from an attribute of God, insofar as it is affected by a modification which is eternal and infinite (by I.P22). It had, therefore, to follow from, or be determined to exist and produce an effect by God or an attribute of God insofar as it is modified by a modification which is finite and has a determinate existence. This was the first thing to be proven. And in turn, this cause, or this mode (by the same reasoning by which we have already demonstrated the first part of this proposition) had also to be determined by another, which is also finite and has a determinate existence; and again, this last (by the same reasoning) by another, and so always (by the same reasoning) to infinity, q.e.d.

Badiou remarks that this is among the most complex proofs in Part I of the *Ethics*, and that its skeleton is the most extensive. Guéroult, for his part, covers it with uncharacteristic brevity in a little more than a page.[13] If we wander through it and attend to some of its details, it becomes significantly more elliptical than either commentator allows.

What is immediately striking, when one replaces the symbol "P28" in the skeleton with its referent, the text of the proposition, is that it is not clear what exactly is being proposed nor what stands in needs of proof. Each syntactical unit is subject to a procedure of doubling which adds precision to the terms of the proposition at the same time that it obscures just what needs demonstration. This begins with the subject of the sentence, "every singular thing." It is immediately specified by two qualifications: every singular thing insofar as it is finite and has determinate existence. What is the relation between these two and the nature of their difference? Is "determinate existence" not the same thing as being finite? Or is Spinoza, perhaps, operating a distinction between non-existent finite things (essences) and finite existent things such that "existence" means something like "actual"? It's not clear, and in any case, it is not the thing that is being proposed in the proposition. The verb around which the proposition turns is equally complex. Each finite, existing, singular thing is defined by two capacities: it "can neither exist nor be determined to produce an effect (*operandum determinari*) unless it is determined to exist and produce an effect by another cause." What a singular thing can do here is again doubly determined according to existence and determination. But what is the nature of the difference between determinte existence and the "*operandum determinari*"? Retrospectively, one might observe that their identity is a consequence of this proof, but their function in the proposition is fundamentally ambiguous. And that next clause—"unless it is determined to exist and produce an effect by another cause"—is this what stands in need of proof? Apparently not: what needs proof lies inconspicuously in the next, adjunct clause, "which is also finite and has a determinate existence." What is to be demonstrated is not that finite things can neither exist nor produce effects without first being caused, nor that existence and causality imply one another to the extent that one cannot be thought without the other, but that the causes of finite things must also be finite.

At what point does it become clear that this is what needs proof? Only in the demonstration itself, as the work of proof turns around that last clause in its attempt to establish what Badiou calls "closure of the finite in relation to the relation of immediate causality."[14] My point is not that there is a kind of persistent ambiguity to Spinoza's prose, but that the consequence of that ambiguity in this particular case is that the sense of the proposition escapes the border of the proposition. Of course, one would expect that any demonstration would deepen the sense of a proposition by showing the process of its construction. But that's not what is happening here. The basic propositional sense of the utterance itself still demands completion.

In contrast to the proposition, the first sentence of the demonstration seems to be an ideal model for an exclusively "mathematical" image of Spinoza's thought: it gathers together in a synthetic judgment two formerly distinct propositions: (1) whatever has been determined *to exist* has been so determined by God; (2) whatever *produces an effect* has been determined to do so by God. Each, in turn, reproduces in a condensed way the content the Corollary of Proposition 24 and Proposition 26 respectively. The opening sentence, then, joins the two previously established terms together in a new judgment. But even here it is worth observing that the sense of that first word—"whatever (*quicquid*)"—is ambiguous. Does it refer to the finite and singular things of the proposition and thereby collapse the metonymic oscillation between "singular things" and "finite things" (and the different associative horizons each expression opens up) into a more general word, "whatever"? Or does it refer to the total set of things produced by God, both "eternal and infinite" or finite? As it turns out, it is the latter. But the fact that, again, we need what comes later to resolve or even illuminate, what is there at the start indicates signals that to read this first sentence and to progress to the second requires opening up a space of indetermination around that first word, a space which we subject to a procedure of progressive determination. The movement from one sentence to the next is supported by a process of questioning that would constitute the medium of the sequence of propositions.

The real question raised by the first sentence, though, is not the nature of the *quicquid*, but the conditions under which it might retain any sense at all by the end of the proof. What is at stake, the first sentence indicates, is the very sense in which a singular thing can be said to be "determined by God." It thus implicates all of the previous propositions, cited or not in the proof, which turn on the assertion of God's causality, like P18: "God is the immanent, not the transitive cause of all things" or P25: " God is the efficient cause, not only of the existence of things, but also of their essence." Now, the demonstration works by means of a process of elimination which shows, on the basis of previous proofs, that infinite and eternal things cannot be the immediate causes of finite and singular things. A finite, existing, singular thing, it asserts in its pivotal sentence, can only "follow from, or be determined to exist and produce an effect by God or an attribute of God insofar as it is modified by a modification which is finite and has a determinate existence." This sentence does two contradictory things at once. On the one hand it says that the causes of finite things must be other finite things. This would seem to rule out "God" insofar as God is defined as "a being absolutely infinite" and whose attributes express its "eternal and infinite essence" (I.D6). On the other hand, the sentence is at pains to name God as a causal element by proliferating levels of modification: God *or* an attribute modified by a modification. The moment of proof in the demonstration turns around a paradox: it asserts at the same time that the infinite is cause of the finite and that it is not the cause of the finite. It implies in the same statement the identity of substance and mode and the irreducible distance between them.

The resolution of this paradox might take three forms. At the level of the structural distribution of the concept, one could clarify the nature of the difference and identity between substance and mode. At the level of interpretation, one could affirm the paradox or insist, as Guéroult does, that the direction of the proof is not toward the unilateral restriction of immediate causality to finite things, but toward the necessity of conceiving a "double determination," even if such a concept appears at first sight to be an "abuse" of language: one determination which comes from God and one which comes from "exterior causes" (Guéroult I: 340). Or, finally, at the level of reading in the prosaic sense, which is where I wish to limit my argument, one might make a decision about the procedures of progressive specification and the complex temporality of sense, the way in which the movement of reading retrospectively renders problematic without contradicting the opening sentence. Either way, the point I want to make is simple: nothing in this proof is reducible to the symbol 'P28'. The details of the proof transform the skeleton into a discourse in which sense is no longer immanent, one which risks, it its abstraction, falling back into the other abstraction of immediate being.

Put differently: one cannot read the proofs without breaking with the surface of the text and opening a supplementary space of questioning and progressive determination in which the reader performs extensive and unacknowledged background work. In order to represent this background work, one could not merely expand the skeleton for the proof and sneak in a few more definitions. One would have to posit a second table always hovering in the background of the first, one which accounts for the problematic movement of sense across the proof. And this table would have to account for all of those interpretive mechanisms which allow for metonymic associations, the quick work of the mind which converts propositions into their opposite and trades on already established meanings as momentary catachreses and imprecisions on the way to the systemic sense. There is a very different movement of thought at work than composition and resolution, synthesis and analysis. It seems oriented by something quite different: a dialectic of problems and questions which makes the movement of thought the movement of sense.

In the utterance of any given proof on Badiou's table, there always persists a horizon of potentiality, specifically the potentiality for radical, perhaps savage, future specification.[15] One could always insist that it was only for stylistic or pedagogical reasons that Spinoza did not pause to clarify the sense of "cause" in the earlier propositions. But then those are precisely the kinds of things a skeletal reading of Spinoza is trying to avoid, both of which testify to the demands of an apprenticeship and the concrete movement of thought in the act of discovery, or reading.

3

But does this reading of the proof not collapse the context of justification and the context of discovery? And is not it the case that the transcendental-empirical movement of sense that I am tracing here is fundamentally the one that does not matter? All that matters is that, once you have reached the end of the apprenticeship, you think and act in the cold quietness of the stars. To put it differently, the only movement of thought that matters in proof is that in which truth is established. To focus on the details of its genesis is precisely to miss the point. It is this question that I want to address in the third part of this essay, in part by historicizing the concept of proof. Indeed, this raises the question of what happens to history at the level of proof and proof at the level of history.

As Stephen Gaukroger has argued, this distinction between the context of justification and that of discovery or invention was not yet firmly established in the seventeenth century where we see again and again "the running together of questions of deductive inference and the logic of discovery."[16] In fact, if anything was firmly established, it was precisely the contrary of the separation of discovery and justification. As Gaukroger explains, if the two were inextricably bound it was because what mattered in deductive inference was "how inference could be informative." The central question was, "in what way does the conclusion of an argument tell us something different from the premises from which it is deduced?"[17]

This association of deduction, invention and novelty has its roots in antiquity. Consider, for example, Aristotle's well-known opening remarks in the *Rhetoric*:

> Rhetoric then may be defined as the faculty of discovering the possible means of persuasion in reference to any subject whatever. This is the function of no other of the arts, each of which is able to instruct and persuade in its own special subject; thus, medicine deals with health and sickness, geometry with the properties of magnitudes, arithmetic with number, and similarly with all the other arts and sciences. But Rhetoric, so to say, appears to be able to discover the means of persuasion in reference to any given subject. That is why we say that as an art its rules are not applied to any particular definite class of things. As for proofs, some are artificial, others inartificial. By the latter I understand all those which have not been furnished by ourselves but were already in existence, such as witnesses, tortures, contracts, and the like; by the former, all that can be constructed by system and by our own efforts. Thus we have only to make use of the latter, whereas we must invent the former.[18]

You can see the assemblage of deduction, invention and novelty at work here. Rhetoric is the art of discovery, and it deploys its art across all of the others: there are thus means of persuasion specific to geometry and the other arts and sciences, but what they all have in common is the imperative to discover their means of persuasion. Ultimately this means the discovery of *proof* and there are only two places you can discover it: either it is ready made or it is invented through our own effort, either it is pre-established or it is invented by our own power of thinking. Immediately following this distinction Aristotle will institute the more famous distinction between the three kinds of appeal—logical, ethical and pathetic—so it is clear that the word proof has a larger extension than merely logical proof. But what I want to underline here is just this assemblage of proof, invention and our power of thinking: proof as artifice, something made by our power of thought. It is an organization of the mind that was not fully disassembled until the late eighteenth century.[19] When Spinoza was writing, the relations of its central terms were undergoing significant redistribution.[20]

Indeed, by raising the specter of rhetoric in my title, I do not want to bring into focus the questions of the *Theological-Political Treatise* nor Spinoza's inability to ever leave the imagination alone. I mean, first, the necessary play of sense outlined above, and second, the question of the status of invention in Spinoza, a concept which constituted for a long time the zone of indiscernibility between rhetoric and philosophy. I briefly want to track its redistribution in seventeenth-century thought because (a) Spinoza's place in it is not immediately clear and (b) it bears immediately on what the word "proof" means in Spinoza. The best way to track this is to follow the way in which the problem of invention was figured in debates over the nature of method.

As is well known, philosophical method in the seventeenth century had two aspects or modes: synthesis and analysis. Here is one version of the distinction from the Port-Royal Logic:

> Method may be called, in general, the art of disposing well a series of many thoughts, either for discovering truth when we are ignorant of it, or for proving it to others when it is already known. There are thus two kinds of method: one for discovering truth, which is called *analysis*, or *the method of resolution*, and which could also be called the *method of invention*; and the other for helping others understand it when we have already found it, which is called *synthesis*, or the *method of composition*, and which may be also called the *method of doctrine*.[21]

Arnauld and Nicole are summarizing in this passage several presentations of the concept of method in Descartes—most immediately the discussion in Descartes' reply to the second set of objects (which ends with Descartes' presentation of the *Mediations* in the *more geometrico*).[22] If I am using Arnauld's version it is because of the clarity with which he positions the question of invention and ties it back to the medieval thematics of composition and resolution.[23] Invention or discovery belongs to the side of analysis. The act of judgment which resolves complex things into their constituent parts and continues to dissolve, break apart, untie, unfold things until it gets to the most simple and intuitively clear elements. This is its discovery. At this point the process of composition or synthesis can begin which, precisely, says nothing new and hence is not a method of discovery or invention. Synthesis is not a method of invention, but one of doctrine or instruction. It is for helping people learn what you already know, and its benefits are primarily presentational. It might wrest from your reader their assent, Descartes says, but it "does not teach the way in which the thing was discovered."[24]

This restriction of invention to the analytic method, for both Descartes and Arnold, is caught up in the very idea of synthesis. As Arnauld puts it later, the aim of the synthetic method is "to prove all propositions which are at all obscure, by employing in their proof only the definitions which have preceded, or the axioms which have been accorded, or the propositions which have already been demonstrated."[25] The synthetic method is retrospective. It gathers together already established truths. It does not create new ones. It might be useful in the presence of a hostile reader, or in the case of Spinoza's *Principles* a slow reader, but it only—for Descartes—reveals what was "contained in what went before"[26]—and for this reason Descartes thought it was "sterile."[27] On this point, in particular, we are close to one of Descartes fundamental revisions of this concept of method, a revision which is grounded in his criticism of the syllogism.

Stephen Gaukroger has argued that there are three distinct problems with the syllogism for Descartes. The first two appear in an early text, *Rules for the Direction of the Mind*, which it is unlikely Spinoza would have ever seen. The first is that syllogism is circular. "Dialecticians," Descartes explains, "can find by their art no syllogism that yields a true conclusion, unless they first have the material for it, that is, unless they have already learned the truth itself which they are deducing in their syllogism."[28] This is immediately followed by a second problem: syllogism is not generative of new ideas.

> Hence it is clear that they themselves learn nothing new from such a form, and that vulgar dialectic is therefore entirely useless for those who wish to investigate the truth of things. On the contrary, its only use is that now and then it can expound more easily to others arguments already known; hence it should be transferred from philosophy to rhetoric.[29]

This latter point is one that Descartes made on several other occasions, most notably at the beginning of the *Discourse on Method* where again he writes that while the syllogism is useful when one wants "to explain to someone else the things one knows," it is significantly less useful when one wants to "learn them."[30] Deductive inference is circular; it produces nothing new; its function is presentational and pedagogical. It is fundamentally not, then, an agent of invention.

One of the reasons for both of these claims is tied to Descartes' conception of truth. It is after all true ideas that proofs are supposed to produce. As Gaukroger puts it, the argument against the syllogism that Descartes pursues with most vigor is not the argument for circularity or its inability to generate the new. The central problem for Descartes is a third one: it is an "impediment to the conduct of our reasoning."[31] Thus Descartes writes in a letter to Mersenne:

> There is no way to learn what truth is, if one does not know it by nature. What reason would we have for accepting anything which could teach us the nature of truth if we did not know that it was true, that is to say, if we did not know truth? Of course it is possible to tell the meaning of the word to someone who does not know the language, and tell him that the word *truth*, in its strict sense, denotes the conformity of thought with its object, but that when it is attributed to things outside thought, it means only that they can be the objects of true thoughts, either ours or God's. But no logical definition can be given which will help anyone discover its nature. I think the same of many other things which are very simple and known naturally, such as shape, size, motion, place, time and so on: if you try to define these things you only obscure them and cause confusion.[32]

In a way, this passage problematizes both wings of method: synthesis, of course, because synthesis adds nothing; it only alters presentation. But analysis as a method of discovery is suspect here too. The primary advantage of analysis is that it breaks the complex into its simple truths. But the implication here is just that when you reach those truths, they're not true because of the analysis. They're true because you know them to be true. This was already Descartes' position in the *Rules*. Rule three admits only two "acts of the intellect" which lead to truth: deduction and intellectual intuition.[33] Rule 4 insists that "nothing can be added to the pure light of reason without in some way obscuring it."[34] Thus the first rule of *The Discourse on Method*: "never to accept anything as true that I did not plainly know to be true [...] and to include nothing more in my judgments that what presented itself to my mind so clearly and so distinctly that I had no occasion to call it into doubt."[35]

For all of these reasons then—circularity, redundancy and distraction—Descartes severely limits the inventive element of method and decouples it from the process of truth. If invention plays a role at all, it is only in the method of analysis; but this does not characterize or compel truth. It is ultimately the clarity and distinctness of ideas intuited by the mind that characterizes truth.

This, of course, will not stop Leibniz, on the other side of Spinoza, from taking exactly the opposite position. He reverses both terms of the configuration: not only is synthesis not "sterile," it is the locus of invention. "Those who think that the analytic presentation consists in revealing the origin of a discovery, the synthetic in keeping it concealed," he writes, thinking of Descartes, "are in error."[36] Leibniz gives several reasons for this, but the most intuitive—to the point of appearing banal—is just that when you combine two things already well known, you end up with a third, which, precisely, is new.[37] Where does the novelty come from? How do you get out of the most simple? The answer, for Leibniz, is that you pose a question. It is for this reason that Leibniz gathered analysis and synthesis together under a broader art of questioning, a "*methodus quaerendi*."[38]

In short, on one side of Spinoza, Descartes disconnected proof from invention. On the other side, Leibniz reasserted the primacy of invention and tied it to a more general art of questioning. What, then, is Spinoza's position?

4

Almost every response to this question returns, at least initially, to Lodewijk Meyer's "Preface" to Spinoza's *Principles of Descartes' Philosophy*. Meyer quotes Descartes' *Reply to the Second Objection*, and directly reproduces the Cartesian distribution of concepts: invention belongs to analysis; synthesis is pedagogical and presentational. The extent to which this discussion reflects Spinoza's own, though, is radically unclear. What I want to suggest here, is that Spinoza's position is quite different—that on the question of method, Spinoza lies between Leibniz and Descartes conceptually as well as chronologically and takes important elements from each side.

The question of invention is developed in a curious way in the *Treatise on the Emendation of the Intellect*. On several occasions, Spinoza signals that one of the central functions of method is to determine the "right way of discovery [*recta inveniendi via*]" (*TIE* 94). Method should "teach rules so that we may perceive things unknown [*res incognitae*]" (*TIE* 49). The question, though, is how this is situated in relation to the other aspects of method.

Unlike Descartes and Hobbes, Spinoza's other immediate predecessor on this question (and to whom I will return shortly), Spinoza divides method not into two parts, analysis and synthesis, but three.

> Method must, first, show how to distinguish a true idea from all other perceptions, and to restrain the mind from those other perceptions; second,

teach rules so that we may perceive things unknown [*res incognitae*] according to such a standard; third, establish an order, so that we do not become weary with trifles. (*TIE* 49)

Already, in this passage, one can sense an important element of Spinoza's difference from Hobbes and Descartes: the discovery of things unknown does not proceed from confused idea to clear idea as in the analytic method. The question of discovery pertains to the second moment of method, once we can distinguish true ideas from false ideas. I would seem to proceed, then, from one true idea to the next.

It is worth emphasizing, though, that there is no explicit discussion of analytic and synthetic methods in the *Treatise*, and it is not immediately clear where it might fit. If the two appear at all, they appear in their Hobbesian form in the distinction of the last two types of knowledge. One of the ways in which Spinoza formulates the distinction between the last two types of knowledge here is in terms of inference from effect to cause or the perception of an effect through its cause. In the third kind of knowledge, he writes, we "infer the cause from some effect;" in the fourth, we perceive a thing "through its essence alone or through its proximate cause" (*TIE* 19). There are other criteria for these types of knowledge, but these two map almost directly on to Hobbes' distinction between analytic and synthetic methods. Method, writes Hobbes, "is the shortest way of finding out effects from their known causes or causes by their known effects."[39] As a method of invention, analysis regresses from effect to cause, and it grasps this cause as a definition for the thing, and that definition must be genetic. Synthesis moves from definition to definition, consequence to consequence, through a process of composition of truths.

Numerous commentators, following Guéroult, have argued that Spinoza's conception of definition as knowledge by generation is Hobbesian.[40] It is precisely in the context of his theory of definition that Spinoza will raise the question of invention at several points. Consider the following passage: "the right way of discovery [*inveniendi*] is to form thoughts from some given definition. [...] So the chief point of this second part of the Method is concerned solely with this: knowing the conditions of a good definition, and then, the way of finding [*inveniendi*] good definitions" (*TIE* 94). This passage complicates things in ways I cannot do justice to here, but it shows that invention has at least two aspects, both of which are distributed around the nature for a good definition: invention as the formation of new thoughts from a given definition and invention as the discovery of good definitions.

Guéroult draws what seem to be the full implications of the first aspect of invention: forming new thoughts from a given definition. At the beginning of his first volume, he insists that Spinoza's understanding of the *more geometrico* is not Cartesian, but Hobbesian.[41] At the end of his second volume, he indicates that one of the decisive features of this is the relocation of invention:

> For Descartes, genesis is part of analytic geometry which is opposed for that reason to Euclidian geometry, synthetic, static, and non-genetic. And thus he prescribes for philosophy an analytic method, the only one capable of inventing knowledge [*science*], and confines the synthetic method to the subaltern role of simple exposition. [...] For Spinoza, by contrast, genesis is an essential part of Euclidian geometry itself. [...] This is why all knowledge which wants to be true—which is to say adequate—and thus, in the first place, philosophy, must found itself on [genetic definitions]; in short, it must practice a synthetic method which, being genetic from end to end, is able only to produce the true and thus, by consequence, to invent science.[42]

This last point is perhaps the most important—science must be invented—and it is a point to which I will return shortly. But for the moment I merely want to note the precision with which Guéroult describes the repositioning of the problem of invention. A quite different conception of geometry—as a science which proceeds by way of genetic definitions—leads to a quite different consideration of the nature of invention. It is as if invention appears twice in the equation in two different senses—both brought under Guéroult's preferred word: genesis. Genesis appears first in a real definition, which must be grasped as knowledge by generation. It appears a second time as invention, the linking of one proposition of a proof to the next.

One of the virtues of Guéroult's position is that it opens up an interpretive possibility for what strikes me as a difficult problem for reading the *Treatise* in this way if we expect it to be coherent, namely: the *Treatise* develops at the same time a quasi-Cartesian conception of truth which would seem to render synthetic inference "sterile" for precisely the same reasons Descartes gave. Truth needs no sign, Spinoza says. For the "certainty of the truth, no other sign is needed than having a true idea" (*TIE* 35). Or as he will put it later in that work, a true thought is distinguished from a false primarily by "an intrinsic denomination": "the form of the true thought must be placed in the same thought without relation to other things, nor does it recognize the object as its cause, but must depend on the very power and nature of the intellect" (*TIE* 71). The intrinsic denomination of a true idea is not, it would seem, to be given by a relation to other thoughts—which, de facto, excludes any form of inference. On Guéroult's reading, though, this would not be a problem: the genetic definition is accessible only to thought in the act, the fourth kind of knowledge which moves from cause to effect. And this would explain why the movement of proof is never only repetition, but difference as well.

More difficult for this reading, though, is that other sense of invention: arriving at good definitions. Spinoza promises us that he will return to this part of method, but never actually does. At two other moments he seems to signal a return (*TIE* 99 and 107), but these accounts always move on to something else—which is to be expected given the quick disintegration of the text at this point. But this deferral may also be a symptom of the redundancy of the question insofar as the question of invention is just the question of method itself. This is a reading which takes shape if it is positioned in relation to a broader question, to which I have alluded at several points in this essay, namely, the question about the extent to which we can install ourselves immediately at the end of our apprenticeship, in that perfect circuit of proof which moves from genetic definition to genetic definition by means of a synthetic judgment that is genuinely productive and whether this would constitute the "pinnacle of wisdom."

While it is clear that Spinoza's text encourages such an image of thought, it is equally clear—though this is less frequently acknowledged—that this is a rare mode of thought. The things we "have been able to know by this kind of knowledge have so far been very few" (*TIE* 22). The hopeful "so far" anticipates one of the earliest discussions of invention in the text, this time technological rather than logical invention. Spinoza introduces the image first as an argument against infinite regress in method: we do not need another method to tell us our method is good just as "with corporeal tools" we do not need a hammer to first make a hammer (*TIE* 30). But after he makes this point, the metaphor continues:

> But just as men, in the beginning, were able to make the easiest things with the tools they were born with (however laboriously and imperfectly), and once these had been made, made other, more difficult things with less labor and more perfectly, and so, proceeding gradually from the simplest works to tools, and from tools to other works and tools, reached the point where they accomplished so many and so difficult things with little labor, in the same way the intellect, by its inborn power, makes intellectual tools for itself, by which it acquires other powers for other intellectual works, and from these works still other tools, or the power of searching further, and so proceeds by stages, until it reaches the pinnacle of wisdom. (*TIE* 31)

Method is identified here with the progressive invention of new technologies of thought. What is more, though, Spinoza emphasizes the historically situated nature of thought: it is not yet at the pinnacle of wisdom. And rather than leaping history, "the power of searching," it seems, can only "proceeds by stages." It has a history which is the history of invention.

Spinoza then occupies a curious place in the shifting field of relations between deductive inference and invention. On the one hand, he acknowledges the very principle that would render deduction excessive: true ideas are true by virtue of an intrinsic denomination. On the other hand, and this is precisely the point, they can only be *discovered*, in so far as they are invented, and once invented will ground, at a later stage of history, the discovery of still more.

From this perspective, it is illuminating to return to Badiou's chart. The point he wants to make—a Cartesian interpretation of the geometrical method—is just that the proof explains the proposition in terms of what has gone before. The table vividly makes that point according to a visual logic that looks right. The table arguably raises even more forcefully the problem of invention—which is to say the problem by which that single proposition on the far right, Proposition 28, gets pitched out beyond the entire mass of supporting propositions, proofs, corollaries and definitions. It requires a move from that which is established to that which is not yet established—a move in which that which is established transcends itself in the direction of the new. To attend to the details of a proof, then, is to notice that it is not merely a recuperative gesture which becomes clear only after everything is already known. On the contrary, there is an inescapable apprenticeship though which thought learns to create. What's more, as I have shown, this process of recuperation, only proceeds by way of an errant questioning—like Leibniz's—but profoundly un-anticipatable. What then is the movement of proof? Let's say it has, at a minimum, two movements: one of transcendence; one of recuperation; one of difference, one of repetition.

5

What about Badiou's movement from a mathematics of proof to a logical politics? The gesture performs a transfer of the authority of reason from the sphere of mathematical rationality to that of practical and political rationality. Recall that this synthesis constituted the secret of freedom:

> The secret of freedom lies in the full understanding of the logical necessity, and the political consequences are that the secret of victory of weakness and poverty over power and wealth does not lie in a negative revolt but in a positive discipline, or that the force of equality does not resemble the natural force of a storm but the mental inflexibility of a proof. With Spinoza's *more geometrico*, we learn that we have to act, not within the violent disorder of the chaos, but within the cold quietness of the stars.[43]

This is a distinctively Badiouian claim whose clearest formulation is developed at length in his *Metapolitics*. The account of the logical nature of metapolitical truth procedures presented there is undeniably compelling on its own terms. As a reading of Spinoza, this position becomes significantly more difficult to hold—not because there is not a logical politics or that rationality does not pervade the entire theory of the state, but because the complexity of Spinoza's position covers significantly more than Badiou's account would allow, and once again affirms the historically situated nature of political decision. To put it only slightly differently: what I think is missing from Badiou's account is not the *logic* of collective life, but its method.

Moira Gatens and Genevieve Lloyd have argued at length, that Spinoza sharply distinguishes politics and philosophy. "It is highly significant," they write "that Spinoza's earliest writings in political philosophy address not only the condition and causes of political life but also the condition and causes of theological life. For Spinoza these two—politics and religion—are inevitably conjoined." Where philosophy concerns itself with reason, both religion and politics are "necessarily bound up with emotion, superstition and imagination."[44] This position leads them to develop a robust account of the political use of fictions—which, they are careful to clarify, "are not always deliberately fabricated falsehoods propagated by those who stand to gain by them." On the contrary, the "fictions which bind together communities" are "attempts to grasp the complex relations within and between collective bodies, and between the present and the past history of those collective bodies."[45]

The complexity of this position is impossible to summarize here. But such an account seems to have broad implications for how we understand the authority of reason. Specifically: I hope to foreground the centrality of political *invention* in Spinoza. For what seems bracketed in a theory of action which aligns itself only with the "cold night of the stars" is precisely that which was bracketed in the erasure of discovery in proof and its connection with a long rhetorical tradition—namely any thematics of a productive, constituent power, a positive politics of institution.

Notes

1 Alain Badiou, "What Is a Proof in Spinoza's Ethics?" in ed. by Dimitris Vardoulakis, *Spinoza Now* (Minneapolis: University of Minnesota Press, 2011), 41.

2 Badiou, "Proof," 48.

3. Gilles Deleuze, *Difference and Repetition*, trans. by Paul Patton (New York: Columbia University Press, 1994), 40–41 and 304.
4. For a discussion of the fundamental differences of Spinoza's method with contemporary set theory, see Aaron Garrett, *Meaning in Spinoza's Method* (Cambridge: Cambridge University Press, 2003), 158.
5. Alain Badiou, *Being and Event*, trans. by Oliver Feltham (London: Continuum, 2007), 241.
6. Badiou, *Being and Event*, 241.
7. Badiou, "Proof," 45.
8. George Boole, *An Investigation of the Laws of Thought* (London: MacMillan, 1854), 187.
9. Charles Jarrett, "The Logical Structure of Spinoza's *Ethics*, Part I," *Synthese* 37.1 (1978), 46, 56.
10. Friedman, Joel, "An Overview of Spinoza's *Ethics*," *Synthese* 37.1 (1978), 104n3.
11. All references to Spinoza's works are to *The Collected Works of Spinoza*, ed. and trans. by Edwin Curley (Princeton, NJ: Princeton University Press, 1985).
12. See Edwin Curley, "Experience in Spinoza's Theory of Knowledge," in ed. by Marjorie Grene, *Spinoza: A Collection of Critical Essays* (New Work: Doubleday, 1973), 54–55 for a discussion of this passage.
13. Guéroult, Martial, *Spinoza: 1. Dieu* (Paris: Aubier 1969), 338–39.
14. Badiou, "Proof," 44.
15. Aaron Garrett has argued that this process of progressive determination applies even more forcefully to Spinoza's definitions. See Garrett, *Meaning*, 163–75.
16. Stephen Gaukroger, *Cartesian Logic: An Essay on Descartes Conception of Inference* (Oxford: Oxford University Press, 1989), 10.
17. Gaukroger, *Cartesian Logic*, 10.
18. Aristotle, *The Art of Rhetoric*, trans. by J. H. Freese (Cambridge: Harvard University Press, 1936), 1355b.
19. Carlo Ginzberg, *History, Rhetoric and Proof* (London: University Press of New England, 1999), ch. 1.
20. For a broad overview of this process, see Stefanie Buchenau, *The Founding of Aesthetics in the German Enlightenment: The Art of Invention and the Invention of Art* (Cambridge: Cambridge University Press, 2013), ch. 1.
21. Antoine Arnauld and Pierre Nicole, *Logic, or The Art of Thinking*, trans. by T. S. Baynes (Edinburgh: Sutherland and Knox, 1850), 302–3 (translation modified).
22. See Descartes, *Philosophical Essays and Correspondence*, ed. by Roger Ariew (Indianapolis, IN: Hackett, 2000), 159–67.
23. See Garrett's lucid discussion of this in *Meaning*, ch. 4.
24. Descartes, *Philosophical Essays*, 160.
25. Arnauld and Nicole, *Logic*, 311–13.
26. Descartes, *Philosophical Essays*, 160.

27 Descartes, *Philosophical Essays*, 9. Cf. Gaukroger, *Cartesian Logic*, 85.
28 Descartes, *Philosophical Essays*, 23.
29 Descartes, *Philosophical Essays*, 23.
30 Descartes, *Philosophical Essays*, 54.
31 Gaukroger, *Cartesian Logic*, 26.
32 Descartes, *The Philosophical Writings of Descartes: Volume III: The Correspondence*, trans. by John Cottingham et al. (Cambridge: Cambridge University Press, 1991), 139. Gaukroger's discussion of this letter is illuminating. Gaukroger, *Cartesian Logic*, 51–56.
33 Descartes, *Philosophical Essays*, 6.
34 Descartes, *Philosophical Essays*, 8.
35 Descartes, *Philosophical Essays*, 54.
36 Leibniz, "On the Universal Synthesis and Analysis, or the Art of Discovery and Judgment," trans. by L. E. Loemker in *Philosophical Papers and Letters* (London: Kluwer 1989), 233.
37 Leibniz, "Universal Synthesis," 233.
38 Leibniz, "On the Art of Discovery in General," in ed. by M. Dascal, *The Art of Controversies* (Dordrecht: Springer, 2008), 96.
39 Hobbes, Thomas, *De corpore*, in ed. by G. C. A. Gaskin, *The Elements of Law, Natural and Politic* (Oxford: Oxford University Press, 1994), 194.
40 See, in particular, Garrett, *Meaning*, chs 4 and 6.
41 Guéroult, *Spinoza: 1. Dieu*, 13.
42 Guéroult, *Spinoza 2: L'Âme* (Paris: Aubier, 1974), 481–82.
43 Badiou, "Proof," 41.
44 Moira Gatens and Genevieve Lloyd, *Collective Imaginings: Spinoza, Past and Present* (London: Routledge, 1999), 87–88.
45 Gatens and Lloyd, *Imaginings*, 90.

Bibliography

Aristotle. *The Art of Rhetoric*, trans. by J. H. Freese. Cambridge: Harvard University Press, 1936.
Arnauld, Antoine and Pierre Nicole. *Logic, or the Art of Thinking*, trans. by T. S. Baynes. Edinburgh: Sutherland and Knox, 1850.
Badiou, Alain. *Being and Event*, trans. by Oliver Feltham. London: Continuum, 2007.
Badiou, Alain. "What Is a Proof in Spinoza's Ethics?" in ed. by Dimitris Vardoulakis, *Spinoza Now*. Minneapolis: University of Minnesota Press, 2011.
Boole, George. *An Investigation of the Laws of Thought*. London: MacMillan, 1854.
Buchenau, Stefanie. *The Founding of Aesthetics in the German Enlightenment: The Art of Invention and the Invention of Art*. Cambridge: Cambridge University Press, 2013.

Curley, Edwin. "Experience in Spinoza's Theory of Knowledge," in ed. by Marjorie Grene, *Spinoza: A Collection of Critical Essays*. New York: Doubleday, 1973, 25–59.

Deleuze, Gilles. *Difference and Repetition*, trans. by Paul Patton. New York: Columbia University Press, 1994.

Descartes, Rene. *Philosophical Essays and Correspondence*, ed. by Roger Ariew. Indianapolis, IN: Hackett, 2000.

Descartes, Rene. *The Philosophical Writings of Descartes: Volume III: The Correspondence*, trans. by John Cottingham et al. Cambridge: Cambridge University Press, 1991.

Friedman, Joel. "An Overview of Spinoza's *Ethics*," *Synthese* 37.1 (1978), 67–106.

Garrett, Aaron. *Meaning in Spinoza's Method*. Cambridge: Cambridge University Press, 2003.

Gatens, Moira and Genevieve Lloyd. *Collective Imaginings: Spinoza, Past and Present*. London: Routledge, 1999.

Gaukroger, Stephen. *Cartesian Logic: An Essay on Descartes Conception of Inference*. Oxford: Oxford University Press, 1989.

Ginzberg, Carlo. *History, Rhetoric and Proof*. London: University Press of New England, 1999.

Guéroult, Martial. *Spinoza: 1. Dieu*. Paris: Aubier, 1969.

Guéroult, Martial. *Spinoza: 2. L'Âme*. Paris: Aubier, 1974.

Hobbes, Thomas. *De corpore*, in ed. by G. C. A. Gaskin, *The Elements of Law, Natural and Politic*. Oxford: Oxford University Press, 1994.

Jarrett, Charles. "The Logical Structure of Spinoza's *Ethics*, Part I," *Synthese* 37.1 (1978), 15–65.

Leibniz, G. W. "On the Universal Synthesis and Analysis, or the Art of Discovery and Judgment," trans. by L. E. Loemker in *Philosophical Papers and Letters*. London: Kluwer 1989.

Leibniz, G. W. "On the Art of Discovery in General," in ed. by M. Dascal, *The Art of Controversies*. Dordrecht: Springer, 2008.

Spinoza, *The Collected Works of Spinoza*, ed. and trans. by E. Curley. Princeton, NJ: Princeton University Press, 1985.

6

Spinoza: A Different Power to Act

Antonio Negri
Translated by Giuseppina Mecchia

Spinoza is a thinker of power. However, when we delve into the Spinozan notion of being from a political perspective, we are often faced with different interpretations of the relation between being-as-power and the political definition of power. The ontological intensity and the qualification of the political productivity of a "being *qua* power" are not evaluated in the same way. As for me, since the identity of being and power in Spinoza is self-evident, I consider that Spinoza's political thought is predicated on a "constituent" understanding of both the concept and the reality of power, on the basis of a monistic ontology and democratic immanence. I believe that I have always defended this premise in my interpretation: ontological (and therefore constituent) power, political (and therefore democratic) immanence and strategic (and therefore programmatic) monism of *cupiditas* (desire) and its attending *praxis communis*.

Still, the title of this essay is: a *different* power to act. Why do we say *different*?

First of all, the Spinozan concept of power is not properly defined according to the Aristotelian, late Scholastic or neo-Stoic traditions. We can certainly retrace some of these influences. But even if they were there, for Spinoza, at the beginning of the seventeenth century, they were in dialogue—and maybe in contrast—with a concept of divine power (as love) derived from Leone Ebreo and the Neoplatonic tradition as it was received and transformed during the Renaissance. This tradition was also present in the contemporary notions of being in Spanish and Dutch thought that were immediate references for Spinoza (this has been shown, among others, by Saverio Ansaldi in his *Spinoza et le Baroque*).[1] In this context, it is impossible to reduce Spinoza's concept of power to the individual, or to the individual power to act: this would be possible if the Spinozan understanding of power had an Aristotelian origin, or if it could fit into the dynamics of scholastic individuation and found its roots there. But this is not the case. The thought of "power as constitution," on the contrary, does not insist on the mark of the individual, but on the one of singular modes, the incessant expansion of power and the epistemological and ontological tension leading to the composition of the common. It is not even true that (as some interpreters have said) social power is structured and enacted toward and through individuals. To avoid this error, it is not enough to exclude from the Spinozan method the methodological individualism (rooted in the philosophy of Hobbes) prevalent in today's sociological schools. If the dynamic of power is differential, horizontal and relational in nature, if it is never defined or used instrumentally, it is because it is socially constituted, and innovates on simple interaction being always oriented toward the common. Spinozan power is different, first of all, because it is modal and therefore collective, common.

Secondly—and consequently—we cannot equate *vis* and *potentia*. *Vis* will never be collective, common, but *potentia* becomes such: in Spinoza the origin and the structure of institutions constitute a *continuum*, which transforms the interaction of forces in institutions of power. If we considered *potentia* as individual *vis* we would open the way to a mystification of the genealogy of institutions, and we would imagine the interaction among powers as a flat, neutral and mechanical relation that would be temporary and unstable. It would be trans-individual, nothing but a horizontal, geometrical relation. But if this were the case, how could we explain the historicity of the Hebraic institutions in his *Theological-Political Treatise*? How could we grasp the constitution of the "*summa potestas*" in the *Ethics* and the *Political Treatise*? The answer according to the thinkers of "transindividual relations" is to consider power processes in terms of "accumulation." This a very important point, which allows us to conceive a dynamic radically opposed to the various forms of transcendental understanding of power typical of the modern, Hobbesian tradition of political philosophy. The accumulation of goods, or of the effects of social power, offers an excessively monistic perspective, constituting the strongest image of the immanent refusal of any socio-political contract and thereby preventing any possible transfer of power toward political domination. In other words, it is by working on the concept of accumulation of powers that we can get rid of all the political theologies accompanying—as in the case of Schmitt and Agamben, on the right as well as on the left—the post-modern restoration of the concept of sovereignty.

But what are the modalities of accumulation? Generally, they are limited by the unifying trend tying constitutive power to juridical positivity. In many ways this is exact: in Spinoza, the convergence between *power* and *jus* is repeatedly affirmed. But this potential unity should be compared with the affirmation of the *Political Treatise*, which states (going back to the *Ethics*) that the amount of power is proportional to the extension of the union (*TP* 2.13). There is no *zero sum* in the association of singularities and the accumulation of powers: *they produce*. But then, how can we consider transindividual relations or social cooperation as flat, neutral processes? We are faced with a contradictory argument, because the *positive* identity of power and right cannot be reduced to a *positivist* perspective. Therefore, the Spinozan *potentia* is different because it is productive.

On this point, I thought that the third chapter in the first part and the introduction to the second part of Pascal Sévérac's *Spinoza* are very important.[2] The productive understanding of the relation between bodies in Spinoza's rational physics is shown according to the criterion of simultaneous multiplicity. The concept deriving from this relation is far from being defined in passive terms, since it seems to express an action of the spirit or, even better, appears as a finite part of divine power.

There is a third reason to consider "different" the Spinozan definition of *potentia*. It is the refusal of any finalistic determination. It is quite obvious that there is no teleology in Spinozan ontology, but it is just as obvious that the defense of freedom is a value for Spinoza and that it represents the *telos* of both his thought and politics. How, then, can we avoid to consider this thought a teleological *praxis*? And how can we qualify and offer a materialist ontological basis (also from the point of view of a Spinozan "sociology of affects") to the discovery that the social process is not a zero sum phenomenon even from the perspective of power? In fact, power appears within a true strategy of singular resistances, which occurs in the collective, or rather as the process leading from the singularity to the social body that modifies, transforms and shapes collective institutions. In Spinoza, the immanence of the collective (modal, common) is productive beyond the limits of singularities. Laurent Bové showed this very well in *La Stratégie du Conatus*,[3] while Filippo Del Lucchese explained that Spinoza's reprisal of Machiavelli never ends up in "machiavellism" (which designates a neutralizing political science, a positivist formalism, the apology of force and the philistinism of the raison d'état), representing instead an inexhaustible instance of freedom achievable in and trough conflict.[4]

We are now faced with the fourth essential point in our discussion of *potentia*. It is widely known that the constitutive process of *potentia* develops thanks to continuous integrations and institutional creations, from conatus to desire (*cupiditas*) and the rational expression of love (*amor*). The core of this process is desire, because it is the moment when the physicality of appetite (*appetitus*) and the corporeality of *conatus* enter the social sphere and produce the *imagination*. The imagination anticipates the building of institutions, it is the power that intersects with rationality and directs its course, *expressing it*. This is why Deleuze calls Spinoza's thought a philosophy of expression. It is the imagination that leads the singularity from resistance to the common. This is where desire acts, and in this action the "desire that arises from reason cannot be excessive" (*E* IV, P61). Thus immanence triumphs in the most fundamental way and the strategy of desire shows the asymmetry of *potentia* and *potestas*. And indeed, it is the positive asymmetry tied to the excess of *potentia* that the theories intent at neutralizing the radical, transformative aspect of Spinoza's thought want to erase: the perpetual excess of the liberating reason that, through the imagination, constitutes itself at the intersection between the action of desire and the tension of love—on the verge of being, building the eternal. This is still another attempt at grasping the "alterity" characterizing the Spinozan opposition to the onto-theology of modernity.

At this point, we need to pay attention to a rather peculiar fact. Those who try to neutralize the ethical excess of desire in Spinoza, often base their analysis of his political thought on the political treatises, and not on the *Ethics*. We need to remember, however, that Spinoza's political thought is eminently present in his ontology—and therefore in the *Ethics*—more than in any other parallel or later work. In any case, that kind of critique comes to a contradictory conclusion: those who want to isolate political *potentia* ignoring the *Ethics*, can't explain the relation between desire and love, because they forget the excess specific to this relation. Furthermore, love, as *res publica* or *commonwealth*, is greater than what cupidity builds as sovereignty or *summa potestas*. The asymmetry between *potentia* and *potestas*—all skewed in favor of *potentia*—is therefore visible with equal intensity whether we look at it from above—from the perspective of the nexus desire-love, which exalts its productivity—or from below—when *potentia* evolves and acts from a perspective of infinite openness.

We can conclude, then, that the fourth aspect of the way potentiality is imagined and expressed is as an excess that breaks the symmetry between *potentia* and *potestas*. The ontology of *potentia* is therefore marked by the force of love. This ends our discussion of the characters marking the "alterity"—or "difference"—of *potentia*.

We can conclude now with our fifth objection to the detractors of Spinozan power: in Spinoza, politics is not an omnipresent social mediator. It is neither a simple element of action nor the property of a structure. In Spinoza politics is not the mediator of society, but its permanent origin as well as its continual rupture. Politics is a power that exceeds every measure and builds an ontological asymmetry with respect to *potestas*. If this were not true, we would be condemned to *a-cosmism*, and not only—like Hegel thought—with regard to the pantheistic concept of being, but also to politics. And politics can never be instrumental for Spinoza, not because it is marked by the force of ethics, but because even if it derives from the relation and the dialectic between the individual and the collective, in this dialectic (which in fact is not a dialectic) there is always a *surplus* originated by the constitutive process. This surplus creates institutions and communication, being neither individual nor inter-individual; it is not an accumulation of individual segments of substance, but of singular modes of power. Spinoza's monism is sustained by the presence of God. And is not precisely this contention, the attempt *to make God work* in a rigorously immanent sense that makes a heretic of the Amsterdam Jew? The consequence is that positive and negative power, the power "we have over" something, and the power "to do" something are the same for Spinoza, because there is no static antinomy in his thought. But also because, ontologically, *negativity does not exist*. There is only power, that is, freedom, which opposes nothingness and builds the common. "The man who is guided by reason is more free in a state where he lives under a system of law than in solitude where he obeys only himself" (*E* IV, P73). We can then conclude this fifth thesis with the ethical emphasis of Spinozan politics, and the common excess that breaks all determinism or positivism.

What we are going to say in the second part of this paper is best introduced by borrowing the conclusions of Chantal Jaquet in her discussion of the positive role played by the will in Spinoza's thought:

> Determining for the State and determined by it, for Spinoza the will has an eminently political nature. [...] A denomination of *conatus* in its relation with the mind, the will designates the indefinite effort of an idea to persevere in its being. A disposition of the mind striving for duration, the will naturally finds its culmination in the persistence of institutions. Although it does not differ from understanding, it plays a specific role in Spinoza's system. It expresses the idea of law and manifests its spirit.[5]

* * *

At this point, I should say that my interpretation of Spinoza's *potentia* has been very useful to me in creating concepts for the analysis of today's political world. I would like, now, to discuss not so much the legitimacy of such an interpretation, but its usefulness and efficacy. This discussion will be articulated as follows:

A. Considering that *potentia* is productive, collective and common, how can we identify its dissymmetry and excesses? And in particular, if the ontological construction is a social production how can we—within this radical immanence—express the antagonistic relation between *potentia* and power, or rather, from the perspective of the labor/capital relation, between creative activity and the private appropriation of labor? In my opinion, the prospect of a qualified difference within the productive process (or rather, in the relation between "labor productive forces" and "capitalist relations of control") is, as we have seen, perfectly compatible with the strategy of the *conatus*. The latter cannot be neutralized, except by the introduction of "weak" elements in the struggle—that is, elements of abstract composition or reductions in the conflictual nature of the ontological relation, or the confusion between modal differences and substantial individuations. But if in Spinoza's thought the qualification of the relation between powers is conflictual, why should we water it down to a system of equivalencies? Why should we undermine its ability to express meaning through conflict and emancipatory journeys?

B. Maybe things are not that simple. People have criticized me for not having acknowledged the post-structuralist premises of my interpretation of Spinoza (and the essential role that they play in my own political philosophy). It has been said that, like Deleuze, I have used the *mos geometricum* as a key for making Spinozan ontology more dynamic and anti-hierarchical. Additionally, I should also have appropriated Foucault's vocabulary, trying to translate the relation *potentia/potestas* into the couple "biopolitical activity"/"biopower." This would have created an absolute antinomy between *potentia* (ontologically creative) and *potestas* (fixed and/or parasitical). It is not wrong to assume that the thought of Deleuze and Foucault converge in my work and in my use of Spinoza, but like Deleuze said, this convergence is a matter of coincidence, and not of influence. In the case of Foucault, I only plunged into the wild recesses of his work many years after writing *The Savage Anomaly*. The depth of the relation between Deleuze, Foucault and my own Spinozan thought is the reason why the accusation often levied against me of bringing the relation between *potentia* and *potestas* to an antinomic level is simply mistaken. The dichotomy between biopolitics and biopower, which coexist (just like labor and capital), is open and chaotic in Deleuze and genealogically built in Foucault. And indeed, how else could one read the inter-individual construction or the "accumulation" of powers theorized by my interlocutors? What could it express, if not the action of *potentia* within/against *potestas*?

I have insisted a lot both on the interaction and the dissociation of *potentia* and *potestas*, biopolitics and biopower. I have retraced, going back to the "habit" theorized by American pragmatists and the *habitus* of Bourdieu, the building of the relation and the difference between *potentia* and *potestas* from within. The antinomy of these two effects, or characters, of power, which is often considered a limit of my Spinozan arguments, cannot be defined as an ontological dualism or, even worse, a kind of Manicheism. It is a continuously produced struggle, a conflict that keeps being posited and resolved, eternally reappearing on different levels. It is the ethical tension emerging from the difficulties and the obstacles characteristic of the journey going from the *conatus*, through desire, to the expression of love. If the relation between *potentia* and *potestas* is asymmetrical, this is because *potentia*, as desire, is never bad, and is always excessive. Bad is what cannot be realized. *Potentia*, on the other hand, builds the common, that is, it directs the accumulation of passions toward the common. It leads the fight for the common through a continuous production of subjectivities and a loving awareness of reason.

C. But people still ask me what it means to build a "*democratia omnino absoluta*." At this stage of the conflictual enterprise traversing Spinoza's ethical construction, wouldn't the embracing of absolute democracy represent an undue interruption of the continuous process of conflict among singularities (understood as social forces) that characterizes Spinoza's ethical field? Wouldn't we end up building a new political theology? Absolute democracy: on the one hand, this would be built by a multitude drawn toward freedom and the good from below; on the other, this would no longer be a "form of government" but the care for everyone's freedom on the part of all. People tell me that outside sovereignty there is no politics. Talking about absolute democracy (and of a democratic multitude) would therefore be a theological choice, while Spinoza's perspective defines a conflict with no end, no solution, either voluntary or determined. To advance the common emancipation of humanity, aren't we looking for an ontological guarantee that is utopian, impossible to find? The answer is no. We simply affirm that the theory of absolute democracy is, for Spinoza, an attempt to invent a new form of politics, outside the theories of sovereignty and the three classical theories of government (monarchy, aristocracy, democracy). If the absolute, for Spinoza, is the ontological web of free singularities, it is logical and realistic to think that political power—as *potestas*—is the result of an attempt to limit the action of the singularities in their struggle for freedom.

These objections are mainly raised by the critics who emphasize the juridical and positivistic component of the political development of potentia in Spinoza. But in juridical positivism, the juridical realm is not defined as desire, as realistic construction of demands expressed in positive law and institutions: rather, it is understood as secondary power, as "leadership of leaderships" (*Führung der Führungen*). The relation between politics and the juridical order is seen as static, as a condition—so to say—of technological efficacy. But Spinoza is not Luhmann: for Spinoza, a constitution is an engine and not a result, it is a "constituent power" as permanent source of laws, and therefore the juridical order becomes effective through the continuous action of the constituent powers.

D. It is strange to hear these objections precisely when, in globalization, with the relative weakening of nation states and of the common European public law, juridical Spinozism—in its open version—seems to anticipate every alternative theoretical experience now generalized in European juridical doctrines—mostly in Germany, where it has found a constant expression, from the struggle for the law theorized by Jhering to Teubner's constitutionalism without the state. But at this point we need to add that Spinoza's political philosophy, while firmly rooted in modernity, firmly opposes all modern affirmation of sovereign power. Spinoza's atheism is therefore violently attacked mostly on the front of his juridical-political theory, starting from Leibniz and Pufendorf. The latter said, for instance, that Spinoza was a reckless man, *deorum hominumque irrisor*, who had condensed in one volume the New Testament and the Coran. Giorgio Agamben has recently used this quote in his book *Opus Dei*.[6]

E. Should we then consider that the reaffirmation of this quality (atheism) and most of all this interpretation of Spinoza lead us toward a philosophy of history? Some people think so: isn't it the case, they say, that *potentia* is always more productive (and historically more successful) than *potestas*? Isn't it true that the multitude, as political subjectivation of *potentia*, constitutive historical force, creative power, is exalted against the parasitic traits of *potestas*? Once we posit the asymmetrical nature of the struggle and the ontological meaning of antagonism, don't we end up guaranteeing the positivity of the production of the common on the part of the multitude? And vice versa: how do we know and decide whether the multitude, instead of producing democracy, is just a *mob*, that is, an instance of plebeian disorder?

I think that the alternative proposed for the multitude, that is, being a mob or a liberation movement, is ambiguous, or rather—when considered as a concrete ethical choice—a scam. In fact, such an alternative expresses the *a priori* (or at least trivial) pretense that the multitude can more easily be a mob than a liberation movement. It is true that Spinoza denounces the unreasonable and homicidal masses as the *ultimi barbarorum*, but he also states that barbarity is precisely the result of the fear of the masses. The multitude, and not us, has to decide what it wants to be. Each individual has been a scumbag far too often before directing his or her desires toward a reasonable end: this is also true for the multitude, which is not so much a quantitative mass but a network of singularities. If the alternative, instead, is no longer addressed in practical theoretical terms but becomes the object of a transcendental reflection, it ends up silently introducing a transcendental proposal—which goes against Spinozan ontology. We pretend to face a mutilated alternative in order to present once more the Hobbesian alienation of sovereignty as the sole possibility for political construction. Within this alternative dwells—as we have already seen—a juridical positivism closer to the Hegelian philosophy of history and/or positivism (which are transcendental exaltations of the present order of things) than to the ethical experimentations in immanence that Spinoza calls us to realize.

In this respect, we also need to remark a possible misunderstanding about the persistence of institutions as the realistic negation of the resistance and productivity of the multitude. In Spinozan ontology and politics, duration does not mean a blockage, or a withering, of temporality. On the contrary, as Laurent Bové has shown, human freedom, which is the necessary requirement for self-preservation, appears as constituent power in action. "The struggles, the relations of force characteristic of the anthropological condition, develop a dynamic ontology of decision about/on problems—or better, the absolute actualization of power in each singular occasion as an ontology of Kairos."[7] We can then conceive the possibility of a duration where there would be institutions created by the multitude on its road to freedom—with no illusion about either the linearity or the final outcome of this process.

F. This is why we should not talk about a philosophy of history, but rather—on a terrain labored from below, in a strictly monistic composition—of "production of subjectivity." This production is objectively founded, materially constituted and actually operating in Spinozan thought. The social conditions of our existence confirm its reality. The theory of the multitude (and of its march on the "road to freedom") is the simple recognition of a development in material civilization. It proposes an alternative struggle against exploitation and the pursuit of happiness. However—after having affirmed the objective materiality of our argument—it remains true that each philosophy (if it is not of the philistine kind, or stifled by ideological reticence) has to decide whether it wants to side with the oppressors or the oppressed. There might be a Spinozan "optimism of reason" (and even a certain "pessimism of the will"). Because even if we accept the hypothesis that politics is only an attempt at regulation of a constant inter-individual struggle, that is, if we remain within a so-called "political realism" and therefore of a "pessimism of the will," it is impossible to consider it as a flat terrain, negating its libertarian impulses and the possibility that the struggle for freedom may produce new subjectivities and anthropological mutations. Machiavelli always affirmed—according to his own humanistic realism—the positivity of the power to act, Deleuze and Guattari showed it as admirably active and multifaceted in *A Thousand Plateaus*, while Michel Foucault started to constitute the mechanisms of subjectivity from below. Pretending that a theory of *potentia* is only a diagnostic, explicative kind of critique is denying the very essence of Spinozism, which is the *praxis* of desire and rational love, of freedom and the common.

In conclusion, then, what is "different" and new in Spinoza's theory of *potentia*? From a political point of view, it is simply a decisive break with a whole line of thought that emphasizes in an admirable but blinding specular reflex, as Sandro Chignola said very recently, the continuity of the transcendental concept of power from Aristotle to Hobbes to Schmitt. But, as a friend said to me, we have forgotten the declensions of the aorist. And from another, immanent, point of view, the "difference" of the concept of *potentia* resides in the fact that—as Chantal Jaquet reminds us—it builds virtue from below: generosity and inner strength are always incarnated in the *polis*. In sum, all beatitude is civic.

Notes

1. Saverio Ansaldi, *Spinoza et le Baroque* (Paris: Kimé, 2001).
2. Pascal Sévérac, *Spinoza* (Paris: Vrin, 2011).
3. Laurent Bové, *La Stratégie du conatus* (Paris: Vrin, 1996).
4. Filippo Del Lucchese, *Conflict, Power and Multitude in Machiavelli and Spinoza: Tumult and Indignation* (London: Continuum, 2009).
5. Chantal Jaquet, *Les expressions de la puissance d'agir chez Spinoza* (Paris: Publications de la Sorbonne, 2005), 107.
6. Giorgio Agamben, *Opus Dei: An Archeology of Duty*, trans. by Adam Kotsko (Stanford, CA: Stanford University Press, 2013), 108.
7. Laurent Bové, "Le réalisme ontologique de la durée chez Spinoza lecteur de Machiavelli," in ed. by Laurent Bové, *La Recta ratio* (Paris: Presses Universitaires de la Sorbonne, 2000), 59.

Bibliography

Agamben, Giorgio. *Opus Dei: An Archeology of Duty*. Stanford, CA: Stanford University Press, 2013.

Ansaldi, Saverio. *Spinoza et le baroque*. Paris: Kimé, 2001.

Bové, Laurent. *La stratégie du conatus*. Paris: Vrin, 1997.

Bové, Laurent. "Le réalisme ontologique de la durée chez Spinoza lecteur de Machiavelli," in ed. by Laurent Bové, *La Recta Ratio*. Paris: Presses Universitaires de la Sorbonne, 2000, 47–69.

Del Lucchese, Filippo. *Conflict, Power and Multitude in Machiavelli and Spinoza: Tumult and Indignation*. London: Continuum, 2009.

Jaquet, Chantal. *Les expressions de la puissance d'agir chez Spinoza*. Paris: Presses Universitaires de la Sorbonne, 2005.

Sévérac, Pascal. *Spinoza*. Paris: Vrin, 2011.

Spinoza, Baruch. *Complete Works*, ed. by Michael L. Morgan. Cambridge: Hackett, 2002.

7

Commanding the Body: The Language of Subjection in *Ethics* III, P2S

Warren Montag

Although there is arguably no point in the *Ethics* at which the political stakes of Spinoza's philosophy are clearer than in the Scholium to Proposition 2 of the Part II of the *Ethics*, neither is there a point that has proven more resistant to interpretation. Of course, to question the mind's ability to command the body is to question something so tenaciously obvious that the mere attempt to question it can only engender confusion, and all the more so given the theologico-political ends this obviousness serves. But this only partly explains the difficulty in question: we cannot assume it is, or is primarily, intentional, a strategic calculation on Spinoza's part. On the contrary, everything here suggests an enormous effort to inquire into what has developed, through long exposure to conflict, an immunity to inquiry, leaving him to identify and exploit whatever weak points he is fortunate enough to encounter through a process of philosophical trial and error that is inscribed in literal existence of the Scholium. There is no easy summary of his activity; we have no choice but to follow his tracks as he probes the obviousness of the obvious.

To begin, we may contrast the language of Proposition 2 to that of its Scholium. The terminology of the Proposition—"The body cannot determine the mind to think, nor can the mind determine the body to movement or rest or to anything else (if there is anything else)"—is drawn from the lexicon of natural philosophy: motion and rest, as well as determination, that is, causality. In the long Scholium to P2, Spinoza shifts to the legal (that is, political and military) register from which the Stoics, particularly Seneca and, following them, Descartes, tend to draw, above all when they speak of the self-mastery or self-control that alone, they argue, makes something like a genuine ethics possible. This is not simply a change in idiom: Spinoza abandons the language of philosophy (that is, of causality) and abruptly replaces it with a juridico-political vocabulary of command and obedience, grounded in part in the opposition between persons who are *sui juris* (legally independent or autonomous) and those, above all, slaves, who are *alieni juris subjectae* (legally subject to the authority of another person) because this vocabulary embodies the concepts that govern the opposition of mind and body, in practice as well as in theory. Thus, the "prejudices" (*praejudicia*) Spinoza seeks to diminish are neither simply errors, nor are they edifices erected on the basis of the imaginary dimension of human existence. On the contrary, they are indissociable from the great apparatuses of coercion and subjection that have already been determined or judged to be co-extensive with society itself (which means that we should take the term "prejudice" in its literal, legal sense, as a judgment already made, the precedent upon which all that follows must be derived).

Spinoza will repeat for emphasis the terms in which the prejudice is formulated (above all in the history of philosophy): all are drawn from the areas of Roman law in which relations of command and obedience and mastery and servitude are codified. Thus, the mind has "*imperium*" or command over the body, as if the mind were the *imperator* or commander of a body of soldiers. It acts, that is, communicates its will, through a non-verbal signal, the "*nutus*" (literally, a nod), or through a verbal order, edict or decree (*decretum*). These three terms together (*imperium, nutus* and *decretum*) occur forty-one times in the *Ethics* and forty of the forty-one occurrences are in prefaces, scholia or appendices—that is, outside of its formal argumentation. Significantly, seventeen of the forty-one appearances of these terms, that is, nearly half, are found in the Scholium to *E* III, P2. Thus, the notions of self-mastery and self-command are not reducible to the "spontaneous" (and universal) illusions of consciousness that Spinoza examines in the Appendix to Part I of the *Ethics*, namely that, because we are conscious of our desires or appetites but not of their causes, we imagine that we are the cause of our desires and can thus freely determine them. On the contrary, he repeatedly argues in the Scholium that experience is not only *not* the source of these illusions, but opposes them (or at least furnishes examples that can be used to oppose them). Accordingly, Spinoza suggests that the "imperative" we feel to bring about our own subjection (that is, the subjection of our thought, passions or affects, and above all the body itself, by the exercise of *imperium* over them) is linked to (or is continuous with) the historical forms of social and political subjection, including the institution of slavery. We do not need to be reminded that this institution, so central to the development of Roman law as well as to the vocabulary, if not the conceptual apparatus, of early Christianity, was, in a new form of course, rapidly becoming just as central to the emerging empires of Spinoza's own time.

Spinoza's attention to, and emphasis through repetition on, the mediation of the relation to oneself and one's own body through the terminology of legal subjection does not in itself set him apart from Descartes, Hobbes and Locke, even if his use of these terms ultimately sets him in opposition to all of them, who in turn differed from each other. Indeed, Macherey has argued that the "principle objective" of the Scholium is "to create the conditions for a theoretical rupture in relation to the explanation of affectivity" advanced in Descartes' *Passions of the Soul* where the lexicon of the Stoics, again, particularly Seneca, as well as that of the New Testament, particularly Paul's Epistles, plays a far more explicit role than in the *Meditations*.[1] But before I turn to the *Passions of the Soul*, particularly Part 1, which exhibits a concentration of the terms we have noted, I want briefly to examine a critically important passage in the *Meditations*. Its importance derives from the fact that the legal terminology which makes the briefest of appearances there is otherwise nearly absent from the *Meditations* as a whole. The exception is the term "*jus*" or right/law (in the French translation of 1647 supervised by Descartes the term *jus* is uniformly rendered as "*droit*"): it or a variant of it (*jure*) appears precisely three times in the entire text. In two cases, the word is used lightly or ironically (e.g., "opinions are given the right to occupy my mind by custom").[2] The third case, found in the sixth and final meditation ("*De l'existence des choses matérielles, et de la réelle distinction entre l'âme et le corps de l'homme*") is far more interesting, especially in the French version, which includes a legal terminology absent from the Latin: *Ce n'était pas aussi sans quelque raison que je croyais que ce corps (lequel par un certain droit particulier j'appelais mien) m'appartenait plus proprement et plus étroitement que pas un autre* ("It is also not without reason that I believe that this body—which by a certain particular right I call mine—belongs to me more properly and more closely than any other.").[3]

What is striking here is Descartes' invocation of right, specifically property right, as the guarantee that the body with which I am most closely united is really "mine" or my own, as if, to use Locke's phrase, itself probably inspired by Descartes, I must be the proprietor of myself, meaning above all my body, for it to be properly mine and not another's, as if the body from which we derive all our sense experiences, and thus all that we imagine, might, just as it so often deceives us when we perceive things through it, finally itself prove to be a delusion. Descartes resorts to God, who would not deceive us, to prove that his own body is both real and really his. But he has already established ownership of the body in law, rendering the idea that the body is "his" by a certain right enforceable, as if God, as so many critics charged, were superfluous.

As *dominus* (*maître* or *propriétaire* in French), the individual alone has the right (and every right carries a responsibility) of command over his body and its effects on his mind or soul. But the consequence of invoking *jus* for Descartes is that the question of dominion over, or ownership of, the body remains a matter of right rather than fact. He thus defers the more important question of how, or rather to what extent, we can actually command the body and secure its submission to our will, given that it is "a kind of machine equipped with and made up of bones, nerves muscles, veins, blood and skin in such a way that, even if there were no mind in it, would still perform all the same movements as it does now in the cases where movement is not under the control of the will or consequently of the mind."[4] Here, the conception of the body as a machine does not simply furnish an occasion for wonderment at the intricate workmanship it exhibits; this conception also inspires fear, the fear that there exists within us a counter-power that resists the decrees of the will, and struggles, through both open confrontation and subterfuge, to impose its mastery on us. In this way, no doubt, Descartes by rendering the body distinct from, and extrinsic to, the mind, seeks to establish the argument for the immortality of the soul. But the same gesture, however, produces a notion of the body as an alien presence within us, capable of producing effects (ideas, images, passions, desires) in the mind, a machine that often works independently of, and sometimes against, our will or knowledge, perhaps even communicating with or imitating other such machines, as animals without mind or soul, can do. From this arises the notion of the indocile body, the body that resists the discipline that the mind attempts to impose upon it, and will not heed the commands and decrees that the soul issues: the body that refuses the subjection that 2,000 years of philosophy, pagan and Christian, has demanded of it. It is to this problem that Descartes devoted his last work, *Les passions de l'âme*.

Written originally in French and only translated into Latin after Descartes' death, *Les Passions de l'âme* represents the closest thing to an ethics (and perhaps a politics) that Descartes would write and certainly had a profound and profoundly complicated influence on Spinoza.[5] In a sense, the work continues the line of inquiry opened in the sixth Meditation but by inverting its perspective: the problem is not, as in the earlier work, that of knowing our body (so much more difficult to know than the mind) and the bodies outside of it, but rather how to distinguish within ourselves, that is, within our mind or soul, the ideas and perceptions that we receive from the body from those which originate in the mind or soul alone. This is not an easy task: however distinct from our mind, and thus only indirectly knowable it may be, the body is the primary source of the perceptions which in turn give rise to ideas in the mind. Perceptions, as it were, continually occupy the mind in a way we cannot control, except to the extent we can separate thought from perception, the ideas that do not depend on the body and its senses from the ideas derived from them. Only in this way can the soul hope to exercise power over the body. And the exercise of this power—*pouvoir* or *empire* in the original French version and *potestas* or *imperium* in the Latin translation—is not only what allows the human individual to be an "agent" rather than a "patient,"[6] that is, to carry out actions of which he is the sole cause rather than be affected passively by causes external to him, but is that which demarcates what is properly human from that which pertains to "beasts [*les bêtes*]."[7] Accordingly, because the body through its effects is never truly external to the mind or soul but remains internal to it, so the struggle to claim or reclaim the human from the bestial or animal is a struggle carried on within the human itself.

Moreover, "bestial" for Descartes does not designate powerful appetites or chaotic violence. On the contrary, the animal realm is rather a world of soulless, spiritless machines or automatons operating with perfect regularity and according to passions understood as motions unaccompanied by thought. The human body belongs to this world and, insofar as it communicates this mechanicity to the mind, constantly threatens to reduce man to a machine. Ideas that originate in the body but are contained in the mind or soul represent the dangerous paradox or unstable contradiction of the thought of what does not itself think. These are the "imaginations that have the body as their sole cause.... Such are the illusions of our dreams, as well as the reveries we often have while awake, when our thought wanders indolently without by itself applying itself to anything."[8] It is precisely amid the ideas and imaginations that pertain to the body alone that we must seek the power to direct our mind "to apply itself" [*s'appliquer*—a frequent term here], to labor with great exertion against the tendency to indolence that appears to be our normal state, the consequence of the mind's irrelevance to the operation of the body-machine. That power is the will itself: it is this alone that allows us to raise ourselves above the corporeal world of automatons.

Thus, Descartes is haunted by the very images Spinoza will turn to very different purposes in the Scholium to *E* III, P2. Not only do men carry out actions often thought to be determined by the will, such as walking or eating (in addition to such "instinctive" acts such as breathing) automatically, that is, without any exercise of the will, but "it is said that those who walk in their sleep sometimes swim across rivers in which they would drown when awake."[9] The power of the body not under the command of the soul, according to the striking example of the sleeping swimmer, is greater than that of the body subjected to its *potestas*. This is not simply "physical" strength, but the corresponding power to produce motions and emotions in the mind. Accordingly, Descartes takes great pains to explain that "the struggles [*les combats*] that are commonly imagined to take place between the inferior and superior part of the soul" or "between the natural appetites and the will" assume a soul divided into parts or even "*divers personnages*."[10] Against Plato, the Stoics, and nearly every tendency within Christian theology (where the notion of *conscientia* understood as conscience becomes central), he asserts that only a failure to distinguish between the "functions" of the soul and those of the body have prevented a clear apprehension of the danger posed by "the body, to which alone all that can be observed within us that is opposed [*qui répugne*] to our reason must be attributed."[11]

As is well known, Descartes solved the problem of the exteriority of body and soul by maintaining that their opposing forces meet at the point of the pineal gland, the battleground where the stronger stops the effect of the other:

> To conquer [*vaincre*] the passions produced by the body one must enter into combat and test the strength of one's own forces, as well as the effectiveness of the weapons that the soul has at its disposal to overpower the passions. Because so many have failed to distinguish between what pertains to the body and what to the soul, they have waged their struggle entirely within the realm of the passions, among which the soul is condemned to vacillate. From this state of ignorance follows the captivity of the will, and the soul, having surrendered without a proper fight, is made the slave of the body. In order not to be condemned to follow the dictate [*dicte*] of the body and its passions which will, at least in a soul not entirely abandoned to the passions, lead to regret and repentance [*repentir*], but the soul must increase its strength by making its resolutions on the basis of the knowledge of truth alone.[12]

What is at stake in this struggle for mastery, which will decide whether, as is so often the case, the soul, deprived of its freedom, is the slave of the body or whether the body will submit to the soul and obey its commands? It is notable that for Descartes the necessary and victorious combat of the soul against the intractability of the body has little to do with the struggle against the lusts of the flesh so important for Christianity. On the contrary, his example is war, and the conduct of the individual exposed to death in battle. In the face of mortal danger, the body, seeking (automatically, mechanically) to preserve itself, produces in us (that is, in our soul) the passions of fear and a powerful, perhaps irresistible, desire to flee. The soul cannot rely on the will alone to overcome these passions and must apply itself to use its reason to persuade itself that the danger is not as great as we fear and that, in any case, death in battle will bring us a glory whose pleasure we feel merely in imagining it. Flight permits us to survive, but will expose us to the contempt of others and the shame and regret we will certainly feel toward ourselves. Thus, the ultimate sign of the soul's subjection of the body is not its ability to restrain the desires for the pleasures of the flesh (which, we should note, are conducive to the perpetuation of human life), but its ability to expose and perhaps even direct the body to death against its inclination to persist in its own being. The weak, those who prove unable to command themselves and their bodies, are in no way exempt from blame: because "even the weakest souls can gain absolute power over their bodies," their failure to do so is itself an act of will, a deliberate refusal to do what all are capable of doing. To describe so total a subjection, even the phrase "*empire absolu*" will not suffice: Descartes must reach beyond the absolute to the remarkable phrase "*empire très absolu*" to denote a mastery that extends to the very life of the body that, outside of reason, nothing more than an animal or machine, must be compelled to the obedience to which it cannot consent: it must be broken and domesticated, that is, enslaved.[13] And there is no greater sign of the power of the *dominus* over the *servus* than the assertion of the right over life and death.

The notion of command, of imperium, belonged to the Roman military lexicon before it became a political concept—*imperator* denoted the commander of a regiment before it became the name of the emperor. Further, it was, as a conceptualization of one's relation to oneself, a familiar theme among the Stoics. In certain ways, the first part of *Passions* appears to culminate in a doctrine similar to Seneca's famous declaration, "*imperare sibi maximum imperium est.*"[14] For Descartes, however, the self that one must be able to command is the other irreducibly present in the self, where the outside resides in the deepest recesses of its interior. Thus, the body, essentially foreign to the soul, perpetually threatens to submit it to machinic ends and only the soul's ability to command the body finally affirms its existence as separate and superior substance. The struggle for command identifies the body as the element both inside and outside the self that is not merely a resident alien but an internal enemy who must be subdued. At this point, Descartes appears closer to Paul than to the Stoics in his fear of the body's power and of the consequences of its victory over the soul. Thus, Paul declares in 1 *Corinthians* 9:27 (roughly contemporaneous with Seneca's text): "But I keep under my body, and bring [it] into subjection: lest that by any means, when I have preached to others, I myself should be a castaway" (*KJB*). Here, as in *Romans* 7:22–23, the body is at war with the inner man (τὸν ἔσω ἄνθρωπὸν), or the mind (νοός), causing the man to do what he does not want to do and not do what he wants to do, a corporeal law unto itself, opposed to the law of the spirit. The body must be made captive, enslaved and forced to obey the commands of the soul whose power, insufficient to the task, requires the grace that God distributes to those willing to offer themselves as slaves. While the violence of Paul's metaphors (the beating, wounding and enslavement often softened or suppressed by translators) might seem foreign to the lexicon of Descartes' argument, in fact, the movement of *The Passions of the Soul* merely defers this violence, pushing it to the threshold of the outside, evoking the violence of war, which one must stand and face even if death is not merely possible but likely, as the ultimate test of one's imperium over oneself. For Descartes, it is as if submitting the body, and therefore oneself, to death would be the only authentic proof of the "very absolute empire" of the soul over the body. Of course, it is not this that distinguishes Descartes from Paul, but the specificity of Descartes' body in relation to the flesh in Paul's sense. The body for Descartes is, above all, a machine capable of directing itself to greater feats than when directed by the mind, and whose power Descartes thus cannot entirely fail to admire. His body exercises a power, a *potentia* rather than a *potestas*, the ability to act, perhaps to labor, as if it were a *nomos* or *imperium* unto itself, an empire not simply of the machinic body, but of what Descartes' mechanism obscures: the life that resists death. At the unthinkable extreme of Cartesian thought is "the corporeal soul" and the body that thinks.[15]

For Descartes, "none of our internal actions would convince anyone who examines them that our body is anything other than an automaton (*une machine qui remue de soi-même*) within which there is also a soul that has thoughts, except speech (*paroles*) or other signs." Thus, he distinguishes speech produced by the soul from the sounds emitted by animals, determined[16] by passions such as fear or hunger, or those simply imitated mechanically and automatically by parrots or magpies. Even the speech of beings endowed with a soul, however, necessarily bears the imprint of the combat waged by the soul to subdue and gain mastery over the body, which in turn fights to liberate itself from the constraints the soul attempts to impose upon it. Indeed, there is a moment in the text when, in apparently deviating from his purpose, Descartes begins to speak, as it were, from the point of view of the body. In "On Satisfaction in Oneself," Descartes describes the tranquility and "*repos de conscience*" that follow the rational pursuit of virtue and the joy that comes from doing good.[17] But those who lack the knowledge of truth necessary to distinguish and overcome the passions may do what they believe is good, but which is in fact bad. Such persons will feel neither satisfaction nor tranquility, but the passions of "pride and impertinent arrogance" which can too easily be mistaken for satisfaction in oneself.

The example that Descartes provides not only does not confront the obvious problem of self-deception, the fact that we may be made to believe by forces internal as well as external to us that we have a knowledge of the truth and pursue virtue when we do not, and that what we feel is satisfaction when in fact it is something else, but in fact deepens and complicates it. The passions of pride and arrogance are particularly seen among

> those who, believing themselves to be devout, are merely bigoted and superstitious: that is, those who, because they are constantly in church reciting prayers, wear their hair short, fast frequently and give alms, think they are entirely perfect and imagine that they are such great friends of God that they could do nothing that would displease him and that everything their passion dictates to them is righteous zeal, even though it sometimes directs them to the greatest crimes that human beings can commit, such as betraying cities, killing princes, exterminating entire peoples for no other reason than that they do not share their opinions.[18]

The people Descartes describes are proud of their humility, glory in their suppression of pride and are models of discipline and self-command: they tame their bodies through ritual and deprivation and, instead of accumulating wealth in order to purchase the pleasures the flesh demands, take pleasure in the frustration of desire. They impose rigor, if not penury, upon themselves in order to give alms, as if the true object of charity were the deprivation of the giver, rather than the relief of those in need, and mark their rejection of the vanities of this world by cutting their hair short. They have indeed subjugated the body and its pleasures, but their combat with the body, their willingness, indeed their zeal, to compel it to risk death for the true faith, signals their contempt of life, including the life of others, as if the passion commanding them is a self-hatred that cannot finally be distinguished from a hatred of others. It is precisely this passion that can so easily be mistaken for the self-command which "is the only thing that can give us a reason to esteem ourselves, that is, the use of our free will and the empire we have over our desires [*volontés*], for we can be praised or blamed only for actions which depend on this free will."[19] Descartes' striking example reveals quite clearly that we can master ourselves and subjugate the body in the service not simply of reason, but also of a passion that commands us to weaken or destroy ourselves and others, as if life itself were the enemy and that this passion is most likely to adopt the guise of goodness and righteousness. It might even masquerade as reason itself.

But, as we have noted, the very movement of Descartes' philosophy, by identifying the body as the enemy both internal and external to the soul, leads him to acknowledge the power that requires its subjection, as if, once discipline were relaxed, an insurgent body could overpower the incorporeal soul to reclaim its own empire, the empire of the body, which endeavors to persist in its being and resists destruction. Thus, Descartes delivers a concept of the body over to Spinoza, who is able in turn to receive this gift only through the arduous labor of reading *The Passions of the Soul* as carefully as he reads the text of Scripture. Macherey goes so far as to argue that Part III of the *Ethics* is in a certain way "written in the margins" of *The Passions of the Soul*; to see that Spinoza develops a part of Descartes' argument against another part allows us to understand why for Spinoza the critique of the separation of mind from body and even more of the attribution or imputation of causal power to the former over the latter must lead to the idea of conatus: the body often endeavors to persist in its being against the commands of the soul. Thus, the body of the swimmer free from the soul's surveillance swims across a river in which the intervention of the soul would cause it to drown, just as the body resists the death which the soul would command it in order to magnify the glory of the sovereign, as the "Preface" to the *Theological-Political Treatise* explains. For Spinoza, the imaginary notions of the soul's command and the body's obedience, of the soul as master/*dominus* who is *sui juris* and the body as slave/*servus* who is *alieni juris* are not mere illusions to be dispelled by true knowledge or even illusions that pertain to the nature of consciousness itself and thus have a necessary existence. Instead, the imaginary is inscribed in the corporeal realities of subjection, legal and otherwise, and the apparatuses in which they are realized.

Thus, the prefaces both to Part III and to Part V (which represents less a continuation of the former than a kind of revision and expansion of it) are explicitly aimed at Descartes (and particularly *The Passions of the Soul*). The preface to *E* III begins by effecting a critical theoretical displacement, substituting the term "affects" for "passions." In part, Spinoza seeks to avoid the moral condemnation attached to the latter term, but he also makes us see that "passion" (derived from the verb *patio*, meaning to suffer, to bear, to submit to) also refers to the "passivity" of the one who is acted on and who is therefore subject and subjected to something else. The use of "affect" allows him to break with the idea that only from a position of "freedom" in which we are determined by nothing but the undetermined will itself can we be said to be active, and to show in contrast that we are necessarily affected in ways that can make us active and adequate causes of things, as well as in ways that diminish our capacity to act.

He introduces the concept of "affect" by dividing it into two contradictory and incompatible notions embedded in the syntactical pattern of his opening sentences of the "Preface" to Part III: "most of those who have written about the affects and the manner in which men live seem to be discussing, not natural things that follow the common laws of nature, but things that are outside of nature [*quae extra naturam sunt*]." These writers seem to conceive man as an "*imperium in imperio*," who "disturbs [*perturbare*] rather than follows nature's order," and "who has an absolute power [*absolutam habere potentiam*] over his actions and is determined by nothing other than himself." Even before the name "Descartes" appears in the preface, the phrases "absolute power" (although Spinoza for "pouvoir," uses the term "potentia" instead of the term "potestas" used in the Latin translation of *The Passions of the Soul*) and "imperium" clearly refer to Descartes' text, even if Spinoza's critique extends beyond it. The contradiction that Spinoza postulates, moreover, is already present in a disavowed form in the work of Descartes and others. On one hand, the affects are placed "outside of nature," that is, outside of the order and connection of things and ideas, existing in an internal world of the soul exempt from the "common laws of nature," which every "natural thing" necessarily follows. Affects are no longer even "things" but "*vitia*" or "*ineptias*," that is, faults, defects, or absurdities without any positive existence, and therefore not merely unknowable in themselves but unworthy of any attention but that which denounces them. On the other, however, nearly all such writers acknowledge the power of these faults or defects, the force they exercise on even the most disciplined minds, determining them to do the worse while they pursue or imagine they pursue the better, as if those who study the passions denigrate them out of a fear of their very power.

But Spinoza is not content merely to condemn those who condemn the affects. The formula "*imperium in imperio*" in particular condenses into a single phrase a number of apparently diverse lines of Spinoza's thought. Drawn from the legal controversies of feudalism, or rather from the struggles to establish absolute states against the fragmentation of powers characteristic of feudalism, and nearly always employed in a pejorative sense, the phrase describes the contradiction of a legally autonomous state existing within another larger legally autonomous state, internal to it but not governed by its laws. In Spinoza's time, such struggles often focused on the authority of the churches in relation to the state, a particularly urgent question in seventeenth-century Holland where the

Dutch Reformed Church exercised considerable power, including the right to prosecute and punish heretics and those who led immoral lives by means of its own courts.[20] Spinoza's use of this phrase to describe a certain conception of the relation of the human to the natural order, and the phrase "absolute power" to describe the notion of the dominion of the mind over the affects thus inscribes these "beliefs" (as he calls them) in a politico-legal register, which constantly reminds us that, irrespective of their truth, they produce real effects. The importance of Spinoza's use of this terminology here is not that it is (explicitly or implicitly) applied inappropriately to the affects, but that the assumptions underlying the idea of imperium as a political concept as it is commonly understood are themselves wrong.

Neither nature nor the affects constitute an imperium. If by imperium we mean a state whose order rests on commands originating in the will of an *imperator* who, by virtue of right (*jus*) and legal authority (*potestas*), would be able to produce the effect of obedience in those subject to him, Spinoza not only rejects such a notion in relation to the human world but denies its applicability even to God who "was not before his decrees nor can he be without them" (*E* I, P33S2). Even more pertinently, in the case of the *summa potestas* or sovereign power, Spinoza repeatedly warns the reader in both the *Theological-Political Treatise* (Ch. 16–17) and the *Political Treatise* (Ch. 2–3) that despite the legal right of the sovereign to do as he pleases, his actual right extends only so far as his physical, material power. There is nothing that more clearly distinguishes Spinoza's political thought from the theories of such contemporaries as Hobbes and Locke than his declaring absolute sovereignty neither good nor bad, but rather impossible, nothing more than a juridical fantasy of power conceived as the sovereign's property, either voluntarily transferred by his subjects or legitimately (and in certain cases, illegitimately) confiscated from them. The notion of absolute power, however assiduously the sovereign may attempt to put it into practice "remains in many ways purely theoretical" (*TTP*, XVII, 536). No one "can transfer to another his power [*potentiam*] and consequently his right [*jus*] to another to such an extent that he ceases to be a man" (*TTP*, XVII, 536). Thus, according to Spinoza, no living individual is without at least the physical power to persist in his being. This irreducible minimum inheres in life itself, that is, in the living body. The power of the individual body, itself composed of individual things themselves composed of individual things ad infinitum, and the multiplication of these forces in the body of the multitude, constitutes the limit on the sovereign's right and authority not in any legal sense, but according to laws realized in the very power of nature itself. Every state necessarily fears its own people more than any external enemy and tends to avoid provoking their indignation: the freedom that results from this fear is not a right granted to the multitude by law, but their natural right which is always co-extensive with their power. This is Spinoza's Machiavellianism: to be held spellbound by the imagination of either the absolute power of the sovereign or the people is to be disarmed, and the disarmed will come to ruin. There is perhaps no more powerful demonstration of the truth of Spinoza's thesis than the collapse of his own attempt to offer a formal definition of democracy as "*omnino absolutum imperium*," in the *Tractatus Politicus*, an attempt that breaks off with a list of the exceptions to the democratic absolute: women, servants, slaves, foreigners—those who constitute the multitude.[21]

The same Machiavellianism, applied to the notion of an individual's absolute power (both formal and physical, both *imperium* and *potentia*) over the affects, leads Spinoza to conclude that this notion is based on a conception of power that is as false an account of the relation of mind and body as of the realm of the political from which its lexicon is derived. Because power is nothing more than a relation between forces, Spinoza argues that we can understand the extent to which it is possible for the mind to moderate the affects only by determining "the nature of the affects and of their forces" [*affectuum naturam et vires*]. But again, the attribution to the mind of "absolute power" over the body's "affects and actions" is not simply an error, but has what Locke called, in relation to the idea of consciousness, a "forensic" function.[22] It renders us "absolutely" responsible and accountable for the affects and actions, which we nevertheless cannot entirely control, to both man and God (and through the latter to ourselves by means of the conscience that anticipates with pleasure or pain the rewards and punishments to come). Indeed, the history of those who have attempted to understand the affects, is itself a kind of theoretical displacement that allows condemnation to replace knowledge, as if the affects insofar as they exist outside of nature are unnatural, that is, not only beyond nature, but contrary to it and worthy only of denunciation. If this is the case, Spinoza implies, the hatred and contempt the affects inspire in those who write about them are equally unnatural, in part because the anger of those who condemn the affects is itself an affect.[23]

But beyond this paradox lies another: the "passions" most frequently condemned in the writings of moralists are not anger, hatred or self-hatred, but precisely those pertaining to the pleasures of the "flesh" which threaten to subject the mind to the dominion of body. It is this fact that connects the notions of imperium and absolute power in their internal and external senses, applied to the mind and to society as a whole, notions whose relation might otherwise be understood as a division between the literal and the metaphorical. Indeed, the very distinction between the inner and the outer, mind and body, the individual and the political, and in an important sense, theory and practice, collapse and are revealed to be the effect of the perpetual attempt to limit and contain the forces of the body, or at least to insure its obedience: the inside of the process of subjection is therefore not an internal reflection or representation of a more primary outside, but rather represents the continuation of the outside as in a moebius strip, as if the outside folds back upon itself as its own interior. But this process is uneven and contradictory and cannot be understood simply as a means to the end of subjecting the body in order that its forces can be captured and turned to the advantage of the *dominus*. The body inspires through its resistance to the absolute extension of power both fear and hatred, although its resistance is less an active opposition than the obstacle the body poses as a physical, living entity with both needs and limitations on what it can do and endure. It was Descartes who noted the link between self-denial and the extermination of entire peoples, between, on the one hand, a self-discipline so unrelenting that one's own body is an enemy to be conquered and, once conquered, subjected to coercion and constraint and, on the other, a need to command others so absolutely that their very existence finally appears as an act of rebellion. In such a regime, the body's pleasures, precisely because they pertain to the body, are devalued and their effects on the mind regarded as a kind of attack, with the result that even the processes of human reproduction become sources both of sin and the shame and contempt that follow it.

The imputation of responsibility to the individual deemed free thus both blocks the way to the knowledge of humanity understood as a part of nature, and simultaneously attaches a moral or "spiritual" value to pain and weakness the acceptance of which is regarded as the clearest evidence of one's fortitude. Accordingly, Spinoza defines repentance (*poenitentia*) as "a sadness that accompanies an action that we believe to have been committed by a free decree of the mind [*quod nos ex libero Mentis decreto fecisse credimus*]" (E III, Definition of the Affects, 27). What is striking here is Spinoza's omission of the agent of the action, as if to underscore the notion that "we" are not the cause of the action we nevertheless repent. Further, repentance is not merely the passion, or passive affect, of regret, but denotes the bodily practices of penance, that is, self-punishment through the infliction of pain or a compensatory subtraction from oneself. Its logic is that of imputation, both subjective and objective: in one and the same movement we impute to ourselves what is simultaneously imputed to us by others, an imputation whose condition of possibility is the "belief" that bodily acts originate in the decree freely issued by the mind.

Spinoza cuts the Gordian knot in which the lines of individuality, freedom, authority, subjection, accountability, and guilt are so entangled as to seem both inseparable and inescapable with *E* III, P2: "the body cannot determine the mind to think, nor can the mind determine the body to movement or rest or to anything else (if there is anything else)." The effect of this statement about causality is above all a double exoneration, and a lifting of the imputation of guilt: the actions of the body can no longer be attributed to a decision of the mind, while the body in turn cannot be the source of the mind's degradation, perpetually threatening to reduce it to an existence, whether animal or mechanical, that is foreign to its essence. The proposition deprives the very theoretical oppositions of command and obedience, *dominus* and *subditus/servus*, insofar as they are applied to the relation of mind and body, of any explanatory power and instead exposes them as the apologia of a world of subjection. For this very reason Spinoza's project of rehabilitating the body and understanding not only the forms of determination proper to it (only bodies determine bodies), but also the power bodies, as they are affected by other bodies alone, exercise (or could exercise if freed from constraint and coercion), is not merely difficult or objectionable; it is for nearly all of Spinoza's readers unthinkable. It is this fact that confers on the Scholium to Proposition 2 not only its importance, but its formal and rhetorical peculiarities.

The Scholium begins by supplying the positive counterpoint to the negative argument advanced in the proposition: the mind no more determines the body than the body determines the mind, not because spirit and matter are so dissimilar that only the occasion of God's intervention would allow a translation from the one to the other (which also implies a hierarchical order between the two, such that any contact between them would threaten the autonomy of spirit), but because "mind and body are one and the same thing." Spinoza almost immediately refers the reader back to his arguments earlier in the *Ethics* in which he explains the assertion that "the order and connection of ideas is the same as the order and connection of things" (*E* II, P7), and its Corollary: "God's power of thought is equal to his actual power of action." "Certain Hebrews," left unnamed, he tells us, saw "as if through a cloud [*quasi per nebulam*] that... God, God's intellect and the things of which he has intellection are one and the same thing" (*E* II, P7S). The human mind in its actual being, as he explains in *E* II, P11–12, is constituted as "the idea of a certain singular thing existing in action [*actu existentis*]." The singular thing, which in the case of the human mind is the body, thus thinks itself as part of the activity by which it exists. Spinoza's description of mind and body as "one and the same thing," repeated frequently for emphasis, raises the question of why this fact, "which there can be no reason to doubt," is not only doubted, but will appear as an absurdity to his readers, just as it has appeared in the history of philosophy, with the exception of "certain Hebrews" and perhaps a few others, such as Lucretius, as a notion unworthy of consideration.

Spinoza's own position that the mind is the idea of the body and that, as a consequence, whatever limits or diminishes the power of the body to act, necessarily limits or diminishes the power of the mind to think (*E* III, P11), compels us to understand the "prejudices" at work as something more than disembodied "beliefs" that can be changed by better arguments than have so far been advanced. Indeed, the very logic of the position that ideas and things, minds and bodies are "one and the same thing" suggests that prejudice (*praejudicium*) necessarily possesses a physical as well as intellectual existence. Prejudice can neither be an act of the mind alone unaccompanied by the body, nor does it exist in an internal place of freedom where it is formed and unformed without external interference. The judgment that precedes and determines experience must then be understood as a kind of precedent, previously determined and now "in force," because law without force, as Hobbes noted, is mere words. The prejudice to which Spinoza refers is not just any prejudice: in fact it is the iteration of a previous judgment now materialized within the existing practice of law, for which the imputation of the mind's determination of the body is constitutive. Moreover, the imputation or attribution of causality and hence responsibility to the free will of the individual designated as "author" of his actions is just as important in the apparatuses, rituals and ceremonies of Christianity, which constitute the practice co-extensive with its theory or theology. This is what Locke meant when he argued that consciousness has a forensic character: every man must preserve an awareness of what he himself (and no other) has thought and done, to be able to account for himself, as he will be held accountable, on the day of judgment when what was hidden will be laid bare and all hearts will be opened.[24] It is precisely the forensic nature of the dominant conception of the mind-body relation in its political/legal, as well as theological, function that Spinoza hopes to make visible and thus open to change in the simultaneity of theory and practice. For precisely this reason, he is on very dangerous ground and accordingly advances with such caution and subtlety that readers are in danger of missing significant parts of his argument. The appeals to experience with which he hopes to counter the stubborn belief in free will seem designed to side-step the great theologico-political structures (again, both intellectual and material) that the *Ethics* seeks to infiltrate and subvert. In a sense, the most powerful effects of the Scholium are deferred, their meaning realized only in conjunction with later parts of the text.

Spinoza's attempt to determine the content of the prejudice that prevents the apprehension of the fact the mind and body are one and the same thing (and the enormous consequences that follow from this fact) draws its terminology, as in the Preface to Part III, from Descartes, but in ways that illuminate and capture the importance of the semantic field to which the most frequently repeated words belong and which overdetermines their meaning in the Scholium to *E* III, P2. When we read that men are "so firmly persuaded" that the body moves or remains at rest "by the command of the mind alone" [*Corpus ex solo Mentis nutu*], to understand "*nutu*" simply as "command," that is, as the equivalent of "*imperium*," for example, is to miss precisely the sense of the embodiment of command, not only in the materiality of speech, but in a physical gesture whose origins lie in the two great institutions of Rome: slavery and the military. Spinoza shared with Machiavelli a high regard for Quintus Curtius' *History of Alexander*, which showed that every sovereign rules at the pleasure of the multitude whose support is his only fortress when fortune opposes him. But perhaps more pertinently, Quintus Curtius was in his own way a trenchant critic of the very notion of absolute power, which he regarded as a fiction fatal above all to rulers: the diminution of resistance to zero, or close to it, is in the case of living beings exceedingly rare, nothing more than an accident of fortune that cannot endure.

Quintus Curtius captures one of those moments in a scene just before Alexander's triumph over Darius, king of Persia, in the battle of Issus. Darius' colorful and splendid army, bedecked with gold and silver and carrying ornamental weapons, was in fact a collection of armies without significant experience or discipline. In contrast, the Macedonian soldiers, however savage (*torva*) and wild (*inculte*) they appeared, nevertheless "intently watched for a nod from the commander, marched with discipline and knew how to maintain order and to obey every command [*ad nutum monentis intenti, sequi signa, ordines servare didicerunt; quod imperatur, omnes exaudiunt*]."[25] They were so disciplined that they did not require any other signal from their commander than a mere nod to be set into motion. The nod is a bodily gesture, a downward movement of the head, the slightest possible expression of the *imperator*'s will, which precisely demands the full attention of those who must obey him. Obedience to the *nutus* is immediate, even automatic, obedience without hesitation or question. This is what makes the Macedonian army an invincible machine: command without resistance. Quite simply and without reflection the soldiers will die rather than disobey their commander. This moment of absolute power, however, will not and cannot last: fortune, which so favored Alexander, will abandon him, render him unfit to command and deprive him of the ability to set armies in motion with a single nod of his head. But the image of the *nutus* serves Spinoza well in that it captures the ease with which the mind is commonly believed to command the body.

The reality, in contrast, is quite different: "no one knows in what way, or by what means the mind moves the body, at what speed, nor to what degree movement can be attributed to the body." Given the absence of such knowledge, "when men say that a given action by the body originates in the mind, which has *imperium* over the mind, they don't know what they are saying" and have instead revealed their ignorance. At this point, Spinoza appeals to experience: everyone believes the ability to speak or to remain silent, among many other things, "depends on a decree of the mind" [*Mentis decreto pendere*]. Here, he introduces the term *decretum*, the first of fifteen occurrences of the word in the Scholium. *Decretum*, a decree, order, or decision in a legal sense, is derived from the verb "*decerno*," which means to decide or determine a matter in dispute, as in a legal decision or determination pronounced by a judge or a decision or determination made by a person. In the context of the *Ethics*, outside of this Scholium, Spinoza translates *decretum* into the language of immanence: nature is what God, whose existence coincides exactly with the action of decreeing, has decreed, as if his command, "let there be light," rather than producing light in a causal sequence, includes within itself the existence of light, as well as both the seeing of light and the blessing of it ("for it was good"). In the Scholium to P2, however, Spinoza's use of the term decree, added to that of command and absolute power, serves to remind the reader of the way its use to describe mental operations represents a continuation of its use to describe the imposition of sovereign will or decision on the people: a decree is not simply an expression of the wishes of the sovereign power; it is neither a request nor a plea. Rather, it denotes a speech act in which the will of the speaker is expressed in a way that carries the threat of force if it is ignored. In the mental sphere, just as unavoidably as in the political, there arises the question of the nature of this force, of how will it be applied and how effective it can be against the resistance that any disobedience to the decree or command might involve. Unless his imaginary interlocutors can explain the way mental decrees are imposed on the body which is then constrained to obey them, they will be compelled to admit that the movement of the body (including and above all its obedience) is not determined by the mind, but only by another body, itself determined by another body and so on (*E* III, P2D).

But "they," as Spinoza says, will not be so easily separated from the prejudice that we now know is no mere belief, except in the sense that it is the belief coextensive with the operations of subjection, themselves grounded in relations of force: "but they will say that from the laws of nature considered only in its corporeality it is not possible to deduce the causes of buildings [*aedificiorum*] and paintings [*picturarum*]." Such creations are the products of human "skill" [*arte*]. The body is capable of building a *templum*, that is, not simply a structure but a space marked out as sacred, set apart from everyday use, only if it is "determined" and "led" or "guided" (he uses the verb "*duco*,") by the mind, recalling Paul's notion that the body itself is a temple, a possession of God's that we keep in trust, as in 1 *Corinthians* 6:19: "do you not know that your body is a temple of the Holy Spirit who is in you and that you are God's and not your own? (in the Latin of the Vulgate: *An nescitis quoniam membra vestra templum est Spiritus Sancti qui in vobis est quem habetis a Deo et non estis vestry?*)." Here, the separation of spirit or mind from the body, renders the latter a possession of the former, even if the form of that possession is only *usus*, the right to use for a determinate time what rightfully belongs to another, the absolute dominus. The body is then a kind of chattel transferred or loaned out from master to master, a captive (one of Paul's favorite terms) taken in war, now a slave, the property of another and under his jurisdiction. For Spinoza's imaginary interlocutors, the body can no more engage in the work of production and creation without a master than the actual slave seized in Palestine in the first century or in West Africa in the seventeenth.

Spinoza, however, is willing to pose a question that no one up to now has thought to ask: what is the body capable of doing when it is liberated from the master's command? Here, he returns explicitly to Descartes' examples: the body operating according to corporeal causes alone does many things that we cannot yet explain and "among beasts we observe a number of things that far surpass human wisdom." But of the images furnished by Descartes, none so captured Spinoza's imagination as that of the sleepwalker or somnambulist. Descartes' account of the extraordinary feats of somnambulists was itself probably a reference to an examination of the topic by Pierre Gassendi, whose personal inquiries and suggestions toward a classification of what he called "*les noctambules*" were cited by researchers for the next century and a half.[26] Indeed, it appears that the incident of a sleeping man crossing a river is an allusion to one of Gassendi's case studies:

> a man who lived near Digne in Provence had one night while sleeping climbed on to his stilts [which peasants often used to travel through marshes or flooded fields] and crossed a flooded river in a nearby valley. He had just reached the opposite side, when he awakened and was astonished at what he had just done. He did not dare to return across the river until daylight when the flood had subsided.[27]

Why did this particular account, which made its way from Gassendi to Descartes to Spinoza, so captivate philosophers, especially those as opposed as Descartes and Spinoza, with the "Epicurean" Gassendi occupying a kind of middle ground? The prevailing view of somnambulists at the time was that their nocturnal activities were partial, indeed degraded, imitations of their waking lives, mere gestures at the real actions in which the affected individuals engage each day, as if somnambulists, through a kind of reflex, mechanically repeated what the "conscious" man, precisely by means of his consciousness, ordinarily did far more effectively, in a necessarily diminished and weakened form, without the direction and force imparted by the waking mind. Finally, the already diminished power of such reflexes is often exhausted after a short time, leaving the individual to awaken with a sense of confusion and shame. This view of somnambulism assumed the soul or mind's necessary command over the body by treating the phenomenon as the afterlife of the mind's directions, that is, as residual motion imparted by a surplus of force determined by the mind that carried over into and disturbed the state of repose.

For Descartes, the dream reveals above all a remarkable power of the body to accomplish things not normally thought possible with or without the mind's direction: not simply respiration or the circulation of the blood, that is, actions internal to the machine of the body, but external actions exhibiting the great strength, skill and dexterity associated with certain animals. The fact that the dreamer can perform asleep actions that would be impossible were he awake, represents a dramatization of the power of the body to produce "movements of our passions that, although they are accompanied in us by thought" do not originate in the mind, but in the body alone, often against our will and "in spite of us." Let us recall that "it is to the body that must be attributed everything within us that struggles against our reason."[28] When reason sleeps, the body, with an animal cunning that surpasses what is properly human, takes advantage of the mind's somnolent state to elude its direction and disregard the training to which it has been subjected. Such examples show all the more clearly the dangers of the unsubjected body which, if not submitted to the mastery of the mind, will overpower it with inhuman passions and the machinic thoughts that accompany them.

The case of Spinoza is clearly more complicated. To draw on the image of the somnambulist who does more than what he could do while awake is to risk "giving to the superstitious material for new questions," perhaps appearing to affirm the existence of spirits, possession, and so on, as he warns when he abruptly interrupts the account of the Spanish poet in the Scholium to E IV, P39 after casting doubt on the very notion of personal identity. In the case of the

Scholium to *E* III, P2, he has two reasons for taking such a risk, both of which set him against Descartes: the power of the body liberated from the command of the mind for Spinoza reveals the existence of a material regime of constraint and coercion which simultaneously produces an obedient body and the idea of consent or the consenting mind proper to it. Here Spinoza returns to the critique of consciousness articulated in the Appendix to Part I of the *Ethics*: "experience as well as reason shows no less clearly that men believe themselves to be free only because they are conscious of their actions, but ignorant of the causes by which they are determined." But, continuing the sentence, he moves beyond this critique, which can be understood as posing a universal human condition that arises from the mere fact of being conscious, to the singular historical and political forms of this condition: "and that, further, the mind's decrees are nothing other than the appetites themselves and for this reason vary according to the varying disposition of the body." Thus, "the decree, just as much as the appetite of the mind and the determination of the body, are simultaneous in nature, or rather are one and the same thing."

It is at this point that the specificity of the term "*decretum*" takes on its full significance for Spinoza. Fourteen of its fifteen occurrences in the Scholium are concentrated in the last ten sentences, where the effect of repetition (above all in the phrase "*ex libero mentis decreto*" or "by the free decree of the mind") is not only to force the reader to confront the fact that its meaning as an individual "decision" or determination, and thereby as a mental act, cannot be disentangled from its political and legal significance, but also to show that the words we actually use, that is, the words available to us to use, are themselves determined, as if the use of the word "decree" had itself been decreed, together perhaps with the words *imperium* and *nutus* (as well as *dominus*, *servus* and *subjectus*) among others. Spinoza appeals to "experience" which shows that "there is nothing we are less capable of doing by a decree of the mind than to remember." In fact, not only is it "not in the free power of the mind [*in libera Mentis potestate*] to remember a thing," but just as, if not more, importantly, it is not in the free power of the mind to forget it. He then gives us an example of the determinative nature of the "involuntary memory" for what we both say and think: "we cannot speak a word [*verbum*] unless we remember it." Since we cannot, except to a very limited degree, command ourselves to remember, what we say is typically determined by the words made available to us according to a causal order beyond our knowledge or control. Not only can we not use words we cannot remember, but for the same reason do not remember that we do not remember them, a forgetting that is one of the necessary conditions of our belief that we speak freely.

But perhaps even more fundamental to Spinoza's project of examining both the causes and effects of the notion of decree as a variant of command is the idea that there are words and thus sequences of words we are not free *not* to remember and, further, that we are not free *not* to say. We may endeavor or believe that we endeavor to forget them, but, as if in one of the dreams that so fascinated Spinoza, our very attempts to forget them seem rather to preserve them from the oblivion to which we believe we seek to consign them. These are decrees, of course, including the decree prohibiting decrees, that is, the orders or commands, which, unlike the declination of the head or the wave of the arm, must be composed of words. They are the words we cannot forget because they are inscribed in our corporeal reality: "the cause of the mind imagining a body is that the human body finds itself affected and disposed by the traces of an external body [*corporis externi vestigiis*] in the same way that it was affected when certain of its parts were pushed by that body" (*E* II, P2D). We cannot choose but remember precisely those words or concatenations of words that are themselves the *vestigia* or traces of the subjected body and the very process of subjection: these traces are both derived from and preserve the disposition of the constrained body.[29] The body, coerced, subjected to a uniformity and repetition of action, including in the words it utters or writes, bears the *vestigia* that will serve as its memory, like the history recorded in the scars on the slave's back. It is decreed to us that we shall announce, repeatedly, as if we were in danger of forgetting it, that we are not subject to any decree, except that which we impose upon ourselves, even as the very words with which we are ordered to proclaim our freedom, words that it is not within our power to forget, are all drawn, without exception, from the lexicon of servitude and subjection.

It is no wonder then that one of the fears expressed in this Scholium is that of saying too much, of not being able to refrain from saying what one knows or remembers, not knowing what or how much one is saying, or even believing that we have freely decided (decreed to ourselves) to say what we know and remember, that is, to confess. Only after making such declarations do we look back upon ourselves and our actions as if we had been dreaming, exactly as the somnambulist awakens in fear after he has crossed the swollen river. It is here that the notion of somnambulism takes on a double significance: the life in which self-subjection is the surest sign of freedom, in which the mind thinks that it is free only because it remains ignorant of the disposition of the body, its power or weakness, its pleasure or pain, its ability to affect and be affected by other bodies, might itself be understood as the somnambulism of those who dream with their eyes open, who dream that they are awake, dream that they are not dreaming, dream that they are masters of themselves and are determined by their free will alone, the will that is theirs and no one else's, to carry out their "own" desires. This is indeed a dream from which one might awake with terror, but only when it was too late, only if the dead could dream they were alive.

But we should recall that neither of the two references to "somnambuli" in the Scholium, describe an obedient individual dreaming he is free, and seem instead to point back to Descartes' example of a body more powerful when it is free from the soul's command than when it is subjected to it: "somnambulists do in their dreams a great number of things they would not dare to do when awake [*quae vigilando non auderent*]" and "do things while asleep that astonish them when they awake [*dum, vigilant, admirantur*]." To be awake, *vigilo*, is to keep watch, here to keep watch over oneself, one's body, and thus simultaneously to be watched, a notion very close to Locke's definition of consciousness and again directly tied to its forensic function. In the absence of this self-surveillance, the somnambulists (note the plural which Spinoza uses in both passages), here defined as bodies freed from the mind's vigilance, "dare to do things" they would not do when awake. The verb *audeo* is closely related to the "*conor,*" the root of conatus, but while *conor* denotes the act of endeavoring or undertaking, *audeo* is the endeavor to do something that, according to Spinoza's own definition, requires courage or boldness. The affect of "*audacia* is the desire [*Cupiditas*] that incites someone to do something that involves a danger to which his equals [*aequales*] are afraid to expose themselves" (*E* III, Definitions of the Affects, XL). Significantly, Spinoza remains silent about the specific nature of the acts that require such audacity: his somnambulists neither cross rivers nor speak or write words that, awake and watchful, they would not speak or write. They simply "do things." But the things they do—and Spinoza does not question whether it is indeed they who do them—cause them when awake, vigilant, and watchful, to feel wonder (*admiratio*).

A number of commentators have noted that the verb *admiror* plays an important role in Spinoza's thought.[30] He defines admiration as the mind's remaining fixed on a singular thing such that the chain of associated ideas is interrupted and the mind is "distracted." As Pascal Sévérac has argued, however, interruption and distraction, while inhibiting thought, also compel it to overcome its own absorption in a singular idea and, in doing so, to break open and broaden the circle in which it thinks; it is the disruption of obviousness.[31] But there is no disruption of thought without a corresponding disruption of the body, as if the somnambulism which so captivates Spinoza were an image appearing in a dream for the briefest moment, the image that eludes the waking mind that tries to recollect it, growing fainter with each attempt to remember until it disappears altogether and even the remembrance of forgetting it is itself forgotten. It is the idea of the body that eludes the constraints and ignores the decrees of the corporeal regime it serves, the idea of the becoming active of body and mind, a power to act that no regime can reduce to zero because it inheres in the act of living itself.

If these strange and elliptical passages have proved so resistant to interpretation, it is perhaps because the opacity that envelopes them is the necessary condition of their existence, the very power that has allowed them to persist in their being. This is not to say that the opacity of these statements represents a strategic intention on Spinoza's part; on the contrary, they appear to arise precisely from the contradictory and fleeting moments in which he himself glimpses the theoretical and political consequences of his own philosophical discoveries "as if through a cloud." In fact, to call this Scholium opaque is to refer to its silence: not just any silence, of course, but the silence determined by the power not to speak even in the face of the command to do so. But we cannot refuse a command if we do not know it is a command, if we live the decree as fact rather than an order. Spinoza found this silence written in the dreams of somnambulists, a silence that, in making *imperium* audible, imparts to us that quantity of *audacia* that permits us to resist servitude, reject death, and cross torrents to the other side of subjection where life is.

Notes

1. Pierre Macherey, *Introduction à l'Éthique de Spinoza. La troisième partie: la vie affective* (Paris: Presses Universitaires de France, 1995), 59.
2. Rene Descartes, *Meditations*, 1.11. I provide my own translations while consulting the French and Latin texts, which are available at *Descartes' Meditations Home Page*. Wright State University, http://www.wright.edu/~charles.taylor/descartes/ The numerals refer to meditation number, followed by paragraph number.
3. Descartes, *Meditations*, 6.6.
4. Descartes, *Meditations*, 6.17.
5. Perhaps the single most important recent study of Descartes' last text is Denis Kambouchner, *L'Homme des passions. Commentaires sur Descartes*, 2 vols. (Paris: Albin-Michel, 1995).
6. Rene Descartes, *Les Passions De L'âme*, original 1649 edition. http://fr.wikisource.org/wiki/Les_Passions_de_l'âme/édition_de_1649, all translations mine, I.1 (Part number followed by article number).

7   Descartes, *Les Passions De L'âme*, I.16.
8   Descartes, *Les Passions De L'âme*, 1.21.
9   Rene Descartes, Letter to Newcastle, November 23, 1646.
10 Descartes, *Les Passions De L'âme*, I.47.
11 Descartes, *Les Passions De L'âme*, I.47.
12 Descartes, *Les Passions De L'âme*, I.49.
13 Descartes, *Les Passions De L'âme*, I.50.
14 Seneca, *Epistulae Morales ad Lucilium*, ed. by L. D. Reynolds, 2 vols. (Oxford: Oxford University Press, 1965), epistle CXIII.30,
15 Descartes, Lettre Au Marquis De Newcastle, letter November 23, 1646.
16 Descartes, Lettre Au Marquis De Newcastle, letter November 23, 1646.
17 Descartes, *Les Passions De L'âme*, III.190.
18 Descartes, *Les Passions De L'âme*, III.190.
19 Descartes, *Les Passions De L'âme*, III.190.
20 See Jonathan Israel, *Radical Enlightenment: Philosophy and the Making of Modernity 1650–1750* (Oxford: Oxford University Press, 2001).
21 See Etienne Balibar, "Spinoza the Anti-Orwell: The Fear of the Masses," in *Masses, Classes, Ideas: Studies on Politics Before and After Marx*, trans. by James Swenson (London: Routledge, 1994), 3–37; and Antonio Negri, "*Reliqua desiderantur*: A Conjecture for a Definition of the Concept of Democracy in the final Spinoza," in *Subversive Spinoza: (Un)contemporary Variations*, trans. by Timothy S. Murphy et al. (Manchester: Manchester University Press, 2004), 9–27.
22 John Locke, *An Essay Concerning Human Understanding*, ed. by Peter H. Nidditch (Oxford: Clarendon, 1975), II.27.26. See also Etienne Balibar, *Identity and Difference: John Locke and the Invention of Consciousness*, trans. by Warren Montag (London: Verso, 2013).
23 See Macherey, *Introduction à l'Éthique de Spinoza*.
24 Locke, *Essay*, II.27.26.
25 Quintus Curtius, *History of Alexander*, trans. by John C. Rolfe (Cambridge, MA: Harvard University Press, 1971), III, 13–15.
26 Pierre Gassendi, "De la phantasie," in *Abrégé de la philosophie de Gassendi*. Vol. 3, 7 vols. (Lyon: Anisson, 1684).
27 Gassendi, "De la phantasie," 268–69.
28 Descartes, Lettre Au Marquis De Newcastle, letter November 23, 1646.
29 See Lorenzo Vinciguerra, *La semiotica di Spinoza* (Pisa: Edizioni ETS, 2011).
30 See Pascal Sévérac, *Le devenir actif chez Spinoza* (Paris: Honoré Champion, 2005); and Yves Citton, "Noo-politique Spinoziste?" *Multitudes* 27 (Winter 2007), 203–16.
31 Sévérac, *Le devenir actif chez Spinoza*, 300.

Bibliography

Balibar, Etienne. *Identity and Difference: John Locke and the Invention of Consciousness*, trans. by Warren Montag. London: Verso, 2013.

Balibar, Etienne. "Spinoza the Anti-Orwell: The Fear of the Masses," in *Masses, Classes, Ideas: Studies on Politics Before and After Marx*, trans. by James Swenson. London: Routledge, 1994, 3–37.

Citton, Yves. "Noo-politique Spinoziste?" *Multitudes* 27 (Winter 2007), 203–16.

Del Lucchese, Filippo. *Conflict, Power and Multitude in Machiavelli and Spinoza*. London: Bloomsbury, 2011.

Descartes, Rene. "Descartes, Lettre Au Marquis De Newcastle," in *Oeuvres et lettres*. Paris: La Pléiade, 1937. http://www.ac-grenoble.fr/PhiloSophie/logphil/oeuvres/descarte/newcastl.htm (accessed December 29, 2014).

Descartes, Rene. *Les Passions De L'âme*, original 1649 edition. http://fr.wikisource.org/wiki/Les_Passions_de_l'âme/édition_de_1649 (accessed December 29, 2014).

Descartes, Rene. "Meditations," in *Descartes' Meditations Home Page*. Wright State University, http://www.wright.edu/~charles.taylor/descartes/ (accessed December 29, 2014).

Gassendi, Pierre. "De la phantasie," in *Abrégé de la philosophie de Gassendi*. Vol. 3, 7 vols. Lyon: Anisson, 1684.

Hobbes, Thomas. *Leviathan*. Pelican: Middlesex, 1968.

Israel, Jonathan. *Radical Enlightenment: Philosophy and the Making of Modernity 1650–1750*. Oxford: Oxford University Press, 2001.

Locke, John. *An Essay Concerning Human Understanding*, ed. by Peter H. Nidditch. Oxford: Clarendon, 1975.

Macherey, Pierre. *Introduction à l'Éthique de Spinoza. La troisième partie: la vie affective*. Paris: Presses Universitaires de France, 1995.

Morfino, Vittorio. *Il Tempo e l'occasione: l'incontro Spinoza Machiavelli*. Milano: LED Edizioni, 2002.

Negri, Antonio. "Reliqua Desiderantur: A Conjecture for a Definition of the Concept of Democracy in the Final Spinoza," in *Subversive Spinoza*. Manchester: Manchester University Press, 2004, 9–27.

Quintus Curtius. *History of Alexander*, trans. by John C. Rolfe. Cambridge, MA: Harvard University Press, 1971.

Seneca. *Epistulae Morales ad Lucilium*, ed. by L. D. Reynolds, 2 vols. Oxford: Oxford University Press, 1965.

Séverac, Pascal. *Le devenir actif chez Spinoza*. Paris: Honoré Champion, 2005.

Spinoza, Baruch. *Complete Works*, trans. by Samuel Shirley. Indianapolis, IN: Hackett, 2002.

Vinciguerra, Lorenzo. *La semiotica di Spinoza*. Pisa: Edizioni ETS, 2011.

8

Interrupting the System: Spinoza and Maroon Thought

James Edward Ford III

The Maroons know something about possibility.

Fred Moten and Stephano Harney, "The Undercommons"

Caliban or the Maroon?

In "Interruption of the System," Chapter 5 of *Savage Anomaly*, Antonio Negri interrogates imagination's centrality to liberatory and repressive political projects. He begins the chapter with a curious epigraph taken from Spinoza's letter to Peter Balling. Spinoza writes of an "unpleasant dream," saying the "images ... remained before my eyes just as vividly as though the things had been real, especially the image of a certain black and leprous Brazilian."[1] By speaking of "Spinoza and Caliban" in that chapter, Negri puts forward the hypothesis that Caliban is the figure in Spinoza's dream, in order to insist on the global reach of Spinoza's ideas, even crossing racial lines that were newly forming in Spinoza's day.[2]

I find it laudable that Negri says, "Caliban is our contemporary hero."[3] Only when Spinoza shifts from the "first" to the "second foundation," that is, from utopian mysticism to his vaunted constitutive materialism, does Negri reference Caliban. This is a welcome turn away from Lewis Feuer's hypothesis in 1957 that Spinoza dreamed of Henrique Dias, the "Negro leader" of the most accomplished and celebrated regiments in the Portugal's defeat of the Dutch.[4] Feuer suggests that the Jews who survived Diaz's defeat of the Dutch brought back many misrepresentations of him as a "Negro terrorist," instead of a freedom fighter, and that Spinoza could not shake these stereotypes. Even if racism partially fuels Spinoza's shock at dreaming of a black rebel, Negri affirms the image's relation to Spinoza's philosophy.

Nevertheless, in a work concerned with Spinoza abandoning philosophical idealisms for constitutive materialism, is Caliban appropriate for marking the specific instance of the transition, of the "crisis," carrying "the possibility of a philosophy of the future" of Spinozan thought and its legacy? To this question, I would have to answer: No. While Caliban epitomizes and resists the Cartesian instrumentalization of the body during European colonial expansion, Caliban is not the most compelling figure for the transition into the materialism Negri espouses in Spinoza.

I support Negri's motivation for turning to Caliban but assert that he chose a less effective figure for his hypothesis. A more effective figure for hypothesizing about Spinoza's dream, his materialist shift and the global reach of the multitude, would be the Maroon—an African who has joined a community of other Africans escaping enslavement in the New World. Maroon communities developed everywhere Africans were sold into slavery in the Americas. Maroon derives from the Spanish *címarron* or "runaway cow." Despite this derogatory misnaming, *marronage* identifies an ongoing praxis in which what the collective builds matters more than the enslavement they are escaping. Shifting away from Feuer's hypothesis on the return of repressed stereotypes, and yet again from Negri's celebration of a fictive figure who is merely insubordinate but not revolutionary, I turn to the Maroon, whose legacy in the history of thought, art, and actual history offers a much stronger complement to Negri's reading of Spinoza.

Typically, the Maroon receives attention in Critical Race studies—as well as Black Studies, Latin American Studies and Hemispheric Studies. Negri's reference to Caliban amounts to an invitation for Spinoza scholars to think of Spinoza at the intersection of philosophy, politics, race and global capitalism, though his invitation has rarely been taken up three decades since the publication of *Savage Anomaly*. In arguing that the Maroon complements Negri's and Spinoza's work more than Caliban, I stage an encounter between Spinoza scholarship, leftist historiography and critical race studies. I charge this essay's circuitous route to the need to situate Spinoza's writings, Negri's *Savage Anomaly*, and Shakespeare's *The Tempest* in the economic and theological-political context of the Dutch Golden Age; and to compare Caliban and the Maroon, whose intellectual legacies articulate distinct responses to colonialism's expropriative measures. Despite the countless recuperations of Caliban, due to his centrality to Shakespearean performance culture, Caliban symbolizes individual acts of the subordinated that remain mired in what Frantz Fanon calls *ressentiment* or what Spinoza called "melancholy." The Maroon actively attempts to overcome the *ressentiment* induced through enslavement in ways that converge with Spinoza's philosophy.

Turning to the Maroon takes seriously Negri's claim that "idealism is contrary to the utopia, *which is humanistic and revolutionary and which wants to be confronted with real things.*" Considering the geopolitical and cultural tensions invoked by Spinoza's dream, it is interesting to read *Bodies, Masses, Power*, where Warren Montag mentions the close ties the elders in the Jewish community who excommunicated Spinoza had with Dutch Pernambuco until the colony's collapse in 1654 due to "Portuguese reconquest, slave revolts and persistent low-intensity war with the rather large Maroon communities." Montag adds that "what haunts Spinoza [in his dream], and the conflicts internal to his work attest to this, is precisely his kinship with this outcast [the Brazilian Maroon], the fact that they are 'objective allies' in a common struggle."[5]

I join Montag and others like Michael Rosenthal who use the language of "haunting" to provoke a more direct engagement with how race informs Spinoza's philosophy.[6] I also join scholars like Jimmy Casas Klausen who, in *Fugitive Rousseau: Slavery, Primitivism, and Political Freedom*, reads Western philosophy through the lens of critical race studies. Klausen "situates Rousseau's political theory in the frame of a black Atlantic world that would have been broadly recognizable to him and refracts his arguments through the long tradition of the concepts of slavery and freedom—particularly *marronage*."[7] Klaussen admits "confusions and blind spots" in Rousseau's philosophy. But he argues that Rousseau "is reaching for a language that comes to terms with the centrality of domination in constituting the institutions of political modernity" and the "counter discourse of unfreedom" undergirding the West's global redefining of the human.[8] I read Spinoza in a similar way, seeing there is no way the philosopher who radicalized the philosophical concept of "the multitude" could have been inattentive to living in a Dutch Golden age depending upon chattel slavery's unparalleled profitability. While Caliban helps one think through the "counter discourse of unfreedom" developed in Spinoza's philosophy, the Maroon, as a figure of thought and historical agent, comes closer to achieving what Negri calls "a systematic dissolution of the world, to guide it to the truth of ethical action, as an affirmation of life against death, of love against hate, of joy against sadness, of sociability against degradation and solitude."[9]

Race and the theological-political

In *Savage Anomaly*, Negri says Spinoza lived during the "Dutch Anomaly," when the Netherlands "reached its cultural peak" startlingly "soon after its creation." Negri rightly mentions the Dutch bourgeoisie's rise despite the capitalist "crisis" impacting much of seventeenth-century Europe, and notes that, culturally, "Holland" still carries "the freshness of the great humanism and the great Renaissance" with "the love of freedom."[10] Negri sketches how the Dutch's cultural development outside absolutist monarchy was facilitated through "the capitalist order of profit and the savage adventure of accumulation on the seas."[11] More should be said about the Dutch Empire's "constructive" and "savage" "appropriative" dimensions to clarify the material and intellectual connections between Spinoza and the Afro-Brazilian population giving rise to his dreams.

Stealing most of their colonies from the Spanish and the Portuguese, the Dutch had possessions in Southeast Asia, which included part of the current Philippines, Malaysia and Indonesia with Jakarta as its capital. In Africa, Dutch control of Benin, Togo and Nigeria secured the trading of enslaved Africans to their plantations in the Americas. In the Americas, the Dutch claimed Saint Maarten, Curacao, Aruba, Bonaire in the Caribbean and, of course, Brazil. This does not suggest complete or consistent success in the Netherland's competition with other colonizers. But when Piet Heyn takes the Spanish silver fleet in 1628 and brings it back to the Dutch Republic, allowing for 50 percent dividends to investors, one can understand why the Dutch partly avoided the seventeenth-century economic woes of other European countries.[12]

These "adventures" should not distract from how minority cultures struggled in the Dutch imperial economy. This is where Spinoza's homelessness comes about, seeing that his philosophy diverged with European colonial endeavors and his Jewish community's place in that continental project. Policies across Europe restricting Jews and New Christians to mercantilist occupations inadvertently gave them an important position in the Dutch attempts to capitalize on the slave trade and colonies in the New World. The Jewish and New Christian communities hoped to achieve new political stability by marshaling their mercantilist abilities for Dutch global ambitions. One historian writes: "in the early seventeenth century, Brazil's merchants and sugar cultivators imported up to 4,000 slaves annually. New Christians provided the bulk of these slaves."[13] In 1630s Brazil, "New Christians were developing, owning, and operating 59 [sugar] mills. A further nine mills belonged to Sephardic owners in Brazil around 1645."[14] New Christians often received and sold the licenses authorizing slave trading; they often kept some licenses for family and community members to ensure economic stability. Little evidence suggests Sephardic Jews directly invested in or ran the trade, whether due to abstaining for religious reasons or being legally barred. Still, available materials suggest the strong economic interests seventeenth-century Dutch Jewry had in the slave trade and the New World.

Spinoza's immediate and extended family were merchants working between the Netherlands and Brazil, though Spinoza himself would see no profit from this endeavor, having inherited a failing business from his father.

Yet one would be remiss to frame these tensions strictly through economic interests. The "Dutch anomaly" developed a *racialized* theological-political culture that legitimated its imperial ascent. That culture created unviable conditions, though in different ways, for the *multitudo* that Negri makes central to understanding Spinoza's sociopolitical context. The multitude speaks "to the sense of the multiplicity of subjects and to the constructive power that emanates from their dignity, understood as totality."[15] I concur but place greater stress on thousands in the multitude deemed below dignity in the Dutch cultural hierarchy. This included kidnapped Africans and others, like the Dutch Jewish community, who straddled a moving borderline allowing them dignity in some but not all cases. These are the mildewed, poisoned edges of the Dutch Golden Age's cultural efflorescence.

Reading the multitude with an eye to racial difference and chattel slavery's significance draws out different connotations in *Savage Anomaly* and Spinoza's writings. Consider when Negri claims that Spinoza's *Short Treatise* calls for "a positive utopia," "proposed with exceptional power but tenuously balanced between mystical annihilation and ontological objectivism, in terms that allow for no escape from the indistinct and the indeterminate."[16] In this passage, Negri argues that Spinoza goes beyond the utopianism of his day. In the same way, effectively reading *Savage Anomaly* in relation to race means going beyond Negri. In the context of Dutch imperialism, I propose reading the above passage from Negri in relation to the Jewish and African populations in the New World. Some Jewish leaders envisioned New World colonies as a refuge from persecution on European soil. The Dutch Jewish community formed through immigration from several European countries devastated by anti-Semitic violence and segregation. The community hoped for greater protections elsewhere, in case discrimination in the Netherlands increased.

Yet, this utopianism among Jews in Brazil allowed no "escape" from their "indistinct," "indeterminate" role in the Dutch imperial project. When Negri mentions the speed of the Netherland's rise to nationhood and imperial power, evidenced through its quick jump from "originary accumulation" to a "monetary market" economic structure, he then recalls Holland's "stakes for burning the witches at the beginning of the seventeenth century."[17] To Negri, this historical event attenuates the progressivism many associate with the "Dutch miracle." Silvia Federici suggests otherwise. Although the witch trials may compromise the Dutch's claim to embody Renaissance ideals of freedom, such trials are considered a boon to capitalist development in Europe and the Americas.[18] Negri understates how the trials negate an old standard of freedom and provide a new basis for capitalist accumulation, worker discipline and for taking the lion's share of surplus value from exploited workers. Federici discusses how rhetoric, laws and persecutory measures that applied to New Christians in the Inquisition soon metamorphosed into the witch trials. As W. E. B. Du Bois has argued, starting in 1442, when the first thirty Africans are sold into slavery in Lisbon, the persecutory measures that Federici identifies are transformed yet again.[19] Through the concept of racial difference, European violence targeting European Jews, women and proto-proletarians can now apply to populations across the globe, especially indigenous and African peoples. In the long term, Europe, under the sign of whiteness, will find new levels of racial, economic and religious unification through exporting its epistemological, political and cultural violence to every corner of the globe.[20] From the twelfth to seventeenth century, the Jew or the New Christian remained the stranger within Europe, within whiteness. The New World came to carry such promise for this community that the prominent rabbi Isaac Aboab, the same who taught and, later on, helped excommunicate Spinoza, joined the Jewish community in Brazil after the Dutch's conquest of Portugal's colonies in the Americas.

By turning to this "utopianism," one can assess tensions internal to the multitude that cannot be effectively framed through Caliban's conflict with Ariel. Isaac Aboab and others turn to colonial Brazil for a way out of persecution, yet the communal effort is nestled within and cannot stand separate from Dutch imperial objectives. Put in Negri's terms, Aboab and his community's utopianism prove incommensurate with the "absolute sociability" found throughout Spinoza's writings. The search for a space outside religious persecution would run up against the antiracist revolt of the Africans imported to work sugar plantations. Maroon societies developed as Africans escaped from plantations to form their own short- and long-term collectives revising societal structures and practices from their African homelands. In 1652, the Dutch lost their Brazilian colonies to the Portuguese. Notably, the Portuguese retook their colonies by offering freedom to the Africans who joined them in overthrowing the Dutch. The Dutch could not withstand Portugal's avarice for its former possessions *and* fight-off Africans intent on obtaining their own freedom and freeing other Africans from Dutch enslavement. As one historian puts it, "The end of Dutch colonial rule was a devastating blow to Amsterdam's Jews. ... The Talmud Torah congregation had also placed great hopes in the growing Jewish community in Pernambuco."[21]

Although Aboab and his community's utopian vision depended upon the Dutch political project, the Maroon communities did not have the same dependence on the Portuguese. The Maroons exhibited a different capacity for what Negri calls "counter-Power" based on "resistance" and, most importantly, on "self-organization" that cannot be subsumed in imperialism's terms.[22] The Dutch responded to a force that had been well underway since the 1500s, namely, the Maroon communities or *quilombos* that took shape in colonial Brazil. Several were short-lived, lasting a few months. Several others lasted a few years. Palmares, however, lasted nearly the entire seventeenth century, ca. 1604–1695. Even after the Portuguese reclaimed colonial Brazil and tried to conquer the Maroon societies as well, Palmares "withstood, on the average, one Portuguese expedition every fifteen months" from 1672 to 1694.[23] Contemporary chroniclers noted the Maroons' many "attacks and raids" on colonial plantations. Palmares illustrated an actional response "to a slave-holding society entirely out of step with forms of bondage familiar to Africa. As such, [Palmares] had to cut across ethnic lines and draw upon all those who managed to excape [sic] from various plantations."[24] Palmares proved not to be the replication of African kinship ties but a revision of African political, ethical and cultural structures specific to New World circumstances.

Two years after the Maroons aided in crushing the Dutch colony in Brazil, Isaac Aboab will return to Amsterdam and play a central role, with other leaders in Talmud Torah, in excommunicating Spinoza. If the truth of these groups is in their effects, then Spinoza's excommunication reveals much about his (former) religious community. It reproduces the very solitude it hopes to avoid in Dutch politics. The document announcing Spinoza's ousting only speaks of his "evil opinions and acts."[25] No one knows exactly what these acts are. Steven Nadler has proposed that though Spinoza published the *Theological-Political Treatise* in 1670, Spinoza began sharing nascent versions of his ideas about religion, politics and philosophy in his early twenties. His excommunication was likely a consequence of sharing ideas that questioned the religious principles and, therefore, the political authority of the leaders of Talmud Torah, of the Dutch Calvinists, and even of Dutch Catholics. After seeing the collapse of their hopes of living outside persecution in Europe, the leaders of Talmud Torah would not tolerate claims that might bring further persecution onto the Jewish community.

However, these attempts to minimize persecution are further evidence of having yet to find an effective route of escaping the "indistinct and the indeterminate." These attempts are mere wishes upon a star against a consistent pattern of violence. Moving abroad or finding relevance in the burgeoning colonial economy does not undo the categorical exclusions troubling Dutch Jewry; slavery simply expands the mechanism of exclusion to millions more. But Spinoza's Jewish community never escapes being targeted. Worst of all, Spinoza's excommunication reads like the very exclusions that his community has escaped elsewhere. They have learned to apply the tactics of exclusion that they still fear (with curses that, today, read as if they are relegating Spinoza to the social death commonly projected onto black life):

> Cursed be he [Spinoza] by day and cursed be he by night; cursed be he when he lies down and cursed be he when he rises up. Cursed be he when he goes out and cursed be he when he comes in. The Lord will not spare him, but the anger of the Lord and his jealousy shall smoke against that man, and ... the Lord shall blot out his name from under heaven. And the Lord shall separate him unto evil out of all the tribes of Israel. ... [N]o one should communicate with him, not even in writing, nor accord him any favor nor stay with him under the same roof nor [come] within four cubits in his vicinity; nor shall he read any treatise composed or written by him.[26]

With Spinoza's excommunication, the harshest excommunication out of the forty issued in the seventeenth century by Talmud Torah, this community has imitated the affects of its persecutors. The tension between Spinoza and Talmud Torah reveals something more. Warren Montag suggests that Talmud Torah found in Spinoza's philosophy a rebellious nature similar to the New World Africans opposing slavery. Perhaps Negri suggests something similar in titling his book *Savage Anomaly*. The multitude oscillates between acquiescence, resistance and radical self-organization. Precisely because of the vicissitudes of the multitude, Spinoza's excommunication suggests even more: Spinoza's philosophy suggested a radicalism could emerge from within that Jewish community and revealed the risks they would take in betting their communal future on their contingent economic position and frequent vulnerability to persecution. Spinoza and the Maroons robbed that community of the excuse that complicity in colonialism was unavoidable or even life-affirming.

The question, for the rest of this essay, is whether Caliban or the Maroon better complements Spinoza's rebellious philosophical practice. Ignoring the material effects of different collectives within the multitude in order to assume a general sense of resistance would yield yet another idealism contrary to Spinoza's thought. As I will demonstrate, Caliban's solitude has limits that Negri, Spinoza and the Maroon are interested in overcoming.

Caliban's "Solitude"

In *Savage Anomaly*, Negri says Caliban is a hero symbolizing humanity's secular world-making capacity—"the truth of the world and the positivity, the productivity, the sociability of human action."[27] The "world-making capacity," elsewhere called "the real process of liberation," follows an "ontological operation" in which "human power annuls servitude." Without taking up this "operation," Caliban cannot access said capacity. Put differently, a brief genealogy of writerly recuperations of Caliban, all concerned with racial difference, will confirm that Negri's Spinozist "positivity," "productivity," and "sociability" barely show up in *The Tempest*. Alden T. Vaughan demonstrates that as early as 1938 Anibal Ponce's *Humanismo burgues y humanismo proletario* "favorably identified Caliban with the exploited masses."[28] But 1950 marks the seismic shift of the interpretative terrain with Octave Mannoni's *La psychologies de la colonization*, translated in English as *Prospero and Caliban: The Psychology of Colonization* (1956). "Mannoni forcefully and explicitly identified Caliban with colonized and exploited people in general," Vaughn says.[29] Many have recalled Fanon exprobating Mannoni for leaving no way out for the colonized in his psychological framework. Fewer have noted Fanon's decision *not* to recuperate Caliban during the quarrel. Considering the many anticolonial writers who recuperate the character from the mid-twentieth century onward, including works such as George Lamming's *The Pleasures of Exile* (1960), Aime Cesaire's *A Tempest* (1969), Edward Kamau Brathwaite's play, *Islands* (1969), poetic works like *The Arrivants* (1973) and Jamaica Kincaid's *Annie John* (1985), Fanon's decision not to join the recuperative effort deserves greater attention.

It is arguable that Caliban remains mired in the Manichaean racial battles Fanon wants the black to abandon, which suggests Caliban does not symbolize the "positivity" of human action. Supporting this argument requires reference to several scholarly works. Recall Fanon saying: "Man's behavior is not only reactional. And there is always *ressentiment* in a *reaction*."[30] "Ressentiment psychology" cannot "integrate experiences of powerlessness" and "poison the ability of the self to function in the present or project an active future."[31] I suggest that Fanon's critique of *ressentiment* is anticipated by Spinoza's critique of bondage, which would include any political subjects and chattel slaves who acquiesce to oppressive conditions. As Spinoza says in *Ethics*, "a free man thinks of death least of all things, and his wisdom is a meditation of life, not of death" (*E* IV, P67).[32] The one who acquiesces acts "like a slave," only "does good from fear of suffering injury" and "is simply driven to avoid what is bad" while "liv[ing] at the command of another" (*TTP* 65).³³ Spinoza inadvertently describes Caliban. Despite how much one appreciates his recalcitrance, Caliban's insubordination works strictly within the confines Prospero has set. Even Caliban's desire for revenge depends upon offering himself as slave to another potential master, as when he beseeches Stefano:

> As I told thee before, I am subject to a tyrant … that by his cunning hath cheated me of the island³⁴

And a bit later:

> by sorcery he [Prospero] got this isle
> From me he got it. If thy greatness will
> Revenge it on him…
> Thou shalt be lord of it and I'll serve thee.³⁵

And when Caliban advises Stephano on the plan of attack:

> … 'tis a custom with him,
> I' th'afternoon to sleep: there though mayst brain him …
> Remember, first to possess his book; for without them
> He's *but a sot, as I am, nor hath not*
> *One spirit to command*³⁶

Caliban's entreaty reveals that he will forego freedom for revenge because, as Spinoza says, revenge is the slave's *modus operandi*. Seeing Spinoza as an intellectual ancestor of Fanon sheds further light on the range of enslavements occurring under colonial regimes, without losing sight of the chattel slave's specific positioning in the process. For now, I continue showing how Caliban holds fast to the reactional psychology Spinoza opposes.

Caliban exhibits a reactional psychology in part through his *type of* productivity. Caliban's productivity must burst the seams of the mechanistic view prevailing over seventeenth-century Europe to serve Negri's purposes. Negri rightly identifies how human *cupiditas* infuses and erupts the barriers of mechanistic philosophy in the "Spinozan machine." Through references to Descartes, Malebranche, Francis Bacon and others, Federici says, "In being divorced from its body, the rational self certainly lost its solidarity with its corporeal reality and with nature." "In the Cartesian model of the person," says Federici, "there is no egalitarian dualism between the thinking head and the body-machine, only a master/slave relation, since the primary task of the will is to dominate the body and the natural world."³⁷ Prospero becomes "seemingly the center of all powers," the "master" performing "bourgeois subjectivity as self-management" and "self-ownership."³⁸ Meanwhile, Caliban epitomizes the overly impassioned slave body. Labor remedies Caliban's passions and fulfills the master's needs. Negri writes that "in Spinoza productive force is subjected to nothing but itself, and, in particular, domination is taken away from the relations of production."³⁹ Caliban's productivity can only be spoken of through the mouth of Prospero—"But, as 'tis/We cannot miss him: he does make our fire/Fetch in our wood and serves in offices/That profit us"—indicating the domination prevailing over the relations of production.⁴⁰ This offers a more nuanced understanding of Federici's reference to Audre Lorde in critiquing unproductive appropriations of *The Tempest* in Latin America: "For Caliban could only fight his master by cursing him in the language he learned from him, thus being dependent in his rebellion on his 'master's tools.'"⁴¹ Caliban's productivity bespeaks his resignation to a limited set of tools and capacities.

But does Caliban's insubordination push him beyond isolation and into the "sociability" Negri proposes? Julia Lupton examines Caliban's "creaturely" status. There, one can find an answer. Negri and Lupton would agree that Shakespeare places Caliban "within the cosmos of Adam, but as its chaotic exception."⁴² One might anticipate Lupton's research dovetailing with Negri's conclusion that "Caliban, alias Adam, poses the problem of reality no longer as totality but as dynamic partiality, not as absolute perfection but as relative privation, not as a utopia but as a project."⁴³ This is not the case. Lupton writes: "As an Adamic figure, the creature resides in a concertedly prenational, universal scene; by definition, the creature belongs to Creation, not to nation. ... At the same time, the creature is not equal to Adam. ... The creature Caliban shares Adam's sexual passion, but remains, like Leviathan, *perennially alone*."⁴⁴ In Lupton's assessment, Caliban is the perversely non-dynamic, *unproductive* version of Adam. Though Lupton's route through the "creaturely" differs from my interrogation of colonialism and capitalist expansion, I agree with her observation about Caliban's unproductive nature—unproductive precisely because it does not actively reach for a new sociability.

The constant turn to Caliban repeats a pattern that Abena Busia, Sylvia Wynter and other black feminist thinkers have observed. For these writers, Caliban's antipathy toward Prospero distracts from the most radical force in the play, Sycorax, the character who most complements the "sociability" Negri has in mind. Federici also takes this position, when she says Sycorax represents a respect for the commons and for "communal ties that, over centuries of suffering, continued to nourish the liberation struggle to this day."⁴⁵ Most importantly for my critique of Negri's turn to Caliban, Federici notes how these communal struggles "haunt" "Caliban's imagination" by turning to the following passage from *The Tempest*:

> Be not afeard, the isle is full of noises
> Sounds, and sweet airs, that give delight and hurt not.
> Sometimes a thousand twangling instruments
> Will hum about mine ears; and sometimes voices,
> That if then had wak'd after long sleep.
> Will make me sleep again and then dreaming,
> The clouds methought would open, and show riches
> Ready to drop upon me, that when wak'd
> I cried to dream again.[46]

Caliban epitomizes the solitude too weak to singlehandedly stop living at another's command, as Spinoza puts it. He dreams of, but does not pursue, a shared life in the common. A reactive consciousness stalls out his efforts to interrupt the system. I find league with Federici because the constant need to recuperate Caliban does not upend this solitude though it does indicate the generosity of the black intellectual tradition.[47]

On Maroon thought

Meanwhile, "maroon thought work[s] outside of the limits of the doxa and grappl[es] with the unthinkables of the system."[48] Caliban only transmutes Prospero's language to curses but marronage "develop[s] both communities of freedom and a language of freedom in the midst of racial slavery."[49] Maroon thought is nothing else but a concern with the ideas and life practices of transforming *ressentiment* into a being-in-common or, put differently, a "being together in homelessness," so mourning turns into being actional.[50] The Maroon surpasses Caliban in the black intellectual tradition and better complements Spinoza's critique of slavery and search for a constitutive materialism. Such an effort only materializes through marshaling the imagination and suggests that Spinoza's ontology, "as an affirmation of life against death, of love against hate, of joy against sadness, of sociability against degradation and solitude," amounts to claiming the Maroon over Caliban but, more boldly, to realizing that Spinoza's ontology partially comes into its own through the end of actual chattel slavery, in his day and ours.[51] As Christopher Winks says, "as both a willed escape from the intolerable conditions of the Plantation-Machine and a flight toward an indefinable, unchartered (and often mobile) space of sanctuary, and perilous freedom, marronage expressed as desire, is a common possession not only of enslaved peoples but of their latter-day descendants."[52] In that unchartered space, the Maroons seek to "experience themselves otherwise" in an "experimental process" "yearning to generate a counterpower, a new arrangement of corporeal forces, and alternate sources of pleasure and agency," to borrow from the thought of Hasana Sharp.[53]

I examine the Maroon as I did Caliban, in terms of Negri's interest in positivity, productivity and sociability. I will draw on historical aspects of Maroon communities and the Maroon's legacy in black diasporic literature. Just as European Marxists have consistently turned to Spinoza to think through crises in radical politics, so black diasporic thinkers have turned to the Maroon to do the same. This is true of Esteban Montejo's *Biografía de un Cimarrón*, a *testimonio* asserting the significance of Cuban Maroon communities to the Cuban War of Independence. In his poem "Le Verbe Marroner," Aime Cesaire uses the metaphor of the Maroon to assert black radicalism's autonomy against the dictates of the French Communist Party. I am most interested in Gayl Jones' remarkable and understudied long-poem, *Song for Anninho*, published exactly the same year as *Savage Anomaly*, and equally concerned with imagination's role in liberatory praxis. Originally, Jones' long poem belonged to a novel-length project tentatively titled "Palmares." Jones stages *Song for Anninho* after Palmares falls in 1695 to the Portuguese. Almeyda survives, though her breasts have been cut off—colonizers commonly mutilated black women in this way for escaping slavery. Zibrata the "wizard woman" finds Almeyda amid the destruction and nurses her back to health.[54] When Almeyda asks if her lover Anninho survives, Zibrata says no and adds, "I cannot find him for you/It is you who must make the discovery."[55] Just as Negri applauds Spinoza for promoting love over hate, so I appreciate Jones' novel for using Anninho to raise a similar question: "*That was the question, Almeyda/How we could sustain our love/At a time of cruelty …/It's hard to keep tenderness when things all around you are hard.*"[56] *Song for Anninho* begins with Almeyda's desire to find Anninho, which becomes synonymous with finding the New Palmares. Almeyda reflects on the previous Palmares and critiques the instances of *ressentiment* that might undermine the New Palmares taking shape. The poem examines reactional attitudes within Palmares that must be transformed into something actional in the New Palmares.

The enslaved are not just caught in an "indistinct and indeterminate" role in colonial regimes. Surely, they are "subject to fortune" like others Spinoza would call caught in "bondage." Unlike Spinoza's Dutch community, however, enslaved

Africans must escape a social indeterminacy based on their frighteningly distinct economic role: their absolute centrality to economic accumulation through being worked to death makes their humanity evermore irrelevant and unrecognizable to European cultures. The Maroon, may be one of the most radical enactments of a principle Spinoza discusses in the *Ethics*: "Whatsoever disposes the human body, so as to render it capable of being affected in an increased number of ways ... is useful to man. ... [C]ontrariwise, whatsoever renders the body less capable in this respect is hurtful to man" (*E* IV, P38). In seeking that which is conducive to "man's social life" against slavery, the seventeenth century's most thoroughgoing incapacitating force (and most antithetical force to the Spinozist project), the Maroon takes seriously the "positivity" Negri finds in Spinoza's conception of human action.

The Maroon fosters this positivity in debilitating conditions through a concept of power quite similar to Spinoza's. Negri notes that Spinoza circumvents the "constitution-mediation" structure providing the "basis of the concept of the bourgeoisie itself."[57] "Mediation" in *Savage Anomaly*, consistently refers to "a function of command" that comprises "the master line of the bourgeois utopia of the market,"[58] as opposed to other forms of mediation, which Negri prefers to call "tension."[59] Such "mediation" appears in the attacks on women, the proletariat and racial others in Europe and, across the Atlantic, on the plantations bringing the Netherlands glory and unsurpassed fortunes. Productivity, in this setup, would mean acting as an automaton following commands. But the productivity the Maroon has in mind makes "virtue" synonymous with "power," as Spinoza does in Definition 8 of Part IV in the *Ethics*. By making "virtue" "nothing else but action in according with the laws of one's own nature" in the *Ethics*, Spinoza converges with the strivings of black culture. From another vantage, one could say that blackness signals collective human perseverance in environments set against one's very existence. Just as Spinoza returns to Tacitus' skepticism to "regard law and right as permanently subordinate to the relations of force" so the Maroon remains skeptical of transferring power to the colonial forces with the most to gain from slavery.[60]

If virtue and power are "coextensive," then the sole individual can have little power or right before colonial conquest's frequent, indiscriminate attacks (which are, subsequently, transmogrified into justifiable efforts of saving the soul of the victim).[61] No Maroon community could sustain itself without this principle. Wherever slavery found a foothold in the Americas one finds fear of slave revolts and Maroon communities. In this way, Maroon thought converges with Spinoza's claim that "people have never given up their right and transferred their power to another" so completely that the government is not "at greater risk from its own citizens ... than from its enemies" (*TTP* 208). The Maroon nuances that thought by fostering positivity from a more aggressive negativity. The multitude includes those who are structurally within the polis but barred from citizenship or even barred from humanity. Living "instruments" escaping, raiding, or even razing their captors' fields all contest the ontology implied by colonialism and Atlantic slavery. This activity, rather than Caliban's curses, enacts the "ontological operation" "annul[ling] servitude" that Negri had in mind.

Spinoza, with his varied terminology for collectivities, and the Maroon, with its multiple social arrangements, both contest liberal philosophy's privileging of the individual.[62] The liberal individual already personifies the gap between virtue/right as power and as legal formality. The slave marks the extreme limit of this gap, in which legality withholds all rights from its subject. The Maroon in the historical Palmares, addressed this gap. One scholar says the Palmaristas "main business" is "to rob" the colonists "of their slaves, who themselves remain in slavery among them, *until they have redeemed themselves by stealing another; but such slaves that run over to them, are as free as the rest.*"[63] In other words, one's place in Palmares depended upon actively stealing oneself and others away from the racial capitalism that had brought them to the New World. Their freedom required action on behalf of themselves and others. I find an analog between Palmares and Spinoza's examination of the Hebrews' first covenant in the *Theological-Political Treatise*. Seeing that humanity's power can only come through God (and therefore nature) alone, the Hebrews' transferring of right to God interdicts any single leader claiming absolute power over the masses. Spinoza sees glimpses of a shared commitment to right expressed through shared power: "The Hebrews did not transfer their right to another person but rather all gave up their right, equally, as in a democracy, crying with one voice: 'We will do whatever God shall say' (making no mention of an intermediary). It follows that they all remained perfectly equal as a result of this agreement" (*TTP* 214). Similarly, the Palmaristas make stealing away a mutual obligation and, therefore, found a distinct sociability in their Maroon community. Freedom, under such conditions, is immanent to its expression rather than an ascribable (or removable) property.

Calling *quilombos* like Palmares spaces of black freedom dodges identity politics. Their scattering from Africa and other places in the New World before reaching Brazil diminishes the need to ally strictly with others of the same ethnicity. Spinoza finds a similar ethos in the scattering of the Hebrews "after they had lost their state and been taken captive to Babylon. Jeremiah taught them that they should strive for the wellbeing of the country into which they had been brought captive. Later, when Christ saw that they were going to be scattered throughout the whole world, he taught them to cultivate piety towards all men without distinction" (*TTP* 243). In the case of Palmares, scholars have stated that the settlement "had to cut across ethnic lines and draw upon all those who managed to escape from various plantations and at different times."[64] Palmares necessarily formed from a cultural "amalgam." The same can be said of virtually all Maroon communities. Maroon communities also cut across class lines. In such communities, "the ideological basis of social banditry varied from its classic form of archaic peasant protest. Nevertheless, the reactions of Brazilian slaves and Brazilian peasants against an oppressive social and economic order were strikingly similar."[65] Spinoza and the Maroon each see the multitude in a diasporic field of belonging that makes subjectivity non-coincident with national, tribal or ethnic identity.

Song for Anninho attends to the complex gender politics haunting Spinoza's multitude. The poem also emphasizes gender's complex relation to race and class. By choosing a female protagonist for *Song for Anninho*, Jones asks her readers to consider the women who constantly take primary roles in actual marronage and the surrounding lore in the seventeenth and eighteenth centuries. Omise'eke Natasha Tinley makes reference to Maroon revolt in several chapters of *Thiefing Sugar*. In Suriname, the women and genderqueer among the Maroons earned the label "Amazonian" for fighting to dismantle slavery as well as for erotic bonds resisting the plantation's reproductive demands.[66] Tinsley writes that the "colonists' punishments for warrior Amazonianess—*for marronage, the destruction of plantations*—are copious and deeply disturbing, including frequent hanging, quartering, and burning alive," and, I would add, illustrate how Europe translated its gendered violence across the world through racialization.[67] In another chapter, she mentions that "Tacky and Cubah's Revolt in Jamaica initiated rebellions that swept through Bermuda, Dominica, Nevis, British Honduras, Grenada, Montserrat, St. Vincent, and St Kitts."[68] Tinsley writes: "Women like Cubah and Nanny headed rebellions in Jamaica while Cécile Fatiman and Ma Cato provided spiritual leadership to rebels in Haiti and Suriname."[69] Accounts of men raiding plantations for food and women have proven to be overstated in order to besmirch marronage. Women and other gendered figures willingly joined these communities to craft a free life and attack colonialism. Thus, the Maroon figure already has a history of enacting a more expansive gender politics across several centuries, in comparison to Caliban who, as I have stated, remains a putatively masculinist figure that has done little to cultivate listening to the rebel female voice.

Song for Anninho suggests that marronage presses one to take up such listening. Despite seeing the destruction of the most powerful Maroon community of Brazil's present and past, Almeyda does not seek refuge in a fantasy of complete belonging. Throughout the text, language becomes the literal and symbolic means of forswearing a once-perfect origin. At one point, a voice in the poem says, *"Think about language. We will/make words out of words./We will use the same words,/but they will be different."*[70] This imperative tone shows up in italics multiple times. That voice associates language with new creations rather than the signs of things lost but still needed. The poem juxtaposes this generative statement with Almeyda's grandmother's lament: "We lost our language here [in Brazil]," that is, when her grandmother was taken into slavery.[71] Spinoza's exposition of the theory of affects attends to this difficulty as well: "He who imagines that what he loves is affected with pleasure or pain will likewise be affected with pleasure or pain, the intensity of which will vary with the intensity in the object loved" (*E* III, P21). Almeyda challenges the reader to recognize loss without reading it as a final verdict, since her grandmother "was speaking Arabic when she/came here, so she had already/lost her original [language] generations before"[72]—that is, the grandmother could not recognize she already demonstrated an ability to face loss without "poison[ing] the ability of the self to function in the present or project an active future."[73]

Almeyda also recalls Anninho's anxieties over Palmares' vulnerability to the colonial powers. Anninho says "freedom lives in the perpetual threat of destruction. I am free in this world and/Outside, but the others [in Palmares] have freedom always/in Arms."[74] Anninho was born free but joined Palmares to sustain that Maroon community and overthrow slavery. He says: "Those who discover a land, Almeyda, the way/these men know how to discover land, feed other/men to the land. ... But the land knows nothing. ... It takes/whatever it's given."[75] Perhaps a similar anxiety troubles Negri's attributing a particular type of "discovery" to Spinoza's *Theological-Political Treatise*, which "opens a *new world*, which cannot be traversed or even appreciated and valued with the *old instruments*."[76] Negri even contends that Spinoza's "method" "reveals the ontologically pregnant collective force of this *human conquest*, *a conquest that renews being*."[77] Anninho and Negri express their anxiety over colonial power in gendered language. Anninho imagines the land as a woman passively awaiting seduction/violation by colonizing powers (an image Federici critiques in *Caliban and Witch*); Negri associates Spinoza's conceptualization of nature with a pregnancy linked to conquest that implies renewal—another familiar trope in colonial discourse.

Anninho suggests that if Palmares falls, he will be free and other Palmaristas will return to slavery. Anninho really worries because their vulnerability reveals his own, despite whatever rights on paper he might have as a free person in colonial Brazil. Only Anninho's belonging to an assertive collective may ensure that his rights are more than mere words on a page. Ironically, Jones' poem begins with an epigraph of Domingos Jorge Velho, "field master" in the "campaign" that finally destroyed Palmares, which warns Portugal's king not to "think that this war is ended." Without hunting down every "survivor," and building a wall larger than the "Great Wall of China," "another stronghold will suddenly appear" in "Barriga or in any other equally suitable place."[78] Anninho's fears blind him to the fears his greatest enemies have of being overtaken, reiterating Spinoza's claim that fear is a debilitating affect.

Almeyda responds to Anninho with her own sense of "discovery": "Let them take over the old Palmares and we'll have our new one." Almeyda returns to language and the body as literal and metaphorical instances of renewing being without the need for conquest. The appropriate reaction to colonial "discovery," Jones seems to suggest, is a form of "discovery" through *losing* the "globes." Almeyda's mutilation indicates colonialism's brutality and, once again, suggests past loss does not proscribe new attachments. Almeyda faces this through recollecting her grandmother's marriage to "A Dutch mapmaker" only to claim Brazil as her own "part of the world/The landscape and tenderness, the wars too and despair,/the possibilities of some whole living./A new perception."[79] Almeyda's grandmother enacts "new perceptions" beyond the colonial mapping of territory. This claim works outside the logic of private property underwriting colonial accumulation. Almeyda, therefore, admits to their ongoing vulnerability to reconquest, but also withstands the stereotype of the earth as passively awaiting violation or salvation. Maroon women and genderqueer subjects engage these new perceptions while seeking an anti-imperialist geography across generations.

The future possibilities of this new geography show up in Almeyda's dream in *Song for Anninho*. This Maroon's dream is related to but has a different tenor then Caliban's dream or even Spinoza's dream of the Maroon. Almeyda "hear[s] the birds … trying to sing in one voice,/but one discordant voice,/one with many variations. It is a difficult song they are singing," a song that can "tear dreams apart/and make new ones."[80] Perhaps Almeyda hears the same songs that would "hum about" Caliban's ears in sleep, so beautiful that he "cried to dream again." When awake, Caliban perceives himself as trapped within Prospero's language while Almeyda decides, "We must remake our voices." She forswears the revenge Caliban believes is his only option for a merely improved enslavement. This discordance differs from the "untrustworthy" "harmony" "produced by fear" (*E* IV, Ap. 16). Such fear cannot countenance the difference and risk that accompanies genuine possibility. Almeyda hears a song fostering creation because it allows for difference.

The song also pays homage to lost Palmaristas: some say Palmares ended with many of its members jumping off of a mountain cliff to avoid recapture. Gayl Jones makes Almeyda witness to this end. To Almeyda, the birds link mourning to remaking. Admitting instances of powerlessness transforms despair into a meditation on lives lived, informing another life practice for the totality of desires, relations and knowledge exceeding enslavement and excommunication: elegy could be another name for this totality. Spinozist philosophy's objective alliance with Maroon thought coheres in turning excommunication and escape into potentialities rather than the racialized waste of the theological-political. Spinoza's authority stands in stark contrast to the exhausted assumption that European thought has authority *over* non-European populations, their ideas, affects and institutions. Spinoza's authority manifests in sharing power *with* the multitude, which cannot be fully understood without considering racial complexity. Antonio Negri attempted but could not carry out this effort with his provocative turn to Caliban in *Savage Anomaly*.

Song for Anninho makes a considerable contribution to what could be called a treatise on the emendation of Maroon intellect. The resurgence of fascist elements, the continuing superexploitation of the masses by global elites, and the backlash to demographic changes across Western Europe and the Americas, occurring alongside multiple progressive protests, boycotts, sit-ins, die-ins, disbandings of corrupt organizations, suggests the current and future need to rethink authority along these lines. At least since Spinoza wrote his famous works and Palmaristas stole away to the Barriga Mountains, Spinozist thought and the black radical tradition have each stressed an authority defined by turning shared dispossession into the basis for new belonging, privileging active over reactive affects, espousing power coextensive with its expression. Spinoza and the Maroon share a "point of departure from the desire to enhance our pleasure and power the only way it can be done: together."[81] Almeyda's love for Anninho comes to represent that striving for pleasure and power in togetherness. Almeyda closes her poem on this courageous, loving note, signing it from the Barriga Mountains in 1697: "Now I make roads for you, Anninho. I make roads."[82]

Notes

1. Antonio Negri, *The Savage Anomaly: The Power of Spinoza's Metaphysics and Politics*, trans. by Michael Hardt (Minneapolis: University of Minnesota Press, 1991), 86.
2. Negri, *Savage Anomaly*, 86.
3. Negri, *Savage Anomaly*, 98.
4. Lewis S. Feuer, "The Dream of Benedicto de Spinoza," *American Imago*, 14 (Fall 1957), 240.
5. Warren Montag, *Bodies, Masses, Power: Spinoza and His Contemporaries* (London: Verso, 1999), 88.
6. See Montag, *Bodies*, and also Michael Rosenthal, "'The black, scabby Brazilian': Some Thoughts on Race and Early Modern Philosophy," *Philosophy and Social Criticism* 31.2 (2005), 211–21.
7. Jimmy Casas Klaussen, *Fugitive Rousseau: Slavery, Primitivism, and Political Freedom* (New York: Fordham University Press, 2014), 2.
8. Klaussen, *Fugitive Rousseau*, 2–3.
9. Negri, *Savage Anomaly*, 167.
10. Negri, *Savage Anomaly*, 6.
11. Negri, *Savage Anomaly*, 6.
12. Jan De Vries, "The Dutch Atlantic Economies," in ed. by Peter A. Coclanis, *The Atlantic Economy during the Seventeenth and Eighteenth Centuries: Organization, Operation, Practice, and Personnel* (Columbia: University of South Carolina Press, 2005), 4.
13. James C. Boyajian, "New Christians and Jews in the Sugar Trade, 1550–1750: Two Centuries of Development of the Atlantic Economy," in ed. by Paulo Bernardini and Norman Fiering, *The Jews and the Expansion of Europe to the West: 1450 to 1800* (New York: Berghahn Books, 2001), 476.
14. Boyajian, "New Christians," 475.
15. Negri, *Savage Anomaly*, 8.
16. Negri, *Savage Anomaly*, 25.
17. Negri, *Savage Anomaly*, 8.
18. See especially Chapter 5, "The Great Witch Hunt in Europe," and Chapter 6, "Colonialism and Christianization," in Silvia Federici, *Caliban and the Witch* (Brooklyn: Autonomedia, 2009).
19. W. E. B. Du Bois, "The Development of a People," in *The Problem of the Color Line at the Turn of the Twentieth Century* (New York: Fordham University Press, 2015), 251.
20.
    > [The] first major consignment of slaves for the Americas was thus in every sense a European enterprise: the grant of the Flemish-born emperor was to a Savoyard, who sold his rights, through a Castilian, to Genoese merchants—

who, in turn ... have to arrange for the Portuguese to deliver the slaves ... By the end of the sixteenth century, the Dutch, the English, and the French acquire growing stakes in the Atlantic enterprise.

See Lindon Barrett, *Racial Blackness and the Discontinuity of Western Modernity* (Urbana-Champaign: University of Illinois Press, 2014), 19.

21 Steven Nadler, *Spinoza: A Life* (Cambridge: Cambridge University Press, 1999), 116.
22 Negri, *Savage Anomaly*, 112.
23 R. K. Kent, "Palmares: An African State in Brazil," in ed. by Richard Price, *Maroon Societies: Rebel Slave Communities in the Americas* (Baltimore, MD: Johns Hopkins University Press, 1996), 172.
24 Kent, "Palmares," 176.
25 Steven Nadler, "Why Spinoza Was Excommunicated," *Humanities* 34.5 (2013), http://www.neh.gov/humanities/2013/septemberoctober/feature/why-spinoza-was-excommunicated (accessed March 5, 2015).
26 Nadler, "Why Spinoza Was Excommunicated."
27 Negri, *Savage Anomaly*, 98.
28 Alden T. Vaughan and Virginia Mason Vaughan, *Shakespeare's Caliban: A Cultural History* (Cambridge: Cambridge University Press, 1991), 155.
29 Vaughan, *Shakespeare's Caliban*, 155.
30 Frantz Fanon, *Black Skin, White Masks*, trans. by Richard Philcox (New York: Grove Press, 2008), 197.
31 David Marriott, *Haunted Life: Visual Culture and Black Modernity* (New Brunswick: Rutgers University Press, 2007), 233.
32 Baruch de Spinoza, *Ethics*, trans. by Samuel Shirley, ed. by Michael L. Morgan, in *Spinoza: Complete Works* (Indianapolis, IN: Hackett Publishing, 2002), 35.
33 Baruch De Spinoza, *Theological-Political Treatise*, trans. by Jonathan Israel and Michael Silverthorne (New York: Cambridge University Press, 2007), 65. For the purposes of this essay, I found the Cambridge edition of the *TTP* most useful for clarifying Spinoza's critique of slavery in the general sense of political oppression and the specific sense of chattel enslavement.
34 William Shakespeare, *The Tempest*, ed. by Barbara A. Mowat and Paul Werstine, Act 3, Sc. 2, 46–48, http://www.folgerdigitaltexts.org/html/Tmp.html (accessed March 5, 2015).
35 Shakespeare, *The Tempest*, Act 3, Sc. 2, 59–62.
36 Shakespeare, *The Tempest*, Act 3, Sc. 2, 98–103.
37 Federici, *Caliban and the Witch*, 148.
38 Federici, *Caliban and the Witch*, 149.
39 Negri, *Savage Anomaly*, 223.
40 Shakespeare, *The Tempest*, Act 1, Sc. 2, 372–75.
41 Federici, *Caliban and the Witch*, 232.

42 Julia Lupton, *Citizen-Saints: Shakespeare and Political Theology* (Chicago: University of Chicago Press, 2005), 162.
43 Negri, *Savage Anomaly*, 89.
44 Lupton, *Citizen-Saints*, 177 (emphasis added).
45 Federici, *Caliban and the Witch*, 232.
46 Federici, *Caliban and the Witch*, 232; Shakespeare, *The Tempest*, Act 3, Sc. 3, 148–56.
47 Yet I critique Federici for not turning to the rhetoric of marronage more insistently in *Caliban and the Witch*. Still, her work confirms my distinction between Caliban and the Maroon. Federici valorizes past anti-exploitative and antiracist practices in Europe through the frame of New World marronage. Thus, she pushes marronage's influence back to the fourteenth to the seventeenth centuries and even to the immediate aftermath of Rome's collapse: "By the 4th century, in the Roman territories and the new Germanic states, the landlords had to grant slaves the right to have a plot of land and a family of their own, in order to stem their revolts, and prevent their flight to the 'bush' where *Maroon communities* were forming at the margins of empire." Strictly speaking, this is an anachronism. Federici references marronage this single time in *Caliban and the Witch*. Yet, using the term in such a far-flung instance of economic resistance indicates how generally marronage informs the project. Federici remains committed to reframing European gender and labor history without making New World populations a mere derivative of Europe's proletarians. In a text so adamantly committed to a feminist anticapitalist and antiracist politics, *Caliban and the Witch* ends up espousing the Maroon community's *conatus* over Caliban's imaginative (therefore materially real) attachments to his master. See Federici, *Caliban and the Witch*, 23.
48 Anthony Bogues, "Working beyond Criticism: Thinking outside Limits," *boundary 2*, 32.1 (2005), 92.
49 Christopher Winks, *Symbolic Cities in Caribbean Literature* (New York: Palgrave Macmillan, 2009), 71.
50 Stefano Harney and Fred Moten, *The Undercommons: Fugitive Planning and Black Study* (New York: Minor Compositions, 2013), 96.
51 Negri, *Savage Anomaly*, 167.
52 Winks, *Symbolic Cities*, 71.
53 Hasana Sharp, *Spinoza and the Politics of Renaturalization* (Chicago: University of Chicago Press, 2011), 183.
54 Gayl Jones, *Song for Anninho* (Boston, MA: Beacon Press, 2000), 3.
55 Jones, *Anninho*, 6.
56 Jones, *Anninho*, 36.
57 Negri, *Savage Anomaly*, 158.
58 Negri, *Savage Anomaly*, 20.
59 Negri, *Savage Anomaly*, 44.

60 Montag, *Bodies*, 63.
61 Montag, *Bodies*, 75.
62 Montag, *Bodies*, 75.
63 Kent, "Palmares," 180.
64 Kent, "Palmares," 176.
65 Stuart B. Schwartz, "The *Mocambo*: Slave Resistance in Colonial Bahia," in ed. by Price, *Maroon Societies*, 212.
66 Omise'eke Natasha Tinsley, *Thiefing Sugar: Eroticism between Women in Caribbean Literature* (Durham: Duke University Press, 2010), 44.
67 Tinsley, *Thiefing Sugar*, 45.
68 Tinsley, *Thiefing Sugar*, 84.
69 Tinsley, *Thiefing Sugar*, 44.
70 Jones, *Anninho*, 58.
71 Jones, *Anninho*, 58.
72 Jones, *Anninho*, 58.
73 Marriott, *Haunted Life*, 233.
74 Jones, *Anninho*, 43.
75 Jones, *Anninho*, 47.
76 Negri, *Savage Anomaly*, 91.
77 Negri, *Savage Anomaly*, 101.
78 Jones, *Anninho*, 7.
79 Jones, *Anninho*, 13.
80 Jones, *Anninho*, 81.
81 Sharp, *Renaturalization*, 183.
82 Jones, *Anninho*, 119.

Bibliography

Barrett, Lindon. *Racial Blackness and the Discontinuity of Western Modernity*. Urbana-Champaign: University of Illinois Press, 2014.

Bogues, Anthony. "Working beyond Criticism: Thinking outside Limits," *boundary 2* 32.1 (2005).

Boyajian, James C. "New Christians and Jews in the Sugar Trade, 1550–1750: Two Centuries of Development of the Atlantic Economy," in ed. by Paulo Bernardini and Norman Fiering, *The Jews and the Expansion of Europe to the West: 1450 to 1800*. New York: Berghahn Books, 2001.

Du Bois, W. E. B. "The Development of a People," in *The Problem of the Color Line at the Turn of the Twentieth Century*. New York: Fordham University Press, 2015.

Fanon, Frantz. *Black Skin, White Masks*, trans. by Richard Philcox. New York: Grove Press, 2008.

Federici, Silvia. *Caliban and the Witch*. Brooklyn: Autonomedia, 2009.

Harney, Stefano and Fred Moten. *The Undercommons: Fugitive Planning and Black Study*. New York: Minor Compositions, 2013.

Kent, R. K. "Palmares: An African State in Brazil," in ed. by Richard Price, *Maroon Societies: Rebel Slave Communities in the Americas*. Baltimore, MD: Johns Hopkins University Press, 1996.

Klaussen, Jimmy Casas. *Fugitive Rousseau: Slavery, Primitivism, and Political Freedom*. New York: Fordham University Press, 2014.

Lupton, Julia. *Citizen-Saints: Shakespeare and Political Theology*. Chicago: University of Chicago Press, 2005.

Marriott, David. *Haunted Life: Visual Culture and Black Modernity*. New Brunswick, NJ: Rutgers University Press, 2007.

Montag, Warren. *Bodies, Masses, Power: Spinoza and His Contemporaries*. London: Verso, 1999.

Nadler, Steven. *Spinoza: A Life*. Cambridge: Cambridge University Press, 1999.

Nadler, Steven. "Why Spinoza Was Excommunicated," *Humanities* 34.5 (2013).

Negri, Antonio. *The Savage Anomaly: The Power of Spinoza's Metaphysics and Politics*, trans. by Michael Hardt. Minneapolis: University of Minnesota Press, 1991.

Schwartz, Stuart B. "The *Mocambo*: Slave Resistance in Colonial Bahia," in ed. by Richard Price, *Maroon Societies: Rebel Slave Communities in the Americas*. Baltimore, MD: Johns Hopkins University Press, 1996.

Shakespeare, William. *The Tempest*, ed. by Barbara A. Mowat and Paul Werstine. http://www.folgerdigitaltexts.org/html/Tmp.html (accessed March 5, 2015).

Sharp, Hasana. *Spinoza and the Politics of Renaturalization*. Chicago: University of Chicago Press, 2011.

Spinoza, Baruch. *Ethics*, in ed. by Michael L. Morgan, *Spinoza: Complete Works*, trans. by Samuel Shirley. Indianapolis, IN: Hackett Publishing, 2002.

Spinoza, Baruch. *Theological-Political Treatise*, trans. by Jonathan Israel and Michael Silverthorne. New York: Cambridge University Press, 2007.

Tinsley, Omise'eke Natasha. *Thiefing Sugar: Eroticism between Women in Caribbean Literature*. Durham: Duke University Press, 2010.

Vaughan, Alden T. and Virginia Mason Vaughan. *Shakespeare's Caliban: A Cultural History*. Cambridge: Cambridge University Press, 1991.

Vries, Jan De. "The Dutch Atlantic Economies," in ed. by Peter A. Coclanis, *The Atlantic Economy during the Seventeenth and Eighteenth Centuries: Organization, Operation, Practice, and Personnel*. Columbia: University of South Carolina Press, 2005.

Winks, Christopher. *Symbolic Cities in Caribbean Literature*. New York: Palgrave Macmillan, 2009.

9

Spinoza's Biopolitics: Commodification of Substance and Secular Immortality

A. Kiarina Kordela

From tyranny to modern scientific (bio)power

According to Spinoza, the most fundamental law of "human nature" is that "everyone will, of two goods, choose that which he thinks the greatest; and of two evils, that which he thinks the least" evil (*TTP* 203). This law "ought to be counted among eternal truths and axioms" both because it is "the universal law of human nature" and because "reason bids us choose the least of two evils" (*TTP* 203 and 205). Being grounded on both nature and reason, this law constitutes the founding guideline in the formation of that compact humans make by transferring their natural rights to the sovereign: the state. As Spinoza writes, "it is … foolish to ask a man to keep his faith with us for ever, unless we also endeavor that the violation of the compact [*pactum*] we enter into shall involve for the violator more harm than good," and "this consideration should have very great weight in forming a state" (*TTP* 204). Therefore, it appears initially "that the sovereign right over all men belongs to him who has sovereign power, wherewith he can compel men by force, or restrain them by threats of the universally feared punishment of death" (*TTP* 204–5). This is sovereign power, which Michel Foucault has defined "as the right to take life or let live."[1]

Yet, this tyrannical power, Spinoza continues, is ultimately vulnerable, as "no one can long retain a tyrant's sway" for "sovereigns only possess this right of imposing their will, so long as they have the full power to enforce it" (*TTP* 205). If someone else—emerging from the multitude and supported by it—appears in the political scene with more power than the tyrant, the latter will be forced to relinquish his power, for "no one who is stronger than [the tyrant] will be bound unwillingly to obey him" (*TTP* 205). It is due to this limitation that sovereigns can "consult their own interests" only "by [also] consulting the public good" (*TTP* 205).² Thus, power begins to shift from its tyrannical to its ideological and hegemonic forms that we know today, and always in the name of democracy. Hegemony, as we know since Antonio Gramsci, is "linked ... to *consent* as against coercion, to 'direction' as against '*domination*.'"³ That there is no domination in hegemonic power means that in it everybody is (or rather perceives her/himself as) free. For, if, according to Spinoza's definition, "a man is free, in so far as he is led by reason" (*TTP* 276, n. 27), then, "in a state or kingdom where the weal of the whole people, and not that of the ruler, is the supreme law," the sovereigns themselves, on the one hand, are "acting according to the dictates of reason," while, on the other hand, "every member of it may ... live with full consent under the entire guidance of reason," so that "obedience to the sovereign power does not make a man a slave" but a free man (*TTP* 205–6).

Through reason, freedom and obedience coincide. Ultimately, however, even if the motive for the subject's obedience is not reason, this makes no difference, "for it is the fact of obedience, not the motive for obedience" that matters (*TTP* 215). Spinoza elaborates further:

> Whatever be the cause which leads a man to obey the commands of the sovereign, whether it be fear or hope, or love of his country, or any other emotion—the fact remains that the man takes counsel with himself, and nevertheless acts as his sovereign orders.... [A]s a matter of fact, all actions spring from a man's deliberation with himself, whether the determining motive be love or fear of punishment; therefore ... dominion ... extends over every instance in which it can prevail on men to decide to obey it. Consequently, every action which a subject performs in accordance with the commands of the sovereign, whether such action springs from love or fear ... or, indeed, any motive whatever, is performed in virtue of his submission to the sovereign, and not in virtue of his own authority. (*TTP* 215)

Once again, the subject's freedom to decide to obey the sovereign's command coincides with his submission to the sovereign. And although the motive for obedience does not matter, love, rather than fear, is more effective in making freedom and submission overlap. "This point is made still more clear," Spinoza continues,

> by the fact that obedience does not consist so much in the outward act as in the mental state of the person obeying; so that he is most under the dominion of another who with his whole heart determines to obey another's command; and consequently the firmest dominion belongs to the sovereign who has most influence on the minds of his subjects. (*TTP* 215)

In short, on this single page of Chapter XVII in the *TTP* Spinoza has unfolded the ground of the theory of ideology and hegemony, already anticipating Foucault's thesis that modern "[p]ower is exercised only over free subjects, and only insofar as they are free," with the result that "there is no face-to-face confrontation of power and freedom."[4] Such a confrontation between power and freedom becomes actually absurd, since in modern power, in Spinoza's words, "the true aim of government is liberty" itself (*TTP* 259).

This conceptualization of power is from the outset predicated on Spinoza's equation between freedom and reason ("a man is free, in so far as he is led by reason"). And this equation entails that "truth" is to be understood not in a legalistic or moralistic sense—which always implies domination and punishment—but in the scientific sense, postulated by Spinoza's geometric method. This is to say, however much like punishment the result of an act may look, it must be understood not as depending "on the will and absolute power of some potentate" but as "depending necessarily on the nature of the act performed," exactly as "the necessity of a triangle's essence" entails that "the three angles of a triangle are equal to two right angles" (*TTP* 62–63). In Spinoza's famous example, when "God revealed to Adam the evil which would surely follow if he should eat of the tree," Adam should understand "that such evil would of necessity come to pass" (*TTP* 63), in the same way that a mathematical equation brings about a necessary, not contingent, result. As Gilles Deleuze puts it, "because Adam is ignorant of causes, he thinks that God morally forbids him something, whereas God only reveals the natural consequence of ingesting the fruit."[5] The whole *Theologico-Political Treatise* aims at this *scientific religion*, which it produces in order to use it as the blueprint for the construction of its equally *scientific political state*. This state would be the full-fledged realization of what Foucault terms the modern "form of *pastoral* power"—an "individualizing" rather than "legal power," which "is salvation oriented" ("salvation [not] in the next world but ... in this world"), and which at the same time is "linked with the production of truth," including "the truth of the individual himself,"[6] as long as "truth" is understood in precisely the Spinozian scientific sense of logical necessity. Spinoza's coupling of modern power with scientific knowledge also concurs with Jacques Lacan's thesis that the difference between the "classical master" and the "modern master, whom we call capitalist, is a modification in the place of knowledge."[7] With the advent of secular capitalist modernity (since Spinoza's century) we shift from the "discourse of the Master"—in which political authority presents itself explicitly as the Master—to the "University discourse," in which power presents itself as "not knowledge of everything ... but all-knowing [*non pas savoir-de-tout...mais tout-savoir*]." This means that here power pretends to be "nothing other than knowledge," not mastery or power, but *pure* knowledge, which, as such, is said to be "objective knowledge" or "science" or what "in ordinary language is called the bureaucracy."[8] Both Foucault and Lacan refer here to the form of power that by now has become known as biopower. In fact, this is the form of power that Spinoza designates as the "best state of dominion." For, far from threatening the life of its subjects—who, consequently, can only aim "at escaping death"—this kind of power finds its *raison d'être*, in Spinoza's stunningly foretelling formulation, in "making use of life" (*TP*, V, 6). For, again in Spinoza's words, "the ultimate aim of government is not to rule or restrain, by fear, nor to exact obedience, but ... to free every man from fear, that he may live in all possible security" so as "to strengthen his natural right to exist and work without injury to himself or others," and "to develop their minds and bodies in security" (*TTP* 259). In these lines one can easily discern the inception of biopower as a power whose aim, now in Foucault's words, is to "exert ... a positive influence on life," to "optimize and multiply it" through the biopolitical "administration of bodies and the calculated management of life" regarding "propagation, births ... health," and so on.[9] I think that it is to this biopolitical nature of Spinoza's conception of power that Pierre-François Moreau points when he discerns in it the intimation of the modern state apparatuses.[10] And so do also the several references to the numerical and ultimately statistical, rather than juridical, nature of power in Spinoza, from Alexandre Matheron to Lucien Mugnier-Pollet, whose importance Étienne Balibar teases out by stating:

> Here we are at the heart of the endeavor of the *Political Treatise*. The constructions it proposes to us are not so much juridical as numerical or, if you will, *statistical* (preserving for the term its initial double meaning...) ... both as a "science of the state" and as a "science of the population," both from the standpoint of the *imperium* (security, regulation of obedience and of deliberation) and from that of the *multitudo* (effective decision-making, concentration of its power to act). It is a sort of political version of double-entry bookkeeping.[11]

Balibar's remarks also point to the intrinsic intertwining, in fact, overlap of *imperium* and *multitudo*, of authority *and* subjugation, resistance and freedom, as indicated above by both Spinoza's and Foucault's convergence of power and freedom. In biopower it is "impossible to localize the political subject *either in whole or in part,* that is, either in 'the people' or 'the State'" (Balibar 2005, 92). It follows that "each alternate in its own way would then claim to embody or represent the political 'subject,' in which case we have to conclude that this subject is paradoxical as such or that it is a *non-subject* in terms of classical conceptions" (92). And, after all, the constitution of power in Spinoza in terms of a non-classical conception of subjectivity is entirely in sync with the rest of his metaphysics, in which, as again Balibar has stressed, every individual, human or otherwise, is trans-individual.[12] By revealing the structure of power as trans-individual, wherein *imperium* and *multitudo* are constituted in one and the same process and as one and the same "subject," Spinoza's "analysis of political phenomena is the crowning path of a critique of this illusion" in political theory. Spinoza shows us that the "anthropomorphic illusion" is "the fundamental structure of the imaginary, of which the representation of political phenomena occupies a privileged place," up to even the point of "theological anthropomorphism," as in "Hobbes' *Mortal God*" (95). But, what is more, Spinoza shows us that this "anthropomorphic illusion" is operative not only in the realm of politics. In Spinoza, "this trans-individual dimension" is "*always already* embedded in the life of human individuality," which indicates that his "great philosophical project is *to think the human outside of any anthropomorphism*" (95).

Thus, we understand that biopower is the contemporary name for what Spinoza considers the best and "most natural" of all political systems, democracy (*TTP*, XVI, 11)—the system in which power would be in the hands of everybody or, put differently, the multitude would be self-governed. Democracy is the sole government that can fulfill Spinoza's ideal of absolute power, for "if there be any absolute dominion, it is, in fact, that which is held by an entire multitude" (*PT*, VIII, 3).

At this point, then, we are forced to address one of the thorniest questions regarding Spinoza's political theory, namely: what is the status of absolute power or democracy? The most evident alternatives seem to be to consider Spinoza's democracy to be either an ideal in the sense of an unrealizable utopia (something like a Kantian regulative idea) or in the sense of a realizable goal. But these alternatives are further complicated by the possibility that Spinoza's absolute power or democracy is realizable—and even, possibly, necessarily to be realized under certain circumstances—but in a modulation that can hardly be called the realization of a liberating ideal or utopia. Therefore, before we continue to examine what Spinoza's ontology entails about the exact nature of democracy *qua* biopower, let us linger further on its analysis in the *Theologico-Political Treatise* with regard to this particular question.

The fact that modern power involves this overlap of pastoral, salvation-oriented power and scientific truth determines Spinoza's central conceptual strategy in the *Theologico-Political Treatise*. This consists: first, in establishing the opposition between, on the one hand, freedom, consent and reason, and, on the other hand, obedience, ignorance and superstition, not by opposing or even juxtaposing politics to religion, but, on the contrary by locating both series—that of freedom and that of obedience—in each, religion and politics; and then, second, in aligning religion and politics to the point that the perfect political state would mirror the prefect religion, and vice versa. Spinoza unfolds this conceptual scheme first in the context of religion and then projects it to the realm of politics, so that, on the one hand, the obedience to God out of fear comes to mirror the slavish subjection to tyrannical authority, and, on the other hand, the love of God out of knowledge of God, which is a love out "of our free choice," comes to mirror the free submission to democratic or hegemonic authority (*TTP* 62). What the obedience to God out of fear takes as a "Divine command," the free love of God out of knowledge of God understands as "involv[ing] an eternal necessity and truth" (63). What slavish subjects "style God's will or decree," free people recognize as "the necessity of the Divine nature and intellect," which is the ground of any eternal truth (*TTP* 62–63). The obedience to God out of fear, like the slavish subjection to tyrannical authority, considers "the affirmations and negations of God [or the sovereign] … to be not an eternal and necessary truth, but a law—that is, an ordinance followed by gain or loss," up to and including the highest and universally feared punishment that involves the loss of life (*TTP* 63). By contrast, the love for God out "of our free choice" presupposes our knowledge of God, that is, the knowledge of "the existence of God as an eternal truth," which is also the knowledge that "the affirmations and negations of God always involve necessity or truth" (*TTP* 63).

Accordingly, the *Theologico-Political Treatise* seems to aim at showing that both in theology and in political theory, the (scriptural) equation of faith with obedience must be replaced with the equation between faith and love or knowledge of the law *qua* eternal and necessary (scientific) truth. This way, true faith would become indistinguishable from reason (the realm of eternal truths), at the same stroke as obedience and fear of punishment would become concepts no longer applicable to either religion or the state. For, both "Divine" and sovereign "rights appear to us in the light of rights or commands, only as long as we are ignorant of their causes; as soon as their cause is known, they cease to be rights or commands, and we embrace them no longer as prohibitions but as eternal truths; in other words, obedience passes into love of God" or love of the political law, "which emanates from true knowledge as necessarily as light emanates from the sun" (*TTP* 277, n. 28). If this ideal democratic state could be universalized, everyone would be free and subject only to reason, understanding that ostensible prohibitions are actually eternal truths, while authority would represent the most stable form of government, since, unlike coercive tyranny, it would promise the greatest public good to enlightened and free subjects who, as such, could never even conceive of the idea of overthrowing their government.

However, the age-old predicament of humanity, Spinoza laments, is that "there are but very few, compared with the aggregate of humanity," who can "perceive by the natural light of reason that simple obedience is the path of salvation"; the vast majority of people are "taught by revelation only that it is so by the special grace of God" (*TTP* 198–199). As a consequence, although the entire religious project has no "aim beyond inspiring mankind with a voluntary obedience," religion had to introduce "the Holy Scripture or Revelation" and, moreover, has often been forced to bargain for no more than coercive obedience, as did "Moses" who "threatened the people with punishment if they should infringe the law" (*TTP* 183). And Spinoza himself addresses with his treatise only the "Philosophical Reader," who should require neither God's special grace nor coercion for his salvation, while "the rest of mankind" which is infested with "fear" and "superstition," "and those of like passions with the multitude, I ask not to read my book" (*TTP* 11). In other words, deviating also in this from the dominant Enlightenment tradition, Spinoza is not of the opinion that reason can ever succeed in rendering obsolete the Holy Scripture or Revelation or the whatever historically specific imaginary means to obedience—for, clearly, a society that understands itself as secular and enlightened will require other means than Revelation. In fact, in an enlightened society no other means than those (at least appearing to be) based on reason can claim legitimacy.

There remains then one inference: the modern state in which one would not even conceive the idea of overthrowing the political authority—the state of absolute power—would be one in which the means to obedience would pass for operations of reason. It may at first appear that his thesis converges entirely with Moreau's reading of Spinoza's political theory, according to which the main task of politics consists in creating the appearance of reason or, in the English translation of Balibar's rendering of Moreau's position, in producing "*in the imaginary* a simulacrum of rationality."[13] Such a reading could go so far as completely privileging "the *passional* way" and reducing "the 'rationality' of the State or the organization of the multitude…[exclusively to] the appearance produced by the activity or manipulation of the passions"—something for which Balibar reproaches Moreau—as opposed to sustaining the balance between reason and the imaginary.[14]

Whether or not Balibar's criticism of Moreau is fair, the fact is that the present work advances the thesis that Spinoza's democracy or biopower is a form of power in which reason (scientific, bureaucratic, etc., "truth") covers up not imaginary illusions but, on the contrary, real relations of authority and subjection—as it becomes evident particularly from the earlier reference to Lacan's discourse of the university. For we must not forget that the transindividual constitution of both the human individual and political power does not amount to the elimination of power hierarchies—rather, if we are not vigilant this constitution can itself be used as a means for hiding such power dynamics.

Monistic biopower

Turning now to the nature of biopower as it follows from Spinoza's metaphysics, I shall argue that the protection and security of the body and mind in Spinoza's biopower go far beyond Foucault's administration and management of the aging and vulnerable life in duration. If "the love of God is man's highest happiness and blessedness, and [hence] the ultimate end and aim of *all human actions*," and if "in democracy"—Spinoza's ideal and "most natural form of government"— "everyone submits to the control of authority ... not over his judgment and reason" but "over *his actions*," then the highest and ultimate aim of the ideal democratic state is the people's happiness and blessedness (*TTP* 60 and 263; emphasis mine). To be sure, since Spinoza is an non-emanatist monist, blessedness involves not an otherworldly but, to repeat Foucault, a worldly salvation—yet, as we shall see, not the Foucauldian type of salvation which consists in "the 'worldly' aims" of "health ... sufficient wealth, standard of living ... security, protection against accidents," and such.[15] What "renders man blessed and happy," Spinoza writes, is only the "gift" of "our understanding and our knowledge," insofar as they "depend on ... and are perfected by the idea or knowledge of God, and nothing else" (*TTP* 66-67). It is "this knowledge [of God that] contains and involves the true principles of [both] ethics and politics" (*TTP* 67). And, as we eventually learn from the last part of Spinoza's *Ethics*, what gives us access to the knowledge and love of God is neither "imagination" nor "reason" but what he calls the "third kind of knowledge" or "intuition." The distinctive quality of this kind of knowledge is to conceive of the mind and body *sub specie aeternitatis*—something which lies far from the Foucauldian conceptualization of the body and mind as vulnerable.

Let us pursue more closely Spinoza's line of thought in his *Ethics*. In the second part of the *Ethics*, Spinoza writes that the "first kind of knowledge" derives "from singular things which have been presented to us through the senses in a way that is ... without order for the intellect," in other words, a "knowledge from random experience," or a knowledge deriving "from signs, e.g., from the fact that, having heard or read certain words, we recollect things, and form certain ideas of them, which are like them, and through which we imagine the things," we form our "opinion or imagination." Next, reason or the "second kind of knowledge" consists of our "common notions and adequate ideas of the properties of things." While the first kind of knowledge pertains to imagination and "is the only cause of falsity," "knowledge of the second and third kind is necessarily true," with the second pertaining to reason and the third forming what Spinoza calls "intuitive knowledge" (*E* II, P41, P40S2). In the fifth part of the *Ethics*, Spinoza returns to the "third kind of knowledge" to say that it "depends on the Mind, as on a formal cause, insofar as the Mind itself is eternal" (*E* V, P31). In this context, Spinoza introduces the crucial distinction between "duration" and the "species of eternity": "Whatever the Mind understands under a species of eternity, it understands not from the fact that it conceives the Body's present actual existence, but from the fact that it conceives the Body's essence under a species of eternity" (*E* V, P29). Spinoza proceeds to demonstrate this proposition:

> Insofar as the Mind conceives the present existence of its Body, it conceives duration, which can be determined by time, and to that extent it has only the power of conceiving things in relation to time. ... But eternity cannot be explained by duration. ... Therefore, to that extent the Mind does not have the power of conceiving things under a species of eternity. (*E* V, P29Pr)

So far the demonstration concludes that, as long as the mind conceives its Body in duration, it cannot conceive of it under the species of eternity, and that duration cannot explain eternity. What can explain eternity is rather the identity of God and Nature (the famous "Deus, seu Natura," "God, or Nature" Spinoza talks about in the Preface to Part IV of the *Ethics*). This is the identity of God with everything that exists, Body and Mind. To follow further Spinoza's line of thought, therefore, we must now go back to the second part of the *Ethics*, where he advances the position that—given that God is Nature—"the very necessity of God's eternal nature" entails that it "is of the nature of Reason to perceive of things under a certain species of eternity," and hence "to regard things as necessary, not as contingent." This also means that "the foundations of Reason are notions ... which explain those things that are common to all, and which ... do not explain the essence of any singular thing" but of the universal, which therefore "must be conceived without any relation to time, but under a certain species of eternity" (*E* II, P44C2 and Pr.). Reason and its common notions explain things under a certain species of eternity only insofar as they explain things as universal and necessary. Like a geometrical law or a pure structural formula, reason or the second kind of knowledge grasps what is common in all things (e.g., in all triangles) but, to repeat, not what is "the essence of any singular thing" (e.g., a singular triangle). But, if we now return to part V of the *Ethics* we see that, as a transition toward (re-)introducing the third kind of knowledge, Spinoza writes: "*Nevertheless, in God there is necessarily an idea that expresses the essence of this or that Body, under a species of eternity*" (*E* V, P22). For, "God is the cause not only of the existence of this or that Body" within duration "but also of its essence" *sub species aeternitatis*, insofar as this singular essence is "conceived through the very essence of God…by a certain eternal necessity" (*E* V, P22Pr.). Now, even though the essence of singular determined things (finite modes) is conceived under a species of eternity, it must not be conflated with substance itself. In Spinoza's words, "*[t]he being of substance does not pertain to the essence of man*," for "the being of substance necessarily involves existence," so, "if the being of substance pertained to the essence of man, then substance being given, man would necessarily be given…and consequently man would exist necessarily, which is absurd" (*E* II, P10 and Pr.)

Here we are arriving at an important criterion distinguishing the second from the third kind of knowledge. Although both are the source of truth and consider things under a species of eternity, their objects or domains do not coincide entirely. Reason is at once far more encompassing and more limited than intuition, as the former accounts for everything that follows from the necessity of God—whether directly or indirectly—whereas intuition accounts only for what follows from God indirectly, which is to say only for things and ideas with actual existence. These latter things and ideas have "God…[as] a cause not insofar as he is infinite, but insofar as he is considered to be affected by another idea of a singular thing which actually exists, and of this [idea] God is also the cause, insofar as he is affected by another third [idea], and so on, to infinity" (*E* II, P9). The corollary to the proposition preceding the above proposition distinguishes between the objects of reason and those of intuition as follows. Within reason "singular things do not exist, except insofar as they are comprehended in God's attributes," that is, "their objective being, *or* ideas, do not exist except insofar as God's infinite idea exists"—i.e., for reason, it suffices that things and ideas follow from the necessary nature of God in order for them to "exist." By contrast, intuition pertains to "singular things [that] are said to exist, not only insofar as they are comprehended in God's attributes, but insofar as they are said to have duration" (*E* II, P8C). Thus, in Spinoza's own example, we can know from reason (specifically, geometry) that "the rectangles formed from the segments of all the straight lines intersecting" within a circle "are equal to one another," and that, therefore, a circle contains "infinitely many rectangles that are equal to one another"; "[n]evertheless, none of them can be said to exist except insofar as the circle exists"—i.e., insofar as they follow by necessity from the nature of the circle (the equivalent of God's attributes in the afore-cited passages). In short, for reason, all these infinite rectangles "exist." By contrast, "of these infinitely many [rectangles] let two only... D and E, exist"—and the reader of the *Ethics* can see the two intersecting lines, D and E, drawn within the circle. The "ideas" of these two rectangles "also exist now, not only insofar as they are only comprehended in the idea of the circle, but also insofar as they involve the existence of those rectangles" and "[b]y this they are distinguished from the other ideas of the other rectangles" (*E* II, P8S). In other words, while reason considers things as eternal insofar as they are simply necessary (as are the infinite equal rectangles within a circle), intuition considers things with regard to their *singular* essence, that is, not simply with regard to what follows by necessity from the nature of God but also with regard to that which determines their existence or non-existence. For "to the essence of any thing belongs that which, being given, the thing is [NS: also] necessarily posited and which, being taken away, the thing is necessarily [NS: also] taken away" (*E* II, D2). In other words, unlike reason which disregards the question of existence and focuses entirely on universal necessity, intuition links the existing mode with its singular necessity, that is, its essence *sub species aeternitatis*.

As Yirmiyahu Yovel puts it, "particular essences are eternal while minds are perishable"; therefore, the third kind of knowledge—which for Spinoza constitutes the path to a secular conception of "salvation"—"consists in uniting the two, the perishable mind and the eternal essence" (1989, 170). Beyond reason, which is not concerned with the actual existence of things, "[w]e conceive things as actual in two ways: either insofar as we conceive them to exist in relation to a certain time and place"—that is, through imagination or the first kind of knowledge—"or insofar as we conceive them to be contained in God and to follow from the necessity of the divine nature" not only in universal terms but also in terms of their singular existence—and this is intuition or the third kind of knowledge (*E* V, P29S). This is why, in Balibar's words, far from referring "to a *general idea* of humanity, an abstract concept under which all individuals are subsumed and their differences neutralised," essence "refers precisely to the power that *singularizes* each individual" (1998, 107). So, returning to the demonstration of Proposition 29 in part V, now we can see why—after having just stated that the Mind in its capacity of conceiving the Body in time cannot explain eternity—Spinoza can proceed to add:

> But because it is of the nature of reason to conceive things under a species of eternity ... it also pertains to the nature of the Mind to conceive the Body's essence under a species of eternity ... and beyond these two, nothing else pertains to the Mind's essence .... This power of conceiving things under a species of eternity pertains to the Mind only insofar as it conceives the Body's essence under a species of eternity, q.e.d. (*E* V, P29Pr.)

The third kind of knowledge addresses not the empirical life as we conceive it within time, but rather it is the kind of knowledge in which the "*Mind knows itself and the Body under a species of eternity*" (*E* V, P30).[16] To recapitulate, a singular essence is the eternal immanence of substance in that singular mode, or it is substance *insofar as* it is eternally the immanent cause of that *singular* mode, or, yet again, it is the eternal expression of substance through that singular mode.

Now let us recall that substance itself has been defined already on the first page of the *Ethics* as "what is in itself and is conceived in itself," (*E* I, D3), which means that "substance cannot be produced by anything else" and, therefore, it is "the cause of itself" (*E* I, P7, Pr.). In turn, as the very first definition of the *Ethics* states, "[b]y cause of itself I understand that whose essence involves existence" (*E* I, D1) Since the essence of nothing that is actualized and exists in the duration of perishable modes can necessarily involve existence, it follows that substance cannot be reduced to anything actualized. Rather, it must be the very *potentiality* or *power* (*potentia*) of actualizing itself.[17] That whose essence necessarily entails existence is self-actualized, that is, it is the sole cause of itself. And, as we have seen, this is what differentiates substance and its essence from any singular essence, insofar as the latter is not self-caused and its essence does not necessarily involve existence. It follows that, insofar as a mode's singular essence is the eternal expression of substance through that singular mode, *singular essence must be the potentiality or power of actualizing whatever that mode can actualize.*

Returning to biopower, it follows that the singular essence of a human being consists in the power of its Body and Mind to actualize whatever they can. In other words, the Body and Mind in Spinoza's biopower concern not a *bios*, that once born, is exposed to disease and accidents, but *bios* as a singular expression of *substance*, that is, to quote Gilles Deleuze, of the "full, unvarying *power* of acting."[18] Following Spinoza's metaphysics, at stake in *bios* is the *power* of the living Body and Mind to actualize their singular essence, that is, their potentiality as singular modes.

Marxian monistic biopower and secular immortality

This power, of the living Body and Mind to actualize their potential is what Karl Marx called labor-power. And the reason why, even though labor-power has always existed, it was first Marx who focused on it as a central object of analysis is that in capitalism labor-power acquires an exceptional importance. Within the capitalist mode of production, which accompanies modern power, "labour-power ... as," in Marx's words, the "*capacity* of the living individual"[19] to produce "is his [the laborer's] vitality itself," that is, it "is not materialized in a product, does not exist apart from him, thus exists not really, but in *potentiality*, as his *capacity*."[20] Yet, once "it has been solicited by capital," that is, once it is commodified, this potentiality "becomes a reality." In other words, capitalism, Paolo Virno continues, amounts to the unprecedented social actualization of the "commerce of potential as potential."[21] Capitalism amounts to the commodification of potentiality. And, given that commodification notoriously entails the elimination of singularity—as concepts such as alienation indicate—what is at stake through the commodification of singular essences concerns ultimately the commodification of substance. Consequently, a Spinozian-Marxian theory of biopower is concerned with the double *commodification of potentiality qua singular essence and of potentiality qua substance*. And since both pertain to eternity, this theory of biopower is concerned with the *commodification of eternity*.

A few propositions after the one distinguishing eternity from duration in Part V of the *Ethics*, Spinoza alludes to one of the side effects of the commodification of substance by adding the following intriguing scholium:

> If we attend to the common opinion of men, we shall see that they are indeed conscious of the eternity of their Mind, but that they confuse it with duration, and attribute it to the imagination, or memory, which they believe remains after death. (*E* V, P34S).

Here Spinoza, who, as we have seen, does not shy away from intellectual snobbery, is willing to grant the consciousness of the fearful and superstitious members of the multitude general access to eternity—yet, such knowledge can only lead them to confusion, and so they mistake eternity for immortal afterlife, the infinite continuation of the life of their particular, individual bodies or minds.

And thus we have arrived at Spinoza's theory of the secular illusion of immortality. Let us recall that the ultimate aim of government is salvation, understood as a secular or worldly salvation. Now, in principle, salvation should be obtained only through the knowledge of God, which is accessible only to the third kind of knowledge that alone conceives of bios under a species of eternity. However, the vast majority of humanity, the multitude, mistakes eternity for immortality (just as it requires Scriptures, of the religious or secular/ideological type). It follows that Spinoza's *biopower* concerns not just the wellbeing and productivity of living individuals and collective bodies (modes), but, above all, the fact that *these same actual bodies and minds that exist in time and are the modes of an eternal substance are (mis)taken to be immortal.*

In short, once, with Spinoza, God is equated with Nature and hence truly secularized, the belief in immortality—itself a misconception of salvation—can survive only through a "confusion": the slippage from eternity to infinite duration. This slippage is enabled by the fact that the unprecedented, specifically modern, commodification of eternal substance entails as its corollary the equally unprecedented accumulation of *surplus-value*, which results in nothing less than the *introduction—in the world of actual, empirical, worldly life—of a temporality of theoretically infinite duration.*[22] For, being by definition the unlimited reproduction of ever more value—"value which is greater than itself"[23]—surplus-value functions as a kind of temporal valve, as it were, that, as Éric Aliez puts it, "open[s] up the duration of the durable" to infinity within social reality.[24] From then on, the primordial nature of the durable to remain, however long-lasting and resilient it may be, always confined within its limited duration is undermined, gradually allowing for the fantasy of the imaginary limitless duration of actual bodies and minds. The theoretically infinite duration of surplus-value allows for the pernicious slippage from bios under a species of eternity to the (fantasy of the) immortality of our actual bodies and minds. In its biopolitical twist, capital procures a temporality that functions as a surrogate for the species of eternity, and thereby entices subjects to seek their salvation in the very generator of this temporality—surplus-value. The secular (pastoral) biopolitical imperative becomes: consume, invest and act in any way that perpetrates the accumulation of surplus-value, so as to be saved![25]

To recapitulate, Spinoza intimated the secular biopolitical mechanism of fostering an illusion of immortality, even after "God is dead," or, rather, in the Lacanian correction of Nietzsche, even after "God is unconscious." Spinoza did so through his observation that people mistake eternity for immortality, and this not because they necessarily believe in a creationist God, and paradise and hell. Rather, what enables this mistake is a cognitive slippage relating to the difficulty of thinking in terms of the third kind of knowledge, compared to the easiness of thinking in terms of the imaginary. Here I have spelled out this slippage between these two Spinozian kinds of knowledge in terms of their respective temporalities, which are also distinct temporalities within the capitalist mode of economic exchange. Spinoza's substance and singular essence, like Marx's labor-power, are potentialities whose temporality is eternity—nothing changes in potentiality ever, since potentiality is itself not static but change: change does not change. Eternity is the temporality in which the third kind of knowledge operates. Surplus-value, by contrast, involves no qualitative change but merely quantitative accumulation, and for this it requires diachronic time (you have to wait some time until your investment procures profit). And since surplus-value is by definition ever greater than itself, it requires an infinite, or at least indefinitely progressing, diachrony. This is the temporality of imagination. This imaginary self-perpetuating diachrony constitutes the perfect blueprint for the illusion of the immortality of a mode—that is, of a living being in diachrony, whose essence does not involve existence. Through the temporality of surplus-value, the illusion that diachrony can continue for ever, modes (actually living bodies and minds) end up imagining that we can go on living for ever, as if our essence necessarily involved existence.

Between the capitalist biopolitics of infinite duration and a biopower of eternity

The above entails that at least one reason why Spinoza's project of the ideal democratic state continues to be thwarted by the ever-expanding state of global capital is that fear and superstition continue to cater to secular versions of misconceptions of salvation and fantasies of immortality. If so, then it is the underside of Spinoza's religious, political and scientific utopia—the continuation of fear and superstition in its modern, secular versions, as traced here and as it still needs to be traced further—that can point to the path of challenging the biopolitical authority of capital.

Now as then, in modern biopower or in tyranny, the ultimate object of universal fear remains death. Tyrannical power was largely sustained by the religious mitigation of this fear through the promise of the immortality of the soul in the transcendent realm of the heavens. The parallel developments of the capitalist economy and secularization, with their concomitant folding of transcendence within immanence—from Spinoza's "God or Nature" to the commodification of eternity—amount to the earthly absorption of heavens: the folding of eternity (albeit in an alienated form) within the plain of temporal immanence. This is to say that, even if only in a perverted way, in this respect capitalism itself is monistic. However, capitalism involves, and is defined by, a further aspect: the accumulation of surplus-value, as a result of the social actualization of the commerce of the potential *qua* potential. This latter aspect, as we have seen, triggers the slippage from eternity to (the fantasy of) infinite duration (within temporality, of course), thereby constituting the core of the secular superstition that capitalist biopolitics exploits. Herein lies the capitalist distortion of monism.

Bringing once again Marx and Spinoza together, we can spell it out more precisely. Labor-power is the sole "use value which the worker has to offer."[26] Whereas in all other economic transactions, "the one side (capital) ... stands opposite the other side as *exchange value*, and the other (labour) stands opposite capital, as use value," in "the relation of capital and labour" an exceptional phenomenon occurs, as "exchange value and use value are brought into relation," so that they are not simply each other's opposites but, rather, just as "[t]heir unity ... immediately splits ... their difference immediately coincides."[27] Once the laborer's use-value (labor-power) is commodified, it encounters capital not just as its opposite (use-value) but also directly as exchange-value, and, in fact, as the very unit of exchange-value, for, in Marx's words, although "use value as such does not stand in a connection with exchange value ... it [the use-value of labor] becomes a specific exchange value only because the common element of use-values—labour-time—is applied to is as an external yardstick."[28] *Qua* labor-power in itself, labor is use-value, but *qua* labor-time—which is how it counts once commodified, that is, once it exists *not in itself* but *for* capital—labor is exchange-value. And if labor is one locus of the overlap of use- and exchange-value, money is its counterpart. For "[m]oney ... as currency"—that is, as the object *used* for all economic exchanges—"loses its *exchange value* as intrinsic quality, and becomes *mere* use value," that is, the "use value for determining the prices etc. of commodities"; therefore, since money is also a use-value, "[m]oney itself ... is a commodity."[29] It follows, Marx continues, that "the opposite of capital cannot itself be a particular commodity, for as such it would form no opposition to capital, since the substance of capital is itself use value."[30]

What, then, can be the opposite of capital? Marx responds:

> The communal substance of all commodities, i.e. their substance not as material staff, as physical character, but their communal substance as *commodities* and hence *exchange values*, is this, that they are *objectified labour* [i.e., labor-time]. The only thing distinct from *objectified* labour is *non-objectified* labour, labour which is still objectifying itself, *labour as subjectivity*. Or, *objectified* labour, i.e.

labour which is *present in space*, can also be opposed, as *past* labour, to labour which is *present in time*. If it is to be present in time, alive, then it can be present only as the *living subject*, in which it exists as capacity, as possibility.[31]

While objectified or actualized labor (present in space) is essentially capital, self-objectifying labor or labor as subjectivity can exist only as capacity, as the perpetual sheer possibility of actualizing itself—as labor-*power*. Thus, "the real *not-capital* is *labour*," that is, "*productive labour*," which can be said to be present in time, but only insofar as this is the time not of actualized space (and, hence, the linear time of use-value) but the time of virtual space, which is eternity.[32] But capital's legerdemain consists in feeding on the appropriation of precisely its true and sole opposite—this labor-power *sub species aeternitatis*—by commodifying it, that is, by forcing it out of eternity into the infinite diachrony of surplus-value. The commodification of substance is the precondition for the existence of capital: "Capital ... exists only in connection with *not-capital*, the negation of capital, without which it is not capital."[33] The biopolitical slippage from eternity to infinite diachrony and its illusion of immortality aims at the oblivion of labor as "the real not-capital."

The distance between this capitalist perversion and Spinoza's monism corresponds to the difference between the capitalist biopolitics of infinite duration and a biopower of eternity.

However, the difference between the two is not as clear-cut as in this last statement for, as we have seen, in commodifying, and thereby alienating, the singular essence, capitalism commodifies a perverted version of substance and its temporality: eternity. This means that capitalism produces and circulates in the market substitute forms of eternity in the form of what Lacan called "imitation" or "semblance of surplus *jouissance*" (Lacan 2007: 81). But I leave this for further examination.[34]

Notes

1   Michel Foucault, "*Society Must Be Defended*": *Lectures at the Collège de France, 1975-6*, trans. by David Macey (New York: Picador, 2003), 241.
2   Unless otherwise noted, brackets in citations are mine.
3   David Forgacs (ed.), *An Antonio Gramsci Reader: Selected Writings, 1916-1935* (New York: Schocken Books, 1988), 423.
4   Michel Foucault, "The Subject and Power," in ed. by Brian Wallis, *Art after Modernism* (New York and Boston, MA: The New Museum of Contemporary Art and David R. Godine, Publisher, Inc., 1999), 417-33, 428.

5 Gilles, Deleuze, *Spinoza: Practical Philosophy*, trans. by Robert Hurley (San Francisco, CA: City Lights Books, 1988), 22.
6 Foucault, "Subject and Power," 422.
7 Jacques Lacan, *Book XVII. The Other Side of Psychoanalysis*, ed. Jacques-Alain Miller, trans. by Russell Grigg (New York: W. W. Norton, 2007), 31..
8 Lacan, *Le Séminaire. Livre XVII: L'envers de la psychanalyse, 1969–1970*, ed. Jacques-Alain Miller (Paris: Seuil, 1991), 34; *The Other Side*, 31.
9 Michel Foucault, *The History of Sexuality: Volume 1: An Introduction*, trans. by Robert Hurley (New York: Vintage Books, 1990), 136–40.
10 See Pierre-François Moreau, "La notion d'Imperium dans le Traité politique," in Ed. Emilia Giancotti, *Proceedings of the First Italian International Congress on Spinoza* (Naples: Bibliopolis, 1985), 355–66.
11 Étienne Balibar, *Masses, Classes, Ideas: Studies on Politics and Philosophy before and after Marx*, trans. by James Swenson. New York: Routledge, 1994, 22–23. Balibar is also right to remark that in this context "Negri is wrong … to argue that the Spinozist notion of 'constitution,' insofar as it represents the development of the power of the multitude, does not leave any room for the idea of mediation." To be sure, "Spinoza challenges the juridical mediation of the contractual type as the real or imaginary foundation of sovereignty," but this only "in order better to develop… an analysis of institutional mediation" (1994, 23).
12 See Étienne Balibar, *Spinoza: From Individuality to Transindividuality* (Delft: Eburon, 1997).
13 Balibar, "Potentia Multitudinis," Quae Una Veluti Mente Ducitur: Spinoza on the Body Politic," trans. by Stephen H. Daniel, in *Current Continental Theory and Modern Philosophy*, ed. Stephen Hartley Daniel, Evanston: Northwestern University Press, 2005, 86. See also Pierre-François Moreau, *Spinoza, l'expérience et l'éternité* (Paris: Presses universitaires de France, 1994), particularly 427–65.
14 Balibar, "Potentia Multitudinis," 88. This conclusion is decisively substantiated also by Spinoza's double generation of the City (or the foundation of society) out of both rational and imaginary reasons (see Spinoza *E* IV P37 and its two demonstrations and scholia; and Balibar's relevant extensive commentary in Balibar, *Spinoza and Politics*, 78–88). The political in Spinoza cannot be reduced to only one of these two sides.
15 Foucault, "Subject and Power," 422.
16 Deleuze, *Spinoza*, 63.
17 Of course, substance is also its own effects, that is, everything that is actualized, nature *qua natura naturata*, in distinction to substance as *potential* or *natura naturans*.
18 Deleuze, *Spinoza*, 63.
19 Karl Marx, *Capital: A Critique of Political Economy, Volume 1*, trans. by Ben Fowkes (London: Penguin Books, 1990), 274; emphasis mine.

20 Karl Marx, *Grundrisse: Foundations of the Critique of Political Economy (Rough Draft)*, trans. by Martin Nicolaus (London: Penguin Books and *New Left Review*, 1993), 267; emphasis mine.

21 Paolo Virno, *A Grammar of the Multitude: For an Analysis of Contemporary Forms of Life*, trans. by Isabella Bertoletti, James Cascaito, and Andrea Casson (New York: Semiotext(e), 2004), 84.

22 Several crucial remarks are required here, though, not being central to the present argument, I will keep them brief, while referencing further relevant readings. As Lacan has pointed out, surplus-value is not to be understood as a purely economic category, its equivalent on the level of thought and human subjectivity being what he calls "surplus-enjoyment" (see Lacan, *Book XVII*, particularly Chapter vii). We first find the logic (though not the term) of surplus-enjoyment in Aristotle's analysis of chrematistics (χρηματιστική) a kind of a miniature version of capitalism manifest in antiquity in the marginalized practice of exchanging money not for the acquisition of goods but for the purpose of profit making. By being constantly frustrated—since, the quest here being always for ever more profit, no acquired profit can satisfy one's craving for enjoyment—surplus-enjoyment perpetually renews its urge in an (imaginarily) infinite duration (see Aristotle, *The Politics*, trans. by T. A. Sinclair, revised by Trevor J. Saunders (London: Penguin Books, 1992), particularly Chapters I viii–I x; 75–87). More generally, Marx's theory of commodity fetishism indicates that no category is ever purely economical or purely a category of thought and subjectivity. For, according to the theory of commodity fetishism, objective relations are the relations of their producers, so that, as Étienne Balibar puts it, "there is no theory of objectivity without a theory of subjectivity" (Étienne Balibar, *The Philosophy of Marx*, trans. by Chris Turner (London: Verso, 2007), 64; see also Marx, *Capital*, particularly the chapter "The Fetishism of the Commodity and Its Secret," 163–77; for my thoughts on these topics, see A. Kiarina Kordela, *$urplus: Spinoza—Lacan* (Albany: SUNY Press, 2007), which expands further on the relation among Marx, Lacan and Spinoza's *Ethics*; and *Being, Time, Bios: Capitalism and Ontology* (Albany: SUNY Press, 2013), which elaborates on the centrality of commodity fetishism in secular epistemology, as well as on monistic biopower).

23 Marx, *Capital*, 257.

24 Éric Aliez, *Capital Times: Tales from the Conquest of Time*, trans. by Georges Van Den Abbeele (Minneapolis: University of Minnesota Press, 1996), 7.

25 Beyond such directly market-related biopolitical administrations of surplus-enjoyment, science, at least in its popularized forms, significantly contributes to fostering illusions of earthly immortality, whether directly of the body (e.g., through the increasing development of anti-aging technologies, the promise of the cure of all diseases) or of the mind (e.g., digital immortality—see http://www.huffingtonpost.com/2013/06/18/mind-uploading-2045-futurists_n_3458961.html—a notion already largely popularized through films, video games and other popular culture).

26 Marx, *Grundrisse*, 267.
27 Marx, *Grundrisse*, 267–69.
28 Marx, *Grundrisse*, 269.
29 Marx, *Grundrisse*, 268.
30 Marx, *Grundrisse*, 271.
31 Marx, *Grundrisse*, 271–72.
32 Marx, *Grundrisse*, 274 and 272.
33 Marx, *Grundrisse*, 274.
34 For my attempt to examine the biopolitical function of the commodification of eternity see Kordela 2017, particularly Chapter 7, "The Other Side of Value: Labor and Enjoyment."

Bibliography

Aliez, Éric. *Capital Times: Tales from the Conquest of Time*, trans. by Georges Van Den Abbeele. Minneapolis: University of Minnesota Press, 1996.

Aristotle. *The Politics*, trans. by T. A. Sinclair, revised by Trevor J. Saunders. London: Penguin Books, 1992.

Balibar, Étienne. *Masses, Classes, Ideas: Studies on Politics and Philosophy before and after Marx*, trans. by James Swenson. New York: Routledge, 1994.

Balibar, Étienne. *The Philosophy of Marx*, trans. by Chris Turner. London: Verso, 2007.

Balibar, Étienne. "Potentia Multitudinis, Quae Una Veluti Mente Ducitur: Spinoza on the Body Politic," in ed. and trans. by Stephen Hartley Daniel, *Current Continental Theory and Modern Philosophy*. Evanston: Northwestern University Press, 2005, 70–99.

Balibar, Étienne. *Spinoza: From Individuality to Transindividuality*. Delft: Eburon 1997.

Balibar, Étienne. *Spinoza and Politics*, trans. by Peter Snowdon. London: Verso, 1998.

Deleuze, Gilles. *Spinoza: Practical Philosophy*, trans. by Robert Hurley. San Francisco, CA: City Lights Books, 1988.

Forgacs, David (ed.), *An Antonio Gramsci Reader: Selected Writings, 1916–1935*. New York: Schocken Books, 1988.

Foucault, Michel. *"Society Must Be Defended": Lectures at the Collège de France, 1975–6*, trans. by David Macey. New York: Picador, 2003.

Foucault, Michel. "The Subject and Power," in ed. Brian Wallis, *Art after Modernism*. New York and Boston: The New Museum of Contemporary Art and David R. Godine, Publisher, Inc., 1999, 417–33.

Foucault, Michel. *The History of Sexuality: Volume 1: An Introduction*, trans. by Robert Hurley. New York: Vintage Books, 1990.

Kordela, A. Kiarina, *Epistemontology in Spinoza-Marx-Freud-Lacan: The (Bio)Power of Structure*. New York: Routledge, 2017.

Kordela, A. Kiarina. *Being, Time, Bios: Capitalism and Ontology*. Albany: SUNY Press, 2013.
Kordela, A. Kiarina. *$urplus: Spinoza—Lacan*. Albany: SUNY Press, 2007.
Lacan, Jacques. *Book XVII. The Other Side of Psychoanalysis*, ed. Jacques-Alain Miller, trans. by Russell Grigg. New York: W. W. Norton, 2007.
Lacan, Jacques. *Le Séminaire. Livre XVII: L'envers de la psychanalyse, 1969–1970*, ed. Jacques-Alain Miller. Paris: Seuil, 1991.
Lloyd, Genevieve. *Spinoza and the Ethics*. London: Routledge, 1996.
Marx, Karl. *Grundrisse: Foundations of the Critique of Political Economy (Rough Draft)*, trans. by Martin Nicolaus. London: Penguin Books and New Left Review, 1993.
Marx, Karl. *Capital: A Critique of Political Economy, Volume 1*, trans. by Ben Fowkes. London: Penguin Books, 1990.
Moreau, Pierre-François. "La notion d'Imperium dans le Traité politique," in ed. by Emilia Giancotti, *Proceedings of the First Italian International Congress on Spinoza*. Naples: Bibliopolis, 1985.
Moreau, Pierre-François. *Spinoza, l'expérience et l'éternité*. Paris: Presses universitaires de France, 1994.
Spinoza, Baruch/Benedict de. *A Theologico-Political Treatise and a Political Treatise*, trans. by R. H. M. Elwes. New York: Dover, 1951.
Spinoza, Baruch/Benedict de. *The Collected Works of Spinoza*, ed. and trans. by Edwin Curley. Princeton, NJ: Princeton University Press, 1985.
Spinoza, Baruch/Benedict de. *Die Ethik: Lateinisch/Deutsch*, trans. by Jakob Stern. Stuttgart: Reclam, 1990.
Virno, Paolo. *A Grammar of the Multitude: For an Analysis of Contemporary Forms of Life*, trans. by Isabella Bertoletti, James Cascaito, and Andrea Casson. New York: Semiotext(e), 2004.
Yovel, Yirmiyahu. *Spinoza and Other Heretics: The Marrano of Reason*. Princeton: Princeton University Press, 1989.

Biographical Notes

Aurelia Armstrong teaches philosophy at the University of Queensland. She has published essays on Spinoza, Nietzsche, Foucault, Deleuze and Feminism. She is the editor (with Keith Green and Andrea Sangiacomo) of *Spinoza and Relational Autonomy* (Edinburgh University Press, forthcoming) and is completing a monograph with the working title *Spinoza's Practical Philosophy*.

Cesare Casarino is Professor and Chair of the Department of Cultural Studies and Comparative Literature at the University of Minnesota. He is coauthor, with Antonio Negri, of *In Praise of the Common* (2008), author of *Modernity at Sea: Melville, Marx, Conrad in Crisis* (2002), co-editor of *Marxism beyond Marxism* (1996) and of *Another Mother: The Symbolic Order of Italian Feminist Philosophy* (2018), as well as author of numerous essays on literature, cinema and philosophy. He is also senior coeditor of the journal *Cultural Critique*. At present, he is at work on several book projects, on Spinoza and Marx, on Pasolini and Gramsci, and on the relation between cinema and biopolitics in Deleuze and in HIV/AIDS artwork.

James Edward Ford III currently teaches at Occidental College. His first book *Thinking through Crisis: Depression-Era Black Literature, Theory, and Politics* is forthcoming from Fordham University Press. He has published in *Novel: A Forum for Fiction, Black Camera, Biography: An Interdisciplinary Quarterly* and *The Black Scholar*. He has several articles forthcoming in *Cultural Critique, The Political Companion to W.E.B. Du Bois* and *Systems of Life: Politics, Economics, and the Biological Sciences*.

Joe Hughes is Senior Lecturer in English and Theater Studies at the University of Melbourne. He has written widely on contemporary European thought. His most recent book is *Philosophy after Deleuze* (Continuum, 2012).

A. Kiarina Kordela is a professor of German and Director of the Critical Theory Program at Macalester College and honorary adjunct professor at the University of Western Sydney, Australia. She is the author of *$urplus: Spinoza, Lacan* (SUNY Press, 2007), *Being, Time, Bios: Capitalism and Ontology* (SUNY Press, 2013) and *Epistemontology in Spinoza-Marx-Freud-Lacan: The (Bio)Power of*

Structure (Routledge, 2018). She is also the coeditor of *Freedom and Confinement in Modernity: Kafka's Cages* (Palgrave-Macmillan, 2011). Her work on a wide range of theoretical fields has been published in several collections and journals, including *Angelaki, Cultural Critique, Differences, History of Human Sciences, Parallax, Philosophy Today, Political Theory, Rethinking Marxism* and *Umbr(a)*. Her forthcoming work includes essays on "Spinoza," "psychoanalysis," and "biopolitics" for critical companions to theory, Marx, and psychoanalytic politics, respectively.

Warren Montag is the Brown Family Professor of Literature at Occidental College in Los Angeles. His most recent books include *Althusser and his Contemporaries* (Duke University Press, 2013) and *The Other Adam Smith* (Stanford University Press, 2014). Montag is also the editor of Décalages, a journal on Althusser and his circle, and the translator of Etienne Balibar's *Identity and Difference: John Locke and the Invention of Consciousness* (Verso, 2013).

Antonio Negri is the author of more than thirty books including *Empire* (2000) with Michael Hardt. He has published three books on Spinoza, *The Savage Anomaly: The Power of Spinoza's Metaphysics and* (1991), *Subversive Spinoza: (Un)Contemporary Variations* (2004), and *Spinoza for Our Time: Politics and Postmodernity* (2013).

Juan Domingo Sánchez Estop is an independent searcher and writer. For five years he taught history of modern philosophy. He translated Spinoza's *Correspondence* into Spanish and has published articles on Spinoza. He has been exploring for several years, under the inspiration of Foucault, Althusser, Carl Schmitt and Marx the main categories of the liberal discourse and written on "Governance," "Terrorism" and "Exception." This work is reflected in his book *La dominación liberal* (Madrid, Tierra de Nadie, 2009). He is currently working on Spinoza in Althusser and collaborates with the "Centre de Philosophie" of the Free University of Brussels (ULB).

Dimitris Vardoulakis is deputy chair of Philosophy at Western Sydney University and director of *Thinking Out Loud: The Sydney Lectures in Philosophy and Society*. His books include *The Doppelgänger: Literature's Philosophy* (Fordham University Press, 2010); *Sovereignty and Its Other: Toward the Dejustification of Violence* (Fordham University Press, 2013), *Freedom from the Free Will: On Kafka's Laughter* (Albany, NY: SUNY, 2016), and *Stasis before the State: Nine Theses on Agonistic Democracy* (Fordham University Press, 2017). He is also the editor of *Spinoza Now* (University of Minnesota Press, 2011); and, with Andrew Benjamin, of *Sparks Will Fly: Walter Benjamin and Martin Heidegger* (SUNY, 2015).

Index

Note: Page references with letter 'n' followed by locators denote note numbers.

Agamben, Giorgio, 9, 82 nn.8–9, 136, 142, 145 n.6
Aliez, Éric, 210, 215 n.24
Althusser, Louis, 5, 87, 97, 98, 107, 109 nn.8–10, 110 n.20
Ansaldi, Saverio, 145 n.1
Arendt, Hannah, 108 n.2
Aristotle, 1–2, 11–15, 17, 18, 20, 23, 26, 27 n.4, 28–9 nn.10–16, 29 nn.25–8, 82, 122–3, 132 n.18, 134, 144, 215 n.22
Armstrong, Aurelia, 1, 3, 54 n.31
Arnauld, Antoine, 132 n.21, 132 n.25
Augustine, 3, 19–21, 23, 29 nn.30–3, 30 n.36, 101, 102, 104, 110 nn.16–17

Bacon, Francis, 182
Badiou, Alain, 1, 5, 6, 113–19, 121, 130–2, 132 nn.1–2, 133 nn.5–7, 133 n.14, 133 n.43
Balibar, Étienne, 171 n.21, 200, 201, 203, 204, 207, 214 nn.11–14, 215 n.22
Bennett, Jonathan, 54 n.26
Berlin, Isaiah, 52 n.1
Bogues, Anthony, 194 n.48
Boole, George, 116, 132 n.8
Bossuet, Jacques-Bénigne, 110 n.14
Bourdieu, Pierre, 141
Bové, Laurent, 137, 143, 145 n.3, 145 n.7
Buchenau, Stefanie, 132 n.20

Casarino, Cesare, 1, 4, 83 n.13, 84 n.22
Cicero, 89, 101, 109 n.5
Citton, Yves, 84 n.22
Curley, Edwin, 132 n.12

Del Lucchese, Filippo, 16–17, 19, 28 n.8, 29 n.20, 29 nn.22–4, 29 n.29, 137, 145 n.4

Deleuze, Gilles, 1, 4, 42–3, 54 nn.24–5, 57, 58, 71–6, 79, 81 n.1, 83 n.14, 83 nn.16–21, 114, 116, 132 n.3, 138, 140–1, 144, 199, 208, 213 n.5, 214 n.16, 214 n.18
Den Uyl, Douglas, 33, 36–9, 52 n.2, 53 nn.4–6, 53 nn.8–9, 53 n.11, 53 n.14, 53 nn.18–19
Descartes, René, 2, 5–7, 91, 93, 123–8, 130, 132 n.22, 132 n.24, 132–3 nn.26–30, 133 nn.32–5, 147, 149–57, 160, 163, 165–7, 169, 170–1 nn.2–13, 171 nn.15–19, 171 n.28, 174, 182
Doueihi, Milad, 30 n.36
Du Bois, W.E.B., 178, 192 n.19
Duso, Giuseppe, 110 n.15

Euclid, 128

Fanon, Frantz, 8, 161, 174, 182, 193 n.30
Federici, Silvia, 177–8, 182–4, 189, 192 n.18, 193 nn.37–8, 193 n.41, 194 nn.45–7
Feuer, Lewis Samuel, 52 n.2, 173, 174, 192 n.4
Ford III, John Edward, 2, 8
Forgacs, David, 213 n.3
Foucault, Michel, 4, 9, 30 n.41, 57–8, 71, 74, 75, 81 nn.2–3, 98, 140–1, 144, 197, 199–200, 204, 213 n.1, 213 n.4, 214 n.6, 214 n.9, 214 n.15
Friedman, Joel, 132 n.10

Garrett, Aaron, 132 n.4, 132 n.15, 132 n.23, 133 n.40
Gassendi, Pierre, 171 nn.26–7
Gatens, Moira, 133 nn.44–5
Gaukroger, Stephen, 132 nn.16–17, 133 n.31

Giancotti-Boscherini, Emilia, 82 n.6, 109 n.4
Ginzberg, Carlo, 132 n.19
Guattari, Félix, 144
Guéroult, Martial, 118, 120, 127–8, 132 n.13, 133 nn.41–2

Hardt, Michael, 81 n.4, 83 n.13
Hegel, Georg Wilhelm Friedrich, 5, 100, 102, 139, 143
Hick, John, 29 n.34
Hobbes, Thomas, 3, 5, 19, 22–5, 29 n.35, 30 nn.37–9, 69, 94, 99, 100, 102, 103, 107, 109 n.11, 110 nn.18–19, 126–8, 133 n.39, 136, 143–4, 149, 158, 162, 201
Hoffheimer, Michael, 27 n.3
Hughes, Joe, 1, 5–6
Husserl, Edmund, 91–2

Israel, Jonathan, 171 n.20

James, Susan, 54 n.34
Jaquet, Chantal, 139, 144, 145 n.5
Jarrett, Charles, 132 n.9

Kambouchner, Denis, 170 n.5
Kant, Immanuel, 3, 14, 19, 24–5, 30 n.40, 82 n.9, 102, 107, 201
Kisner, Matthew, 55 n.35
Klaussen, Jimmy Casas, 192 nn.7–8
Kordela, A. Kiarina, 9, 82 n.9, 215 n.22, 216 n.34

Lacan, Jacques, 60, 82 n.9, 199–200, 204, 210, 213, 214 nn.8–9, 215 n.22
Leibniz, Gottfried, 5, 126, 130, 133 nn.36–8, 142
Lloyd, Genevieve, 131, 133 nn.44–5
Locke, John, 5, 100, 102, 149, 158, 159, 162, 169, 171 n.22, 171 n.24
Lord, Beth, 27 n.3
Lordon, Frédéric, 82 n.9, 84 n.25
Lucretius, 70, 83 n.11, 162
Lupton, Julia, 183, 194 n.42, 194 n.44

Macherey, Pierre, 149, 156, 170 n.1, 171 n.23

Machiavelli, Niccolò, 5, 8, 16, 100, 102, 108, 109 n.13, 137, 144, 159, 163
Maimonides, 37
Maine, Henry Sumner, 110 nn.21–4
Malberg, Raymond Carré de, 110 n.14
Malebranche, Nicolas, 182
Marx, Karl, 5, 9, 81 n.4, 88, 98, 102, 107–8, 110 n.25, 209, 211, 212, 214–15 nn.19–20, 215 nn.22–3, 216 nn.26–33
Matheron, Alexandre, 200
Montag, Warren, 2, 7, 175, 180, 192 nn.5–6, 195 nn.60–2, 195 n.81
Moreau, Pierre-François, 200, 203–4, 214 n.10
Morfino, Vittorio, 109 n.13

Nadler, Steven, 179, 193 n.21, 193 nn.25–6
Negri, Antonio, 2, 4, 6–8, 12, 27 n.1, 28 n.8, 81 n.4, 82–3 n.10, 83 n.13, 87, 91, 99, 102, 109 n.6, 144, 171 n.21, 173–83, 185–7, 189, 191, 192 nn.1–3, 192 nn.9–11, 192 nn.15–17, 193 n.22, 193 n.27, 193 n.39, 194 n.43, 194 n.51, 194 nn.57–9, 195 nn.76–7, 214 n.11
Nicole, Pierre, 132 n.21
Nietzsche, Friedrich, 210
Norris, Christopher, 26 n.1

Plato, 27 n.5, 28 n.13, 37, 100–1, 110 n.15, 152

Rancière, Jacques, 12, 27 nn.5–7, 29 n.17
Rawls, John, 14, 15, 25, 29 n.18, 30 n.42
Rice, Lee, 45, 47, 54 nn.27–9
Ricœur, Paul, 88, 108 n.3
Rosenthal, Michael A., 38, 53 n.13, 175
Rousseau, Jean-Jacques, 5, 100, 102, 175

Sánchez Estop, Juan Domingo, 1, 4–5
Sangiacomo, Andrea, 54 n.33
Schmitt, Carl, 99, 109 n.11, 136, 144
Schrijvers, Michael, 45, 47, 54 n.30
Seneca, 171 n.14
Sévérac, Pascal, 145 n.2, 171 nn.30–1
Sharp, Hasana, 185, 194 n.53
Smith, B. Steven, 33, 37, 52 n.2, 53 n.10

Steinberg, Justin, 38–41, 53 nn.16–17, 53 nn.20–3
Strauss, Leo, 27 n.1

Thucydides, 29 n.35, 30 n.39

Vardoulakis, Dimitris, 1–3, 28 n.7, 84 n.24
Vinciguerra, Lorenzo, 171 n.29

Virno, Paolo, 209, 215 n.21

Wartofsky, Marx, 53 n.12, 54 n.26
Weithman, Paul J., 110 n.17

Yovel, Yirmiyahu, 207

Žižek, Slavoj, 82 n.9